*This book
made possible
through generous gifts
to the
Nashville Public Library
Foundation Book Fund*

Alone! Alone!

BY THE SAME AUTHOR

Annie Besant

One to One: Experiences of Psychotherapy

The Ruffian on the Stair

Alone! Alone!

Lives of Some Outsider Women

Rosemary Dinnage

NEW YORK REVIEW BOOKS

New York

THIS IS A NEW YORK REVIEW BOOK

PUBLISHED BY THE NEW YORK REVIEW OF BOOKS

ALONE! ALONE!
LIVES OF SOME OUTSIDER WOMEN

by Rosemary Dinnage

This edition published in 2004
in the United States of America by
The New York Review of Books
1755 Broadway
New York, NY 10019
www.nybooks.com

Library of Congress Cataloging-in-Publication Data

Dinnage, Rosemary.
Alone! alone! : lives of some outsider women /
Rosemary Dinnage.
p. cm.
ISBN 1-59017-069-5 (hardcover : alk. paper)
1. Women—Biography. 2. Women authors—Biography.
I. Title.
CT3203.D57 2004
920.72—dc22

2003027805

ISBN 1-59017-069-5

Printed in the United States of America on acid-free paper.

April 2004

1 3 5 7 9 10 8 6 4 2

The "Alone, Alone!" that echoed through the house, rustled down the stairs, whispered from the walls, and confronted me, like a material presence.

—Alice James

Contents

ACKNOWLEDGMENTS

Though now much altered, most of the essays in this book began as contributions to journals, in particular *The Times Literary Supplement*, the *London Review of Books*, and *The New York Review of Books*. I would like to express my thanks to the editors of these journals for permission to draw on previously published material; and, for particular encouragement both past and present, to thank John Gross, John Sturrock, John Ryle, and, of course, Barbara Epstein of *The New York Review of Books*.

Introduction

WHEN I MOVED a few years ago from the much-loved London house where I had lived for some forty-five years and in which my children were born, I had a huge mass of papers to sort and to pack. Some of these papers were notes for books that other responsibilities had never given me time to finish, but most were dog-eared copies of the articles and reviews that I had written over the years, mostly for *The New York Review of Books* and *The Times Literary Supplement*. As I scanned through them I saw whole streams of thought, preoccupations, changes of mind, flashes of novelty, agonies of work. Writing about books had educated me—to the extent, I swear, of taking a couple of postgraduate degrees. (It is pleasant being wrongly called "Dr. Dinnage" when I am in the United States; kindly Americans aren't aware that in my youth it was almost unknown for girls to stay on at Oxford for postgraduate work.) How else then would I have known anything about evolution, for instance, if I had not had to assess a biography of Darwin, or grasped a glimmer of $E = mc^2$ except by reviewing a life of Einstein? (From this I also learned that great scientists can be lousy husbands.)

When I started reviewing books I was a single parent, working part-time as a research officer for a child development agency. Before that I had done bits of work that put food on the family table: translating books for £100 each, typing, scrubbing—near enough to the nickel-and-dime existence. As a research officer, however, there was writing to do, which slid into book reviewing and articles. As I had just finished another first degree, with an emphasis on child psychology, pursued in the evenings when the children were in bed, "bringing-up-baby" books were usually assigned to me. I accepted this as my lot. But I was able to move on from them—and I owe much to John Gross, then editor of *The Times Literary Supplement*, for encouragement and later for an introduction to *The New York Review of Books*. Happy day! Working on the *Supplement* under John's editorship was far from uneventful.

In the early days I took on a rather lowly kind of literary journalism: reviewing (anonymously, too) minor novels. Reviewing fiction is particularly difficult anyway, and drags one into a thicket of dreadful adjectives (deft, suspenseful, heartwarming, unforgettable, and so on). Reviewing first novels is particularly agonizing: they are written in sweat and tears, and no decent reviewer wants to discourage eager talent. I hope I never broke anyone's nerve. There was one lesson I learned from this novel-reviewing—the importance of *stamina*. I remember a number of exciting first novels from that time whose authors have now somehow faded out of sight.

You certainly need stamina to be a literary journalist or critic, especially when running a home and holding a job as well. Though I broadened out from the bringing-up-baby subject, it was sometimes by accepting, with a sinking feeling, whatever was assigned to me (a book on the spiritual aspect of menstruation and a novel by Umberto Eco stand out as particular heart-sinkers). There is a curious aspect to frequent reviewing: it sometimes feels like writing a diary or a running commentary of evolving ideas. "You remember what I was saying last week about early psychoanalysis," you want to say. "Well, this week I've been reading a novel that points in the same direction..."—but last week's target was one journal, this week's another, with no particular likelihood that the same people read both. Incidentally, it is remarkable how many people will say, "I saw your piece in *The Observer* last week," and follow it up with "But I didn't read it" or "I can't remember what it was about." Then why mention it?

But all the time one is learning while writing. A laboriously thought-out essay—and I have always written with labor—may change one's own current of thought. A long discussion of the Freud–Jung correspondence somehow enabled me to have a completely new glimpse of how one person can unconsciously manipulate another. This was an unsigned piece, as the policy of *The Times Literary Supplement* at the time was anonymous reviewing (this caused a lot of exciting bitchery among fellow academics trying to guess who wrote what). To me, as an extremely shy writer, this policy was in fact a help while it lasted. It was something to hide behind. I am not sure that I could have, at first, made bold assertions above my own name.

Do I regret that the 800,000 words or so of literary journalism that I sifted through were not, instead, two or three solid books of academic research? On the whole, I think not. I have always wanted to write clearly and simply, even—if it is appropriate—amusingly. I detest academic jargon as a creeping disease, and have found over the years that by no means all of the impressive academic works that appear are hard-hitting and long-lasting. And I like variety—to be hopping, in my own mind, from subject to subject and fitting them together. I have always enjoyed sewing patchworks; this collection might be seen as a kind of patchwork. In a good patchwork, however random it seems, each design and color relates to the whole.

While I was packing up files and papers in order to move house, I scanned through them with curiosity to see what patterns and themes emerged over the years. Editors get in the habit of sending out to each member of their team a certain kind of book. I had been sent a great deal of material on psychoanalysis to review, partly because I had been in analysis (not such a common thing in Britain in the 1960s and 1970s), and partly because analysts themselves don't want to review books: firstly, they can make more money in the fifty-minute hour than in the hours needed to slave over an article, and secondly, they tend to write in impenetrable jargon. So I had a great deal of material in this field stashed in my great-aunt's traveling trunk, which is where I kept all the copies. I had written in some depth on fiction as well, especially since *The New York Review of Books* gave me the space to expand, among other subjects, on the mixed bag of novelists I most admired: John Updike, in particular, and those polar opposites Anita Brookner and Iris Murdoch. But above all, I had enjoyed reading and writing about biographies, teasing out the shape and direction of a life.

There seemed to be a particular kind of biographical material, too. It sometimes seemed to me that the policy of editors was: if it's about misery, send it to Dinnage—it's her speciality. Frustration, bereavement, early death, depression, tragedy, and general gloom all came my way. I could understand the annoyance of the versatile actor who is always cast in the same type of part.

At Oxford we had a lecturer, Lord David Cecil, who talked a lot about the "inner life." "Romanticism is about the inner life," he often declared in his curious lisp. Of course this is a toe-curlingly embarrassing phrase now, along with the "inner child" and the "true self," but I am not sure that any more acceptable phrase has been coined to take its place. What my search through great-aunt's trunk revealed was a leaning toward writing about this inner world, whether through Freudiana or biography. In addition, I have always liked weirdness, oddity, outsiderism, nonconformity. So I arrived at the idea that a collection of pieces on women who, by choice or circumstance, defiantly or sadly, stood outside the boundaries of the ordinary could be of interest.

I have to make the confession here that I am very ignorant of "women's studies" and "gender politics"—I'm the wrong generation, you see, and perhaps even the wrong nationality. I don't think that Britain has ever had quite the "girly" culture, the Mom-ism, that American women have had to rebel against. As a wartime evacuee in the United States during World War II, I used to read avidly magazines with titles like *Woman's Home Journal*, which were all about how to make lighter, spongier cakes and how to run up a frilly apron on the sewing machine. Fascinating! I had never actually seen my mother make a cake (the cook did that), but it sounded more fun than Latin grammar, and I rather fancied the pink apron instead of the subfusc Oxford gown. When I came back to England, though I was not old enough to be drafted into the armed forces, I was perfectly accustomed to the fact that women were having to do war work just as much as men—though less dangerously. In the Battle of Britain, I knew, the chances of a young airman, perhaps twenty or twenty-one, staying alive for long had been slim. When, much later, I read my father's letters home from the front during the First World War, read about the Battle of the Somme where he got his wound, the gas attack that he survived with all his brass buttons turned green with mold, I felt even more that life could be unfair—to men.

As for education, about which Virginia Woolf wrote so piercingly, I in my later generation never much wanted to go to university, preferring the idea of escaping from home—traveling, painting, meeting exotic men. But if in the 1940s you had grown up in a university family and passed examinations pretty easily, you were destined to be one of the rather rare women who took up a university place.

Lastly—and childhood impressions, we know, are paramount—I grew up without seeing any particular signs of oppression by males. My mother was perhaps an even more forceful character than my father; my aunts' generation, deprived of husbands by war, got cheerfully on with work in teaching and nursing; my grandmother was a bit of a tyrant.

Hence I shrank from feeling capable of assessing the great wave of feminist literature, especially after a chance suggestion that Charlotte Brontë in some ways adored men brought down a ton of bricks on my head. All that was "not my scene," in the phraseology of the times.

Age, the sight of wrinkly old stars fathering babies, and a rereading of Trollope, the most tender and sensitive of men who nonetheless supported the Victorian status quo for women, have brought me around a little—but I arrive late, panting slightly, to the back of the crowd. The essays collected here stand as they were written, and at best I hope that a naiveté about feminist theory and a genuine lack of bias may have some novelty value.

Some few of the women I have written on truly seem to have been victims of men; about most of them, I am not so sure. Those that I have designated "Solitaries" were, I think, either born to be loners—the extraordinary Simone Weil, the autistic child Nadia—or were made so by early circumstance. Both Gwen and Augustus John were deeply marked by being orphaned early and brought up by unsympathetic caregivers. Besides, both had a touch of genius, and the commitments of genius have never made for a cozy life. The difficulties experienced by Gwen John's contemporaries among women artists are more typical of the price to be paid then for keeping up even a standard of competence in their profession.

Those included in the group "Muses and Partners" are not isolates in the same way, although—the theme of all the sketches essentially being loneliness—we all know that loneliness can exist within a partnership. Perhaps this is especially the case for partners of the eminent: the wives of Churchill and Verdi have left some evidence of this. In the case of Ottoline Morrell and Dora Russell—two incidents in the complicated love life of Bertrand Russell—it is up for discussion who oppressed whom, if anyone at all. Russell was another casualty of early bereavement, like the Johns; one might turn the tables and say that he was himself the victim of the dutiful but overly God-fearing grandmother who was left to bring him up.[1]

1. See Andrew Brink, *Bertrand Russell: A Psychobiography of a Moralist* (Humanities Press International, 1989).

Three muses—Kamila Stosslova, Marta Abba, and Olive Schreiner—I find especially interesting, embodying as they do what psychoanalysts would call "inner objects" rather than real, fleshly partners. "You are my creature, my creature, my creature," Pirandello writes to "his" actress. She must live inside his creative imagination, and never move from there, and then he can write his plays: "The one who dictates inside is you; without you, my hand becomes a stone." It is a remarkable declaration. It has no reference to the needs of the real person who lives her life outside his mind, and it is good to know that after his death Marta Abba escaped her role and married a rich American businessman, whom we may hope was more concerned with diamond bracelets than inner inspirations. Creators—writers, artists, composers—are ruthless about finding a way to keep their creativity alive. Flaubert wrote to his (occasional) mistress Louise Colet that it didn't matter whether the two of them actually met: the important thing was that she was *there*. In the margin of this letter she put several exasperated exclamation marks. With Olive Schreiner and Havelock Ellis it was an unusual case of mutual muses: they petted and nursed one another through their exchange of letters, but found themselves short of conversation when they were actually together. Full letter-writing is now, I suppose, rare. How do the telephone and computer affect these sensitive interchanges? And is a book or music perhaps always composed *for* someone, albeit unconsciously?

Turning to the women I group as "Seers" and "Exotics," I like to think of this heterogeneous group as a kind of party: virginal birth-control expert Marie Stopes chatting with hard-working prostitutes, transvestite Eadie discussing visions with Annie Besant, Enid Blyton planning a visit to a witches' coven. Is it frivolous to include (and inevitably make some fun of) sacred monsters like Stopes and Blyton? I hope not. To become the fantasists they were, they had to be isolates; the oddity is that through a different part of their personality they became extremely successful women rather than bag ladies.

They could put their self-deluding "inner life" into the service of others or, in Blyton's case, into making money.

The "Reinventors" in section V were forced by life to build up a new persona, an armor, for public presentation. Remarkable among them was Isak Dinesen, previously Karen Blixen. In a startling way she truly reinvented herself after she lost home, income, lover, and health and began to write. The rather pretty young Tanne became the extraordinary-looking old lady who spun her chilling little tales of fantasy and exchanged, it would seem, vulnerability for a glitteringly cool heart. Whether Dame Rebecca West, that formidable but nevertheless vulnerable *grande dame*, would have appreciated being linked with Dinesen I am not sure. It might have depended on her mood.

Finally there are the trapped—if not necessarily defeated—ones. Margaret Oliphant was trapped by death, deaths of the children to whom she had sacrificed her talent. But she had a longer span than the thirty-five years Katherine Mansfield was allotted. "Talk to ME," she wrote home, after a night of coughing up her lungs: "I haven't ONE single soul." And then, Alice: Might Alice James have gone on to a happier existence if modern medicine had been available for her? Perhaps not: social custom was against her, temperament was against her, family was against her. In some curious way, she and her brothers Wilky and Robertson were designated sacrifices for the greater glory of the family survivors, Henry and William.

These, then, are the lives of some women who, especially acutely, felt alone. Behind them I have sometimes glimpsed not an oppressing male but the figure of Miss Havisham, that ferocious nineteenth-century goddess of betrayal and power.

—Rosemary Dinnage

I

SOLITARIES

I

AMOROUS AND PROUD: GWEN JOHN

AUGUSTUS JOHN, AROUND a century ago, was on the way to becoming the most celebrated English artist of his generation, while Gwen John would have been known only as Augustus's sister who also did a little painting. The lordly Augustus himself used to say (half-seriously?) that in the long run he would be known as just the brother of the more famous Gwen. His work was bold and flashy, hers low-toned and subtle. By now the tables have almost turned: Augustus has fallen (too far, in my view) in critical opinion, while Gwen has consequently risen. They were orphaned young, and both, in absolutely opposite ways, were solitaries.

Augustus, famous for drink and womanizing and bohemian outrageousness, shared with his sister a certain commitment to truth, and his summing-up of her says the essential. "Gwen and I were not opposites but much the same really," he wrote,

> but we took a different attitude. I am rarely "exuberant." She was always so; latterly in a tragic way. She wasn't chaste or subdued, but amorous and proud. She didn't steal through life but preserved a haughty independence which people mistook for humility. Her passions for both men and women were outrageous and irrational. She was never "unnoticed" by those who had access to her.

For those who associate Gwen John chiefly with the severe self-portrait in London's Tate Gallery she may have a governessy, spinstery Jane Eyre image—which in a sense is accurate enough. A Brontë heroine might also, in the Paris art world of the 1890s, have thrown off her clothes at a party to show that she had the figure for an artist's model, or slept in the woods for a week outside her lover's house to catch a glimpse of him.

In the late nineteenth century the four John children had grown up unmothered, Augusta John being much away taking cures for a mysterious Victorian illness, of which she died when Gwen was eight. They were not unfathered, but evidently wished they were, and spent their lives in flight from Edwin John's repressive personality: Thornton and Winifred escaped to unconventional lives in America, and in old age Thornton was writing that Augustus was still "trying to solve the mystery of our father's character." What they did have was the wild Pembrokeshire countryside; Gwen liked to swim naked, and off the most dangerous rocks. It is always a surprise to be reminded by fiction how much the corseted nineteenth-century woman walked and rode and climbed (Elizabeth Bennett's muddy petticoat, even the Princess Casamassima walking from Hampstead to Hackney); and Gwen John, spending all her adult life in Paris, nevertheless often lived like the gypsy Augustus pretended to be. How many rucksacked travelers today manage to spend their nights in the Luxembourg Gardens, how many pram-pushers (she took a hand with one of Augustus's children) ever sit down on doorsteps when tired?

When Mrs. John died, she left Thornton (nine), Gwen (eight), Augustus (six), and Winifred (four). Augustus's own eldest child was to lose his mother at almost the same age as his father had. It is a pity that no more could be found out about Augustus's mother; a book could be compiled on the unknowability of mothers of the famous. Everyone pays lip service to the idea that early childhood is crucially important, but biographies don't—presumably can't—incorporate this assumption. One poignant glimpse comes from the diaries of

Edna Clarke Hall, a student contemporary of Augustus and Gwen. Clarke Hall was told: "A very nice lady was Mrs John. She painted all around the walls of their nursery just to amuse the children."

What the children's early years were like we cannot really know. We know that their mother was the daughter of a prosperous plumber, one of a huge family in which several children died. She played Chopin and was a talented amateur painter; she married Edwin John when she was twenty-five. She must have been gone often, as she was traveling in search of a cure. In 1884, away from home and aged thirty-five, she died of "rheumatic gout and exhaustion." Oh, to know more!

Michael Holroyd, in his wonderful biography of Augustus,[1] compares the effect of this early bereavement on Augustus and on Gwen. Both of them, as well as inheriting an innate talent, must have in some sense become artists in memory of the mother who had painted their nursery. In many of John's paintings—like the odd *Lyric Fantasy* of 1911–1915, perhaps—Holroyd sees the theme of ideal mother-and-child in ideal landscape. "The deprivation of his mother became the source of that fantasy world he created in its place," he says. "It was an attempt to transmute deprivation into an asset" (though one must say that John's best work is *not* concerned with a fantasy world). Gwen, on the other hand, in pictures of deserted rooms such as *The Japanese Doll* and *A Corner of the Artist's Room, rue Terre Neuve, Meudon*, was painting absence itself. When Augustus said that though he and his sister seemed opposites, they were much the same but "took a different attitude," he must have meant attitude toward loss as well as toward art, though he seems never to have recorded any memory of his mother. In spite of becoming such a roistering character, he was extremely reticent. As Holroyd puts it in the catalog to the 1982 Gwen John exhibition[2]: "Making himself the target of vast

1. Michael Holroyd, *Augustus John: The New Biography* (Farrar, Straus and Giroux, 1996).

2. *Gwen John, 1876–1939*, Anthony d'Offray Gallery, London, 1982.

publicity, he became the hollow man who, though recognized everywhere as the standard celebrity, was without identity: and a painter whose canvasses, as they grew larger, grew emptier." Gwen's pictures, meanwhile, were to grow ever smaller and quieter.

The John children's upbringing may have been dreary within the house (two Salvationist aunts joined the family to help with their care), but happier on the beaches and countryside of Pembrokeshire in Wales. (Nevertheless, Augustus was later to paint in any landscape but that of south Wales.) The family was reclusive and extremely silent, and when Augustus at sixteen went to London to the Slade School of Art he was seen by fellow pupils as exceptionally timid, polite, and tidy. Though traditional in its teaching, the Slade was progressive in being the first college to admit women to full training—and it was the girl students, Gwen and her friends, who were making this the Slade's "Grand Epoch."

Then Augustus had his accident. During his first summer vacation, he dove into a murky Welsh sea and split his head open on a hidden rock. It was a bad wound and for some time he was confined to bed. When he finally did return to college—lo and behold, Augustus was transformed. Transformed in his now bearded appearance and gypsified clothes, in beginning his career of wildness, and even in his work, previously approved of as "methodical" but now much more fluent and assured. So the legend grew up, as summarized on a cigarette card in a series of Fifty Famous People: Augustus John "hit his head on a rock whilst diving, and emerged from the water a genius," it said. Was it anything more than a legend? Without the accident, might he have been like the self-effacing Gwen? In his memoirs John himself dismisses the influence of his accident, and Holroyd ascribes the character change simply to pent-up impatience after convalescence. Adolescents, certainly, do reinvent themselves. Yet this particular change was extraordinary. A friend who returned from abroad was amazed by what he heard: "If you had told me that of any man at the Slade I'd have believed you. But not John." An insatiable restlessness, the restlessness of a hyperactive child, was to determine his whole life thereafter, perhaps even to contribute to the deterioration of his work. Possibly—the brain being so unimaginably complicated—frontal lobe damage from his injury did have a disinhibiting effect.[3] The accident must have stayed in his thoughts: writing in 1908 about himself to Ottoline Morrell (of whom he painted a brilliant portrait), his phrasing was that

> I have always been so excessively anxious to feel myself quite alive that I have plunged with needless precipitation into the most obviously fast flowing channels where there are rocks and bubbles and foam and whirlpools.... This has saved me from morbidity at any rate if it has not improved my complexion.

This flamboyant new Augustus was plunging into early success—a one-man show, travels, infatuations—and at barely twenty-three married his fellow Slade student Ida Nettleship. Before the marriage he had written her a limerick:

There was a young woman named Ida
Who had a porcelain heart inside her
But she met a young card
Who hugged her so hard
He smashed up her crockery. Poor Ida!

And so it was to be. Poor Ida.

Gwen followed her brother to the Slade school, where she and the few other women students there were carrying off prizes. There were various "outrageous and irrational" passions in her life now, for both

3. Oliver Sacks, personal communication.

men and women. In 1904 occurred her extraordinary involvement with the triangle of Augustus, Ida, and his mistress Dorelia, the beautiful and mysterious Dorelia McNeill of innumerable Augustus John portraits. Dorelia tried to escape her fate and went off on a walking trip across France with Gwen—until Gwen, with a steeliness none of the others possessed, persuaded her back into the tribe. There was to be "wonderful concubinage"! Dorelia's first son was born nine months later, Ida's fourth soon after.

Three years later, when Ida made way for Dorelia by dying, Gwen showed the same steeliness in her letter to her lover, the sculptor Auguste Rodin, advising him not to waste energy on condolences for Ida but to save it for their next lovemaking. The brazen Gwen John may be hard to discern in the Tate self-portrait (she was a virginal twenty-four when she painted it), but her letters to the old man, often written at the rate of three a day, some addressed directly to him and some to an imaginary "Julie," were feverish, gross, adoring. At times their bed at his studio was shared with another mistress, a Finnish sculptress. "Aren't you *ashamed* to stand naked before that man?" asked one of the lesbian artists Gwen John posed for. "Oh no," she answered. "I like it very much."

She had written truly of herself that she was "born to love," but it is hard to imagine what she might have made of ordinary marriage. As it was, total dependence on Rodin coexisted with the "haughty independence" her brother described. She seems to have been without self-pity, though at each rupture with Rodin—first his taking of a new mistress, then a three-year gap in the relationship, and finally his death—she was thrown further into isolation. She called this being "tired": "I had a tiring life for some years and so seem only now to begin to paint" (1914); "When one gets tired one loses something which one never gets back" (after his death in 1917). A particularly curious thing, in such a master of line, is the change in her handwriting as seen in letters written before and after the first break with

Rodin—from crisply adult to pathetically schoolgirlish, which became her habitual handwriting.

When she drew, presumably, her hand simply went on knowing what to do. She wrote to a friend about a "quiet part of her mind" where art was, which was undisturbed. It was the need to safeguard this, clearly, that made her a recluse from all except the few people who did not jar on her. With Gwen John it is even harder than with most artists to connect the life with the serene works—pale, elegant images of women, children, flowers, cats, usually in watercolor and gouache.

Though Rodin was unashamedly unfaithful, he showed her a kind of fatherly tenderness as well. Augustus, meanwhile, found her a wealthy American patron, John Quinn, who loved her work; so after great poverty she was able to exhibit and sell quite well. "Acid" was Quinn's word for what he wanted to find in paintings. "There is no harshness, no acid, no pain in his work," he wrote of Augustus John. "Fine draughtsmanship is not enough."

We must see Gwen John's painting in the context not only of her brother's, but of the women artists who were her contemporaries. Ida John was one of the group of talented young women students that included Gwen herself, Edna Waugh (later Clarke Hall), and Gwen Salmond (later Smith). Augustus in his memoirs implies that the latter two were obliterated, as artists, by domesticity; but Alison Thomas's group biography shows that this was not quite true.[4] Both these women made disastrous marriages; both struggled against monstrous odds to keep their work going. Edna Clarke Hall, who survived it all to live to the age of one hundred, left notebooks about her life that Alison Thomas draws on.

These were, originally, high-spirited girls who swam naked off cold English beaches, and tried a little *vie de Bohème* in Paris. Edna

4. *Portraits of Women: Gwen John & Her Forgotten Contemporaries* (Polity, 1996).

had two children, but in middle age she had a kind of breakdown over the bleakness of her marriage. With the help of the psychiatrist Henry Head and of her sympathetic male teachers from the Slade, she set up a studio of her own and maintained a successful reputation as a watercolorist. Gwen Salmond's marriage to Matthew Smith, at the time a nervous aspirant artist, was even more unfortunate. He went on to become a painter of great repute, but along the way dropped wife and children because he felt they were "stifling his career." She always felt crushed by the comparison of her work to his, but did not entirely give up painting. A small exhibition in 1994 in Britain, "Golden Nineties," which contained some work by the Gwen John contemporaries, suggests that in fact they were no more than talented—though under different circumstances perhaps they might have done much better. Painting requires much solitary brooding, and, as Edna Clarke Hall said, after marriage she could "never allow herself to be absent-minded."

Edna wrote in her notebooks about the pleasures of going barefoot on holiday and feeling the sun on her neck: "Curious how exciting it was just to be oneself. Something that is so easily lost." And something we all want to be—not least Augustus's Ida, one of the liveliest of the group, who wrote to Edna in her teens that she planned to have "a studio and ability to paint for myself." Some years later, when she had four babies, she was still pining after "ethics and life and rainbows and colours and butterflies and shimmering seas and human intercourse." But then, in a later letter, we see Ida writing: "Those Johns you know have a hold that never ceases—the ache is always there in place of them when absent."

Her marriage to Augustus had been a runaway affair, and her parents, the artist Jack Nettleship and his wife, were appalled. The young couple lived at first in an empty flat in Liverpool, where John was teaching and where their first child was born. Just over a year later a second son was born, and eighteen months after that a third. By then, stifled in his turn by domesticity, Augustus had fallen in love with Dorelia.

Ida John had of course given up her painting. In a letter she wrote that she was very tired, that she wondered if she could stand much more of the company of babies. Her letters are from someone bewildered by her life. Some days the curtain seemed to lift a little, she wrote to her aunt. "The other days I simply fight to keep where I am.... I can understand the saints and martyrs and great men suffering everything for their idea of truth. It is more difficult, once you have given it some life—to go back on your idea than to stick to it." And to a friend: "I live the life of a lady slavey. But I wouldn't change—because of Augustus—*c'est un homme pour qui mourir.*" And yet—"Isn't it awful when even the desire to live forsakes one?"

Ida had wanted children, had wanted Augustus to have his Dorelia; she even loved Dorelia. A letter she wrote to Dorelia about the struggle with her feelings has more heart in it than any of Augustus's letters:

> I tried not to be horrid—I know I am—I never hardly feel generous now like I did at first... but when I think of some things I feel I suffered too much—it was like physical suffering it was so intense—like being burnt or something... it was nature that was the enemy to our scheme.... At present I hate you generally but I don't know if I really do. It is all impossible now and we are simply living in a convention you know—a way of talking to each other which has no depth or heart.... Nothing can change this fact—that you are the one outside who calls a man to *apparent* freedom and wild rocks and wind and air—and I am the one inside who says come to dinner, and who to live with is apparent slavery.

It was perhaps the imminence of a baby for Dorelia that was too much: "Yet, I do want to be there for your baby. I do want to be good, but I *know* I shan't manage it." So Dorelia's Pyramus was born, in a caravan on the open spaces of Dartmoor. Some six months later Ida had a fourth son, and in 1905 Dorelia had Romilly.

Ida would have liked to leave:

> If I had the money I think I really should do it—but I can't leave him and take his money—and I can't keep the kids on what I have—and if I left the kids I should not find peace . . . how will it end? By death or escape?

She put little blame on Augustus: she had chosen her life, he had never lied to her. But "it's a pity one's got to live with a man." She had her fifth boy, Henry, and fell ill. Recovery from puerpural fever was a hit-or-miss affair at the time—all the more so, presumably, for a woman exhausted by pregnancies. Augustus sat with her and massaged her neck. She was delirious, and laughed a lot, and at half-past three in the afternoon she died.

And Dorelia: within eighteen months of Ida's death Dorelia had the charge of six boys under eight, four of them Ida's (only Ida's last-born grew up with the grandparents). Later she was to have two more children, both girls; John was to have several by other women. Dorelia might seem to be something of a saint; but, as Holroyd makes clear, it was more that she was stoical. She made some attempts to escape, but never quite succeeded. She was to outlive John and die at eighty-seven, cared for by her son Romilly. Holroyd gives one of his bravura summings-up of a life, in this case a chilling one:

> From anything that might cause pain she averted her attention, though she might seem to stare at it without emotion. The range of her interests narrowed. She had stopped drawing, now she read less, and eventually would give up the piano. Nothing got on top of her, nothing came too near. She grew more interested in the vegetable world. The sounds at Fryern matched her

> equanimity: no longer the jaunty duets with Lamb, but a softer noise, the purring, amid the pots and plants, of the sewing-machine as she sat at it, for life as it were.

Gwen was permanently settled in France, partly to escape the influence of her brother, who in his thirties was at the peak of his fame. In these good early years the praise of his work was unstinted. William Rothenstein recorded that "no one living had his range of sensuous, lofty and grotesque imagination." Roger Fry, after seeing the New English Art Club exhibition of 1904, had written that "we hardly dare confess how high are the hopes of Mr John's future which his paintings this year have led us to form." George Moore said he was the wonder of Chelsea, Max Beerbohm that there was no doubt of his genius (and caricatured it). In 1913 an American critic declared him to be one of the three greatest talents among living European artists; the other two were Matisse and Jacob Epstein. The opposition, during these years, came from the old guard, who asked, "What does it all mean?" and complained that "at his worst he can outdo Gauguin."

It was Virginia Woolf who famously announced that "in or about December 1910 human character changed." The occasion was, of course, Roger Fry's "Manet and the Post-Impressionists" exhibition. In his 1996 biography of Augustus John, Michael Holroyd expanded his account of it, to explore John's relation to this first English showing of Gauguin, Cézanne, Van Gogh, and Matisse, as well as to give some idea of the outrage it produced among English philistines. It is a mistake to think that Augustus John's failure (if it was failure) was due to his being a rustic from a provincial backwater. He was well aware of the importance of the 1910 exhibition and the one that followed in 1912, and picked out the Van Goghs, Gauguins, and Cézannes for special admiration. He advised the American collector John Quinn to buy Manet and Degas in 1912. He considered Picasso, whom he had met in 1907, "a wonder"; for a time, in fact—for instance, in the *French*

Fisher-Boy of 1907—his work showed a distinct Blue Period influence. But, perhaps to his own detriment, he was never a joiner or a follower. Even with the Bloomsbury painters, he never had much in common. Though always surrounded by other people and other people's art, John remained a loner: aloneness was a kind of capsule he lived inside.

To the philistines, John was horribly modern: to the cognoscenti such as Roger Fry and Clive Bell, on the other hand, he soon began to seem lightweight and old-fashioned. He painted richly and fluently and fast, but he had that fatal lack of long-term concentration which prevented him from following his work through. His general reputation was not to fade for some further years after that; then, as was said of the Sitwell family, he belonged more to the history of publicity than of art. Now, at thirty, he already had exquisite drawings to his credit—Dorelia caught in pose after pose—and he had done two incomparable portraits of Ida. Within the next few years there were to be other fine portraits—of Yeats, Shaw, William Nicholson, Wyndham Lewis—though later on he was to despise himself for becoming a "mere" portrait painter in order to support the family. There were always to be pictures of gypsies and tinkers, like *The Mumper's Child*—his love of the Romany people was no affectation. And there were the north Wales landscapes painted with fellow Welshman James Dickson Innes. If one takes the close of the Second World War as the beginning of John's decline, he had by then had some twelve exhibitions, and shown over a hundred paintings and drawings at the New English Art Club alone. And it was perhaps his Slade School academic training that, while teaching exquisite drawing, stood in the way of any real interest in the advance of abstraction. If ever anyone fell heavily—and, later, drunkenly—between two stools, it was John.

The reputation for outrage may have been as much a handicap as an asset. It was unaffected and unsought: whether assisted by a bang on the head or not, John was a genuine, not a fake bohemian. Many copied him, in manner and clothes; at art schools, girl students dressed in the Dorelia style; but, like Annie Oakley, John just did what came naturally. He was an icon, a stereotype of the wild artist, but this could make it all the easier for a later generation to dismiss him as a bore. Meanwhile his good friend Matthew Smith, married for a time to Ida's friend, and the contemporary John most admired, crept timidly through his life quite unknown to the man in the street, but has beaten John roundly in critical esteem. John went on producing, went on being a national monument, traveled incessantly, pursued many more women, acquired a fine country house run in amiable chaos by Dorelia, and was awarded the high distinction of the Order of Merit before the end of his life.

Nevertheless, it was, after all, a life of tragedy. Not just because John's work has slipped out of sight—time will adjust that—or even because of family deaths, but because his lifelong experience was of a struggle against melancholy. Witness after witness records what a life-enhancer John was when there was drink and good company around; but in between, there were huge vacancies, what he called "the old *horror vacui*." Katherine Mansfield, glimpsing him at the theater, saw something like a Nash landscape of the Western Front:

> I seemed to see his mind, his haggard mind, like a strange forbidding country, full of lean sharp peaks and pools lit with a gloomy glow, and trees bent with the wind and vagrant muffled creatures tramping their vagrant way. Everything exhausted and finished—great black rings where the fires had been, and not a single fire even left to smoulder.

He was forty at that time; and it was to get worse. The burnt-out inner landscape that Katherine Mansfield had glimpsed kept growing darker. He knew that there was some "damned ancestral strain at work" in his melancholy. He had to struggle through a "mental hail storm," had to keep on the move, had to paint fast because his vitality drained away fast. His self-portrait in old age is of a Lear glaring in horror at the world, suffering a torment he cannot explain.

In France, meanwhile, Gwen dealt with the ancestral strain by—as Augustus said—taking a different attitude. Learning to be "so strong that people and things could not affect me beyond reason" was very important to her. All three of these women painters—Gwen herself, Edna Clarke-Hall, and Gwen Smith—were painfully influenced by men's opinion of their work, but Gwen John conquered the tendency. After looking at an exhibition of Cézanne watercolors she said, "These are very good, but I prefer my own." While she steadily assumed the role of half-starved, cat-crazed English spinster, the pictures still continued, slowly, to be produced. During the 1930s they grew smaller and smaller and more repetitive in theme, but only in the last few years of her life did she stop working. The command of *tone* that Whistler had admired in her was never shaken, nor was her control of form. She scribbled to herself: "Impose your style. Let it be simple and strong. The short strong stalks of flowers. Don't be afraid of falling into mediocrity. You would never."

One would like to see more of the pictures and sculptures made of Gwen John herself; she must be one of the most painted of painters, for from the time she refused her father's allowance (he told her the dress she had specially sewn for his visit looked like a prostitute's) she was dirt-poor. For many years, until subsidized by the American collector John Quinn, she was an artist's model who also painted a little. But though she posed nude for innumerable third-raters, she never herself drew a man; though she scrutinized the world so carefully, down to the color of "the little ball holding the snowdrop petals," her subjects usually look obliquely away from the spectator. A Rodin "Muse," for which she was the model, looks downward in the same way. It was left unfinished, armless, and was only recently cast.

Did Augustus mean it when he said he would be remembered as Gwen John's brother? Certainly he was never satisfied with his work.

His friend John Rothenstein said that he had "seen him peer fixedly, almost obsessively at pictures by Gwen, as though he could discern in them his own temperament in reverse"—rejoicing, Rothenstein thought, at his own wider range, but also envying "the sureness with which she attained her simpler aims."

But her aims were not simple at all. She fought for her painting techniques, as well as for her chosen life, in a way that neither Edna Clarke-Hall nor Gwen Smith was able to. Whereas Augustus ranged anywhere and everywhere for his material, Gwen stayed in bare hotel rooms, painting the room, or single figures, in the pale tones she admired in Whistler. When the First World War broke out, Augustus tried to persuade her to come back to England, but she stayed on in France; later, he helped her buy a cottage in Hampshire, but she never lived in it.

When her patron, John Quinn, died seven years after Rodin, Gwen John began to paint less and less. Over the years she became reclusive, living in poverty with her cats. When the Second World War broke out, she tried to leave Paris; Augustus, on holiday in Provence with a selection of his grown children, had whistled past the city without stopping en route back to England. His sister made her way as far as Dieppe, and then collapsed in the street. Being without luggage, she was assumed to be a derelict and was taken to the Hospice de Dieppe, where she died quite unknown, leaving her possessions to Augustus's fourth son, Edwin. The whereabouts of her grave is not known; Augustus was to have designed a gravestone, but never got it done. "The greatest woman artist of her age," he called her, "or, as I think, of any other."

2

BLACK SEQUINS AND SEAWEED: STEVIE SMITH

"YOU ARE QUITE potty about death," says Celia to Caz in *The Holiday*:

> How you do go on about death, listen if she can think of one other thing—death, death, death. I see you with black sequins and seaweed clinging to your hair. You are like the child in the story who saw the Italian funeral, very grand it was, and as black as a maidservant's dream of death, and the child cried out, *Che gusto avrei di morir' anch'io*. You, my dear, might have been that little Roman, oh dear, oh dear, the little Roman monster amorous of death, be-jetted, be-feathered, besequined, death, death, death.

And the voice Celia puts on to say it in is "rather peculiar, familiar too, rather lisping and thin, it squeaks a little at high pitch."

Here is the dominant theme, the style, the vocal pitch of that odd fish Stevie Smith (born Florence Margaret in 1902, died in 1971). "A nugget of genius," one reviewer ascribed to her; "nervy, bold and grim," she called herself. Though she wrote three "novels" (more like extended free associations than novels as we know them), she is best thought of as a poet of small, farouche poems illustrated with doodles, a cross between Ogden Nash and William Blake.

Though her reputation has seesawed, there have always been Stevie Smith fans, and for a long time I resisted being one of them; the lisp in the voice, the high pitch, and the squeak seemed to me—that terrible English condemnation—affected. *Faux naif*, quaint, whimsical. But the free-floating imagination, the sure instinct for style, above all the deep note of death, death, death sounding through the wispy poems eventually wins one over. Stevie Smith loved to win admirers; she was abominably lonely as well as fey and funny.

The foundations for that were laid down in childhood, broken by illness and bereavement (perhaps even earlier; she wrote a poem about her weaning—"oh the famishment for me"). Her parents were mismatched and when she was three her father left wife and two daughters and went into the navy, sending occasional postcards and little else.

I sat upright in my baby carriage
And wished mama hadn't made such a foolish marriage.
I tried to hide it, but it showed in my eyes unfortunately
And a fortnight later papa ran away to sea.

There is a suggestion in this, however airily put, that she had felt herself responsible for her father's desertion; and certainly she was a wary, precocious child. The result of never having been really childish was that the child lived on in the adult Stevie Smith, a source both of her talent and her melancholy.

Mother, aunt, and great-aunt set up house with the two children in Palmer's Green, a far-out north London suburb where they had little money, but good schooling. When Peggy (later Stevie) was five she fell ill of tubercular peritonitis and, following the horrible medical custom of the time, was sent away to a nursing home for three years. Her family visited, but it was at this time that the lifelong attacks of desolation must have set in. She describes in the autobiographical *Novel on Yellow Paper* how she cried and refused food and was chilled by indifferent caresses that were so unlike her mother's. It was at this age, too, she says, that she learned to love suicide, and she makes the dubious proposition that all children should be introduced to it at this age:

> To brace and fortify the child who already is turning with fear and repugnance from the life he is born into, it is necessary to say: Things may easily become more than I choose to bear.... That "choose" is a grand old burn-your-boats phrase that will put beef into the little one, and you see if it doesn't bring him to a ripe old age.

When she came back, her mother was already beginning to be ill with the heart disease she was to die of when Peggy was seventeen. In *Novel on Yellow Paper*, again, she describes the torture of watching her mother: "When I saw the suffering of my much loved ma, I could not help her. I raged against necessity, I raged against my absconding and very absent pa, I raged and fumed and spat." And so the mother died; and "the last minute when you are dying, that may be a very long time indeed."

So in the first seventeen years of her life Stevie Smith learned very thoroughly that indeed it is possible that things may become more than we can bear and that it is best to make a servant of death, a deliberate choice. And she clung to safety—her surviving aunt, the suburban home, a monotonous job—for most of her life as a writer. But she must have been learning other things, too, that enabled her to coast so freely with her imagination, to let go and fly. There was much Edwardian suburban security and fun for the two girls—books and church and the countryside and amateur dramatics (she shone at dramatics and at drawing, and was to use both later, in illustrations and poetry readings). Her childhood accounts for the "death, death, death" note, but also for the wit and joy and confident originality.

Unlike her sister, Stevie (as she now became) was not considered clever enough for university, so she went to work as a secretary in a publishing house. There she stayed for thirty years. "Dark was the day for Childe Rolandine the artist/When she went to work as a secretary-typist"; nevertheless for much of her time she seems to have been reasonably happy there. She lived in the Palmer's Green house (as she was to do all her life) with Aunt, "the Lion of Hull," a majestic maiden lady who heated up Stevie's bedtime milk and cosseted and championed her. "Oh how deeply thankful I am I didn't go having an aunt with clever ideas about literature and painting. Oh how I dread these cultured gentlewomen, like you get so many of in America." And yet, "of course my life runs on secretly all the time, as it must, and she has no idea that it does."

Part of the secret life was writing poems, part of it love affairs. There were two men in Stevie Smith's life in her twenties (and possibly none after), men she could not imagine marrying but whom she grieved over. She felt herself to be solo. Opinions vary about her love life; friends have said she was waiflike and spinsterish, but on the other hand she had long slim legs and wrote in *Novel on Yellow Paper*:

> Miss Mogmanimy would enlarge upon how alcohol leads to irregularity in sexual behaviour. Oh what a lovely phrase that is, and how it does not describe the way you feel at parties sometimes, if you have your right friends there, and that lovely feeling, you get quite shot up, and it is lovely oh how I enjoy it.

Ahem, as she was fond of saying.

She submitted some poems to a publisher ("neurotic," "very ultra-1934"), and finally got some into print but was told by the editor to go away and write a novel. In six weeks she produced *Novel on Yellow Paper*, which came out in 1936 with a miniature furor—as if Gertrude Stein had written *Diamonds Are a Girl's Best Friend*, said one newspaper. It also initiated a problem that was to pursue her: friends resented appearing in frank or mildly malicious descriptions, and she was dropped from some guest lists.

Yet she wrote as much to win friends and admirers as for any other reason, Jack Barbera and William McBrien point out in their biography of her[1]; life with Aunt and at the typewriter did not provide much scope for her wit and style, and it was through the writing that she came to know writers and get on a circuit of literary parties and weekend visits. (She was a dreadful guest, jealous of children and animals who upstaged her, demanding of her own way; but she was often asked again.)

Even those who are devoted to Stevie Smith's poems may have mixed feelings about the three novels. *Novel on Yellow Paper* is an extended soliloquy, a ramble; *The Holiday* has more structure—with endless digressions and quotations. She wants to think the book rather than write it: "Oh talking voice that is so sweet, how hold you alive in captivity, how point you with commas, semi-colons, dashes, pauses and paragraphs?" It is a preoccupation that was of her time (Virginia Woolf's *The Waves* came out in 1931). Sometimes whimsy hovers a little too near. But then there are the moments when fantasy takes off, as it does in her long description of a private game she liked to play. You're walking down a long straight road somewhere in France, she says; the road turns into a track, the track into a dried marshland; you turn to the right, and find the house, and go up the path and inside and shut out the wind. You find food and fresh figs and a fire, outside the wind and sea are roaring; you go to the big stone bath with brackish water, and after your bath you put on a heavy toweling gown. You go down the corridor to the room with the straight, hard bed and fine sheets:

---

1. *Stevie: A Biography of Stevie Smith* (Oxford University Press, 1987).

> Ah this is the lovely dark room, and the air is in and about and in through the great open windows, and the grey light is in the dark sky far away. *Ah night space and horror, keep my dream from me.*

It is a lonely fantasy. Comfort turns to a flash of fear.

The year after *Novel on Yellow Paper*, the first collection of poems came out, winning good reviews; the next novel, *Over the Frontier*, was less successful, but Stevie Smith was now quite part of the 1930s literary scene. "She is in love with Death...and with the scenes of childhood," said a critic; "her writing has the air of an odd only, lonely child." She was always very consciously an orphan; and as she grew older got the look of a withered Alice in Wonderland.

In the second book of poems death is much more omnipresent than before; the title poem, "Tender Only to One," means tender only to death. Stevie Smith's death fantasy was not of her mother gasping her life away—that was life, suffering; death is always seen as a wonderful blankness, a deliverance. It is life that is dry, dusty, restless—in *Novel on Yellow Paper* she sees the Devil in garbage, in empty ice-cream cartons; death is coolness and flowing water and cessation. "Oh, beastly mind that shifts so much, that is a tyrant, that runs every way and every way at once," she says; but death

> *is a scatterer*
> *He scatters the human frame*
> *The nerviness and the great pain*
> *Throws it on the fresh fresh air*
> *And now it is nowhere.*

This is all unreal and consolatory; yet there is a kind of hopefulness in seeing death as so benign. And of course there was the side of her that got hopefulness from life as well; Barbera and McBrien tell a story of how Stevie and a friend walked in the stage door of a theater, went up and discovered boxes full of mustaches and false noses, put them on, and "twizzled and twirled" in delight. A late poem called "I Wish" shows us that side. She wishes, at first, that she could find a gray dove's wing to hide her head under; but then she sees reflected in a car's chromium hubcap a whole world stretching out, and she wants to go into that world, where she would find a road and a blue sky and a beach.

She was far from being the realistic kind of suicide who sees that the act is the loneliest thing anyone can do. Yet she did in fact make a suicide attempt. It was in her early fifties, after the distractions of love and first authorship and wartime, when she was beginning to be unfashionable and to find it hard to get published. Barbera and McBrien's *Stevie* is a carefully documented book, and yet the authors say in just one sentence that she tried to slash her wrists at the office. Surely, with such a passionate pursuer of death, we should know more: What preceded it? How seriously did she try? Was anyone there at the time? Who found her and what happened then? At any rate, the attempt was a success in its way, because her doctor ordered a long rest and that she leave the secretarial job, which by now was surely very wearisome. Financially, she managed thereafter by doing book reviews (including one on Simone Weil) and poetry readings.

Although she regularly reviewed novels as well, she began to be sent many books on Christianity by editors. It was a subject that made her endlessly fascinated, ambivalent, angry, and the editors recognized a good source of copy. In general her theme was "This God the Christians show/Out with him, out with him, let him go." The Christian story is a fairy tale, she wrote; God has not been fair to us; he is a murderer of his son. And if the son was human, why did he not experience the sins we have to struggle with? What about the cruelty of Hell? But there was a great longing all the same for submission to a source of love and care, a source that she lost early in life and looked for ever after. In *The Holiday* she wrote:

> I kneel down in the aisle, leaning back on my heels with my head against the pew, I say: the soul does not grow old, the soul sees everything and learns nothing, and I say: How can we come back to God, to be taken into Him, when we are so hard and separate and do not grow.... And I say, if we are to be taken back, oh why were we sent out, why were we sent away from God?

The crucial question was expressed in the Stevie-esque title of one of her poems, "Will Man Ever Face Fact and Not Feel Flat?" Of course there was always room for wisecracks (on the Assumption of the Virgin: "If the universe is expanding is she still Going Up?"). But as usual the pain and the jokes went together. Bravest of all martyrs, she wrote in one of her reviews, are the martyrs to atheism, and perhaps she was thinking of herself. She loved Christianity but felt self-respect demanded that one should forgo it. God made us savage so that we should survive, she wrote; we don't remember that "you put this poison in us":

> *Generally we stand*
> *With the tears on our face*
> *And our hands clasped in anger,*
> *Faithful but unfortunate.*

The great Trappist monk Thomas Merton, who loved Stevie Smith's work, said he found much true religion in it.

In the 1960s began the era of poetry readings, and a revival of fame for her; she proved to be a natural-born star. Through most of that supposedly swinging decade she was nursing Aunt, who lived to be ninety-six, and the poetry readings were her only escapes. She began to chant some of her poems rather than speak them, and this was a great success. A small elderly lady dressed like a schoolgirl and singing odd poems in a flat voice might have been grossly embarrassing, but she brought it off. In 1967 she appeared at a "Psychedelic Feast" of poetry, reading with a number of drunken Beats, and outread them all.

Aunt died in 1968, a release for Stevie and yet a great sorrow. She was only to live three more years herself. Death disproved his benign nature, as he usually does, and came in the form of a brain tumor. Curiously, the letters she wrote when her perceptions were already clouded seem only an extension of the style she had always cultivated—

> (Anyway I've had now to sing glad pleas for happy gladdings of more endless pops & goes. I have signed my name but now I feel awfully frightened. Am I saying wisely in these solemn legalnesses) that any little murder, caused by here & there, has been quite let off by my names having been signed so beautifully!??

Her conversation disintegrated as the source of her jokes, her loneliness, her loves were crushed by the indifferent growth. But once or twice, her friends noted, she said in her old way, "heigh-ho." Heigh-ho for wry amusement, for stoical sorrow.

3

VICARAGE PASSIONS: BARBARA PYM

IN 1966 BARBARA PYM records in her diary that she is reading an account of someone that "made me laugh—people lying ill in the Dorchester and dying in Claridges." "My own story," she goes on, "judiciously edited from these notebooks would be subtler and more amusing." This reinforces the feeling given by the diaries that, frank and entertaining as they are, they conceal as well as reveal. For what is Barbara Pym's own story? Why did she choose the words "subtle" and "amusing" for it, and do they quite fit the life history as told in her diaries and letters?[1] The "story" ostensibly is the quiet progress of an unmarried lady novelist who produced ten books, very gently satiric ones, very English, much concerned with the provision of cups of tea in adversity and the workaday aspects of the Church of England. But seeing it in close-up we can find that there is much more to be known about this writer's life.

The beginning of the story, anyway, is as bright as daylight: the future creator of churchy spinsters and mopish curates was a pretty girl with a passion for clothes, "the flicks," punting, ginger beer and ice cream, and, above all, young men. Her Oxford diaries from the

---

1. *Barbara Pym, A Very Private Eye: An Autobiography in Diaries and Letters*, edited by Hazel Holt and Hilary Pym (Dutton, 1984).

early 1930s might be those of any other ebullient and romantic young sprig. On one page alone, we find her devoted to black velvet dresses, kangaroos, Moll Flanders, Leslie Howard, "Stormy Weather," and peach-colored lace underwear—an admirable selection. "Disgraceful I know but I can't help choosing my underwear with a view to it being seen!" Barbara Pym was ravenously inquisitive about people herself, so we may reasonably be prompted by the peach underwear to wonder: How far did her string of love affairs (sentimental, unhappy) go? The diaries don't reveal it, apart from one entry in 1932, when she was nineteen: "I went to tea with Rupert (and ate a pretty colossal one)—and he with all his charm, eloquence and masculine wiles, persuaded.... [Here several pages have been torn out.]" This would not be worth curiosity today—but it *was* the 1930s.

Soon the diaries' account of Oxford frolics gives way to a very long-term unrequited love, the first and foremost of a series to last thirty-five years. She stalks the streets where she might meet him, he actually speaks to her ("felt desperately thrilled about him so that I trembled and shivered and went sick"), he is offhand with her, he allows her to type his manuscript for him. Here the world of Sandra (Barbara Pym's assumed name at Oxford) takes a first step toward that of the author of novels of pianissimo love and loss. "I'm beginning to enjoy my pose of romantically unrequited love," she wrote—as twenty years later she was to have Belinda, in *Some Tame Gazelle*, musing that "she was now a contented spinster and her love was like a warm, comfortable garment, bedsocks perhaps, or even woollen combinations."

In 1937 Henry Harvey, the loved one, marries someone else and in the diary she inscribes "*So endete* [*sic*] *eine grosse Liebe*." She writes, however, a brilliant series of letters to him, showy and arch and just slightly edged with malice. How seriously did she mean a later diary entry: "It is the only occasion when one really wants a husband—in a pub with uncongenial company and the feeling of not belonging"?

Meanwhile, a couple of years after Oxford, she had written *Some Tame Gazelle*, in which Henry Harvey figures as the mellifluous but ever so slightly ridiculous Archdeacon Hoccleve. It is typical of a Pym novel that all the teasing is benign, and if there is any hostility toward men for their insensitivity, it vanishes on a breeze of the gentlest ridicule. Women do adore these creatures, is her attitude; isn't it a splendid joke? The book was turned down by publishers, and in 1939 she completed another (still unpublished). Writing had by now become her job: "I honestly don't believe I can be happy unless I am writing. It seems to be the only thing I really want to do." But war was to intervene.

In 1941 she moved to Bristol to do war work in the department of censorship, and shared a large house called the Coppice with a dozen others. Here unrequited love reared its head again. One of the women in the house—a close friend—was divorcing her husband, and Barbara Pym fell in love with him. He of course took the relationship more lightly than she did, and after a while broke it off. It is clear that she went on being unhappy for a long time. But the code of the "excellent women" prevailed—"one always has to pick oneself up again and go on being *drearily splendid*." By this stage in the diary we recognize a muting of feelings, a position somewhere between the larky girl of the early pages and the stoical, amused Miss Pym of middle age:

> Oh mumbling chumbling moths, talking worms and my own intolerable bird give me one tiny ray of hope for the future and I will keep on wanting to be alive. Yes, you will be alive, it will not be the same, nothing will be quite as good, there will be no intense joy but small compensations, spinsterish delights and as the years go on and they are no longer painful, memories.

This is very Stevie Smith! The literary paths of Pym and Smith did occasionally cross; but is there a definite influence there? (Pym was the elder by seven years.) On the whole, I would think not—each was such a solo act, such a special individual. Where they overlap is in something peculiarly English: the stiff upper lip, pain borne with a nod to the ridiculous.[2] A Pym character "copes," carries on being "drearily splendid," and Stevie Smith stands tearstained in church, "faithful but unfortunate."

To escape from her situation Pym next joined the WRNS (the women's navy) and spent some time, notably chic in officer's uniform, in the Mediterranean (even this un-Pymlike experience is brought into the books via the naval officer Rocky in *Excellent Women*). Minor characters in the sentimental procession of unrequited loves came and went. In 1946 she was demobilized and took a job, which she was to keep until retirement, as assistant editor of an anthropological journal, and for a few years there are virtually no diary entries.

Probably this was because she was really writing at last. *Some Tame Gazelle*, written before the war, was offered again and this time accepted. It was published in 1950. "Delightfully amusing," wrote one critic, "but no more to be described than a delicious taste or smell." True: the Pym flavor, whether you like it or find it insipid, is almost impossible to pin down; it makes critical adjectives look gross and clumsy, like big hands in a doll's house. Over the next thirteen years six novels came out. It is striking that, with all the experiences that separated the writing of the first novel when she was twenty-three from the next when in her thirties, her style and type of subject did not change a fraction. From the start she knew the kind of books she intended to write.

In 1963 came the blow: Cape turned down her latest novel (it wouldn't sell, it wasn't what the Sixties wanted), and she entered her fourteen-year period of publishing ostracism. "Drearily splendid"

2. There is a much-loved piece of English vernacular: "Well, if you didn't laugh you'd cry, wouldn't you?" It is only, I think, heard from women.

though she was about it, the diaries contain muted protests against her fate. "In the restaurant all those clergymen helping themselves from the cold table, it seems endlessly. But you mustn't notice things like that if you're going to be a novelist in 1968–9 and the 70s. The posters on Oxford Circus station advertising Confidential Pregnancy Tests would be more suitable." "What is wrong with being obsessed with trivia? Some have criticized *The Sweet Dove* for this. What are the minds of my critics filled with? What nobler and more worthwhile things?" "Mr C in the Library—he is having his lunch, eating a sandwich with a knife and fork, a glass of milk near at hand. Oh why can't I write about things like that any more—why is this kind of thing no longer acceptable?" She continued to write and to send manuscripts around to publishers, but without success. At about this time there was another of her sentimental episodes, the basis of *The Sweet Dove Died*: love for a younger man, fruitless and painful.

In 1974, after an illness, she retired from work to share a country cottage with her sister (oak beams, cats, and a church, unfortunately, that was "not very high")—thus fulfilling the picture she drew at twenty-three in *Some Tame Gazelle* of the two of them as cozy village spinsters. Marmalade-making and patchwork are mentioned and there were, no doubt, vicarage jumble sales. And now comes the moment of high drama—and irony—in Barbara Pym's life. It is 1977, the retired Miss Pym is sixty-three; *The Times Literary Supplement* as a New Year's gimmick runs a feature about the most underrated and most overrated living writers. Independently, two literary personages choose Pym as most underrated. The story makes the front page of *The Times*, and the ball begins to roll. Photographers and interviewers come running; more important, a new publisher snaps up her last two unpublished novels, which come out to friendly reviews. One, in fact, is nominated for the prestigious Booker Prize, though it does not win. She even cracks the American market. The irony, though, is that Barbara Pym is soon to have a terminal return of cancer.

She died in 1980, at sixty-six, in a hospice in Oxford, and her books have acquired something of a minor cult readership. Curiously enough, she seemed to foresee the shape of her life. Twice in her unpublished years she toyed with the idea of being rediscovered: "In about ten years' time, perhaps somebody will be kind enough to discover me, living destitute in cat-ridden squalor." And when she was young she liked to play the game of genteel churchy ladies and was fond of calling herself "spinster" (a word that scarcely has meaning now but certainly did in Barbara Pym's day).

Why the sequence of unattainable, yearned-over men in her life? Hilary Pym has described how formidably attractive and well dressed her elder sister was, and photographs confirm it. But the title of one of the novels, *No Fond Return of Love*, sums up a predominating theme in the life and in the books. Seldom does a Pym woman "get the guy" (with what fastidious amusement she would have regarded such a phrase!). When a friend writes that he is going to spend a year at an Oxford college it sparks off a plot:

> Middle-aged unmarried female don waits eagerly for the autumn when a friend of her Oxford days (the well-known poet, librarian and whatever else you like) is coming to spend a year at All Souls (doing some kind of research, perhaps). At first it is all delightful and they go for beautiful autumnal walks on Shotover (?can one still do this) but unknown to her he has been visiting a jazz club in the most squalid part of the town (where is that now?) and has fallen in love with a nineteen year old girl . . . the ending could be violent if necessary—or he could just go off with the girl, leaving the female don reading Hardy's poems.

Of course, it being a Pym plot, the woman has to be hopeful and then betrayed. It seems that in life and in fiction Barbara Pym could not envisage the plot of woman gratified or triumphant. Perhaps she needed so much to write that love affairs were deliberately chosen for their fruitlessness; a friend, she reports, "thinks perhaps this is the kind of love I've always wanted because absolutely nothing can be done about it." Perhaps what she liked most were moments of sentiment; she remarks on "what a great pleasure and delight there is in being really sentimental.... People who are not sentimental, who never keep relics, brood on anniversaries, kiss photographs good-night and good morning, must miss a good deal."

The diaries were not intended for introspection or psychological complication. When they are not concerned with the various men preoccupying her they act as a kind of ragbag for the odd and Pym-like observation. Lunch hours, for instance, she makes rather a specialty of: overheard conversations in the Kardomah café in Kingsway, rambles around City churchyards where shabby dignified women drink coffee from plastic cups. She keeps modestly up with the times: John Lennon, so "like a very plain middle-aged Victorian female novelist"; and "Did you see on the back of the *Sunday Times* today about the girl who is starting the Orlando Press, erotic books written by women for women? What can they possibly be like? (I shall look out for them with interest.)" Christianity in its mundane details is a recurring note: "Buying Christmas cards in Mowbrays [church shop]—one feels one can't push"; "Why should there be a notice to say 'Marmalade for Sale' in the window of the Hibernian Church Missionary Society?"; a sentence for a novel—"If only, Letty thought, Christianity could have had a British, even an English origin! Palestine was so remote, violence on one's TV screen."

Interspersed among the later diaries are her letters to the poet Philip Larkin, first an epistolary admirer and then, after a nervous meeting, a friend. Larkin, something of a male, poetic Pym (or alternatively she was something of a female, prose Larkin), was an ideal correspondent and the letters seem to hover on the verge of laughter. Tongue-in-cheek, surely, was the discussion of Mr. Larkin's Panama hat ("32/6 seems expensive but not when you think of it as an investment"), Mr. Larkin's doctoral robes ("Is there a floppy hat to go with them? A pity you can't be photographed in them for your 1969 Christmas card—or perhaps you have been?"), and Mr. Larkin's holiday ("Many thanks for your letter, and card from Northern Ireland. It seemed a very original place for a holiday...").

Few diaries give us the whole person and the whole life; most diarists make it a receptacle for a particular kind of diary fodder, and this is true here. We have to glimpse the life sometimes across gaps and between lines. For one thing, in spite of the numberless references to things ecclesiastical, we do not know anything about Barbara Pym's faith—whether it was fiery or *terre-à-terre*, whether it had remained solid since childhood or had fluctuated. Clearly it was central to her life. Curiously, the churchy scene—curates to tea, jumble sales, squabbles over the altar decorations—which to the original generation of her readers was so pleasantly familiar, may be as exotically remote as Jane Austen's settings to present-day readers.

So can her book lead us to understand how it was that she saw her story as "subtle" and "amusing"? It might have had the makings of being tragic, but avoided that. Perhaps it was amusing because, at the least, she never ceased to be an entertainer; and subtle, because she was a subtle person. "Comic and sad and indefinite" sums it up best, as it does all our lives:

> "I'm so glad you write *happy* endings," said Mabel. "After all, life isn't really so unpleasant as some writers make out, is it?" she added hopefully.
>
> "No, perhaps not. It's comic and sad and indefinite—dull, sometimes, but seldom really tragic or deliriously happy, except when one's very young."

4

FEEDING ON LIGHT: SIMONE WEIL

IN SIMONE WEIL's short life we encounter a whole new dimension of solitude: of distress that seems to have begun in childhood, leading on to a tragicomic adulthood, and in the end to an access of vision that has inspired readers of the scattered works she left. Her mother's name for her was "the trolless," her students were to call her "the Martian"; but she also attracted the name of "saint." She worked hard for it—perhaps in protest against the brilliance of her elder brother.

The childhood stories about her are in the convention of the lives of saints: the little girl, when the family moves house, refuses to move until she is given a heavier bundle than anyone else; sends her Easter egg to a soldier at the front; declares that "it would be better if everyone was dressed in the same way and for a *sou*." "Simone is a saint," a servant is reported as saying at some point in her childhood, and this, her biographer Simone Pétrement[1] comments, was the first of many times the word was used to describe her. "There are few men or women who would not feel unworthy to touch such a life," she says. The sanctity of her subject is thus clearly in question from the outset, and we know that the biographer's approach will be to some extent at least hagiographical. Let us make out the case, then, for and against Weil's sanctity.

---

1. *Simone Weil: A Life* (Pantheon, 1976).

She was born in 1909 into a non-Orthodox, gifted, and ambitious Jewish family, a month prematurely and only nine months after her brother André—perhaps not a welcome timing. Something of the family atmosphere is suggested in André's remark that at mealtimes both parents left what they thought were the best bits of food for the other, and so no one ate what he enjoyed. Weil *père* was an anxious and hypersensitive doctor with an obsession about hygiene; Mme. Weil —overpowering, says Pétrement tactfully, in her "passionate love of her dear ones and her noble ambitions for them"—reappears frequently in her daughter's life story, following her from place to place surreptitiously to slip food into the empty larder, clothes into the untidy cupboard, money into the purse depleted by donations or absent-mindedness ("and the disorder! For the last eight days of my stay here I've been slaving from morning to night to get things into a halfway decent state!" runs a letter about her daughter at twenty-two). In the Weil household there were no toys or dolls, reports a governess. But where the two children's education was concerned nothing was spared.

Absolute purity, of intellect, habit, and motive, is the theme to which Weil returns again and again in her writings. Purity began in childhood, for in the Weil household a passionate war against germs was waged: kissing was not allowed for hygienic reasons, and when a family friend tried to kiss the child Simone's hand she is reported to have been terrified and screamed for water. As an adult she could not bear to be touched, writes Pétrement, and "often spoke of her 'disgustingness.'" If we also cast a clinically cold eye on the theme of *eating* which runs through Simone Weil's life, from her refusal to take communion to the headline in 1943 of "French Professor Starves Herself to Death," we have to notice that she used to joke as an adult that she had been poisoned in infancy and that "that's why I am such a failure": her mother had fallen ill when Simone was six months old, and a year of feeding troubles and debilitation followed, complete with the doctor's verdict that the child would not live.

The childish escapades of these two anxiously nurtured children took curious forms: they used to knock at the neighbors' doors and beg for food because, they said, their parents were starving them; and even more ingeniously, refuse to wear socks in winter, and then shiver dramatically with cold when out with their mother in public, begging for warmer clothes.

André was brilliant, especially in mathematics, taking the *baccalauréat* at fourteen. His sister has recorded her reaction in her "Spiritual Autobiography":

> At fourteen I fell into one of those fits of bottomless despair which come with adolescence, and I seriously thought of dying because of the mediocrity of my natural faculties. The exceptional gifts of my brother, who had a childhood and youth comparable to those of Pascal, brought my own inferiority home to me.... After months of inward darkness, I suddenly had the everlasting conviction that no matter what human being, even though practically devoid of natural faculties, can penetrate to the kingdom of truth reserved for genius, if only he longs for truth and perpetually concentrates all his attention upon its attainment.

This was to remain the focus of her life—to be a genius at "truth": a passionate, proud, even frighteningly ambitious decision; and the reason why she is still written about when the precocious Pascal of a brother is not.

At sixteen Simone Weil entered the *khâgne*—the formidable preparatory course for École Normale examinations in philosophy—at the Lycée Henri IV, only a year after it was opened to girls. The impression she made on students and teachers is to appear again and again in the life story. Her friend Gustave Thibon (who came to admire her) was to say of their first meeting, "I had the impression of being face to face with an individual who was radically foreign to all my ways of feeling and thinking." Her clothes, for one thing, were always atrocious enough—though they might well have passed in north Oxford—to provoke exasperation as much as hilarity among her compatriots (on a later occasion her students stood guard while they made her put her sweater on the right way around behind the blackboard). At the École Normale it was proposed at one time that the annual skit be built around her, rather than around the staff in traditional fashion. The first impression, says Pétrement, was "that some common element of humanity was missing in her.... Many of her old classmates, when they finally read her writings, were surprised to discover that she was so human." Yet the photographs show a lively, cheeky child and an adolescent face that, without the glasses, could as easily have modeled itself into that of a *grande amoureuse* as of the archetypal spinster schoolmistress.

She passed well—though as always at the cost of overwork and blinding headaches—into the École Normale, and adequately well out of it, having earned the nickname of the Red Virgin for her political views. Posted to teach in Le Puy, she involved herself heavily in trade union work, workers' education, and demonstrations—not at the time as respectable as they are now—that led to a local uproar. Not the least of the opposition's case in the *affaire Le Puy* seems to have been that Mlle. Weil had been seen shaking hands with an unemployed stone breaker in front of her *lycée*; her defendants, on the other hand, argued for freedom of opinion for state employees, and her pupils signed a petition in favor of their teacher. "The proletarians don't need a Joan of Arc. Let her do her job and stay in her place" was the reaction of a left-wing colleague; another commented more charitably, "These are the things one does when young, and they are beautiful rather than useful."

Two further teaching posts followed without scandal, though her relations with colleagues were usually hostile. Most of her pupils failed their examinations. The *professeur*, wrote an inspector summoned specially to assess her work, although clearly of intellectual distinction, spoke confusedly and without lifting her eyes from the page, while her students "strained to take notes about which they understood nothing."

Toward the end of her Le Puy period she went down a coal mine, and the article she wrote afterward shows that her political thinking was already sensitive: it is the nature of the work and the machinery, she argued, that is oppressive, and it is not easily altered by crude political changes. In view of her inability to compromise on any point she was not, of course, a Communist Party member even at this time. Her view of the USSR was always consistent: "a bureaucratic, military, and police dictatorship that has nothing socialist or communist about it but the name."

The need to understand at first hand how industrial working conditions could be made tolerable was the theoretical reason for her decision to leave teaching for a period of manual work in factories. To hold political opinions without relevant practical experience was, she felt, totally hypocritical: that none of the Bolshevik leaders had set foot in a factory, or had any direct experience of the worker's life, made politics "a sinister farce." Beyond this genuinely felt belief was a driving need to *experience* rather than to cerebrate: "To act as much as I can. And that is all." So runs one of the conclusions in the moving and painful examination of herself that she wrote around this time, in which she accuses herself above all of "idleness"—irresponsibility, the substitution of thought for action. And still further beyond this motive we can discern the wistfulness of a longing for community: when a friend described a feeling of joy and belonging at the sight of a lighted factory at night she wrote back that this "went straight to my heart. I felt the same as you, ever since I was a child." And so at twenty-five, having applied for leave to "study industry," with the help of some influence from friends she was hired as a power-press operator. "It won't be possible to stop her. It is better that she do it with you; at least the experience could be kept under some sort of surveillance" was the comment that accompanied her engagement—the kind of comment that was to accompany other ventures.

The months of factory work (broken by periods of sick leave) turned out as might have been predicted: ineffably clumsy, exhausted, unable to keep up the minimum piecework rate, finding none of the "fraternity" she had expected, she discovered that external circumstances can annihilate the soul as well as the body, and that she was not only the most inefficient of workers but lacked the energy to study conditions or conceive of ways to ameliorate them. The discovery that unskilled industrial work fostered not comradeship and revolt but cowed self-interest increased her political pessimism. Pétrement believes that the experience marked a turning point: the mischievousness, the energy, the wish to *épater le bourgeois* were left behind; the mood darkened. Weil wrote that from her factory experience onward she felt branded with the mark of "slave."

But the longing to be a participant in no way diminished; six months later, during her Easter vacation, she went to work on a farm. The experiment was not a success: "When we offered her a fine cream cheese, she pushed it away, saying the little Indochinese were hungry." Also, Mlle. Weil never changed her clothes, could not milk a cow, and deeply embarrassed the farmer's family by asking them to "sum up their desires." All in all it would be appreciated, said Mme. Belleville, the farmer's wife, if she could go and do her work somewhere else. So much study seemed to have driven the poor young lady out of her wits.

Meanwhile the Spanish Civil War had broken out. In 1936, Weil crossed into Spain; unknown to her, the Weil family trailed behind, ever anxious to forestall the trolless's latest prank. Speaking not a word of Spanish, she proposed herself at once for a mission behind the Fascist lines to look for the leader of the POUM, who had disappeared.

She was angry when her unsuitability for the job was pointed out, but managed to attach herself to a small commando group. After a few days with them, left behind with the cook because her rifle shooting was a danger to one and all, she walked into a frying pan of boiling oil and burned herself badly. She reached Barcelona, where her parents were desperately looking for her, and within six weeks of the start of the venture the reunited family was back in France.

From now until the outbreak of the Second World War three years later, Simone Weil virtually abandoned paid work, although there was a brief period of teaching. But with each term she renewed her application for sick leave: her burns were still uncomfortable, she suffered from "anemia and fatigue," and in particular her headaches had become crippling and continuous. Throughout this period she poured out a stream of writings on current issues, most of them unsent letters and unpublished drafts for articles: on industrial relations, on colonialism, on pacifism. The drift of them all, ultimately, is pessimistic: there is never a solution since for any decision, any taking sides involves compromise and "impurity." The Spanish struggle should be abandoned because neither side is pure in heart; Hitler cannot be resisted by those with the stain of colonialism on their hands; relations between labor and capital are insoluble—"social order, though necessary, is essentially bad, whatever kind it may be...."

Her own personal state of mind is revealed in a letter that was probably written during these years:

> My situation is the following. I am not up to doing anything, whatever it might be, and this goes for all kinds of work. I cannot do any work without a great effort, without the anguish of the swimmer who wonders whether he will have the strength to reach the shore.... Since nonetheless I live, reflect, go forward, I become more and more aware of what I carry in my belly; and if I must speak to you with complete sincerity, I have the

> conviction that it contains the germs of great things. This contradiction involves a despair.... So then, as you say, there is no way out. Or rather this is the way out: keep on pushing myself as long as it will be possible for me—and when the disproportion between the tasks that have to be accomplished and my ability to work will have become too great, then die.

As she abandoned hopes of personal or social solutions she was turning more and more to the *vie intérieure* and to Catholicism. It was during these years that she began to experience the mystical intimations she describes in *Waiting on God*, and to keep her notebooks. The question of baptism into the Church preoccupied her more and more, but she maintained to the end that she must stay outside it. Partly it was a question of intellectual flaws in the Church's teaching. But, more flatly, she wrote that "I feel it is not permissible for me. I feel it is necessary and ordained that I should be alone, a stranger and an exile in relation to every human circle without exception."

The course of Weil's life after the outbreak of war is probably the best-known part of it. André Weil had deserted to Scandinavia (for which he was later to be brought to trial in France). Simone refused to leave Paris, and the desperate Weil parents refused to leave *her*; she capitulated on the day before the Germans reached the city and, without even returning for luggage, the family managed to get places on a train for Vichy. After Vichy came Marseilles, and the important meeting with Father Perrin, to whom she was to address most of her religious writings; a spell of agricultural work, more successful than the first one; North Africa, and then a liner for New York, from where she believed it would be easy to get to England and be assigned to Resistance work. During this time she was bombarding the authorities with two plans that she passionately believed in: in 1939, a plan to parachute troops into Czechoslovakia to foment a Czech uprising (yes, all those involved would die, she admitted, but "they will die with dignity"); later, a scheme for taking a corps of nurses to the front to treat the wounded on the spot. The sine qua non of both plans, of course, was that she be included in the mission. The authorities paid not the slightest attention; "but she is mad" is De Gaulle's reported comment. At the end of 1942 she succeeded in getting a passage for England.

She was to live for another nine months. In London she was given an office and the job of reporting on projects for the postwar reconstruction of France. In this office she wrote and wrote, sometimes through the night: about justice and charity, the irreducibility of good, the needs of the soul, sin and human obligation, grace, necessity, punishment, responsibility, charity. This was tolerated. But her interminable pleas to be sent to France for the Resistance were not so indulgently treated by her busy superiors. To the self-evident fact that she would get herself captured at once and endanger others' lives she turned deaf ears and eyes blinded by obsession. At home she slept on the floor as usual, ate little, and wrote reassuring letters to her parents in New York.

In the end she realized she was not going to be sent to France. She fell ill; an early stage of tuberculosis was diagnosed and she was taken to a hospital. She grew worse; and when she refused the lung operation prescribed for her—the most difficult patient he had ever had, the doctor commented—she was discharged and removed to a sanatorium. She died there within a month.

The coroner's verdict—"the deceased did kill and slay herself by refusing to eat while the balance of her mind was disturbed"—was both true and not true. From the time that she left France she had indulged her disinclination to eat by refusing to take more than the French civilian would be getting at home. "To Simone, eating seemed a base and disgusting function," recalled her friend Bercher; she had been delighted when he told her about the metabolism of the hibernating animal and about a nun who had lived for years on nothing but the eucharist—but "when I told these stories to Simone...I had the sensation that I was both giving her pleasure and doing her *harm*. That was how it was with this creature who was at war with her own life." At the sanatorium she would take nothing with milk in it, and at the end almost nothing at all. Yet she wanted food. Before dying she asked for a *brioche*, and for *pommes mousseline* prepared by a French cook. But in England in 1943 these were not available—any more than the absolutely disinterested political program, the perfectly loving friendship, the totally rational religious dogma had been.

Three things stand out from Weil's life story. One is that although, as Pétrement sums up, she never ceased to fight oppression, always obstinately looked for truth, loved beauty, and was generous with her time, money, and effort; although a number of people recognized and appreciated her qualities; yet she was also continually ridiculous, and left confusion and exasperation everywhere behind her. Out for a walk with an acquaintance, she saw a peasant plowing and insisted on taking a turn; she overturned the plow at once, much to the owner's fury. In Marseilles, given Resistance pamphlets to distribute, she dropped the lot in the street in front of the passersby. Her friend Thibon, a genuine but a clearsighted admirer, describes her arrival to start work on his farm: finding his modest house too comfortable, she insisted on sleeping out-of-doors, to the accompaniment of much argument; finally a half-ruined hut was found and "we settled her in there, not without a few complications for everyone. It would have been so much simpler otherwise!" Again and again we read of the connivance of family or friends to suggest that the special cut of meat that was all she would touch was a cheap one, that the private hospital room had been ordered by the doctor. To do ordinary work, eat ordinary food, be ill in an ordinary place, were the least of her self-abnegating desires, but they were beyond her. And yet Thibon came to appreciate her quality, "a limpid mysticism" and understanding of religion.

Secondly we are aware—in her life, it must be stressed, not in her best writing—of a blind spot so large that at times it covered up her whole vision. She who so lucidly described in her writing the need for obedience, the temptations of spiritual pride, was in life blind to her own powerful will, her self-contempt, her ambition, and her obsessions. "If she's an angel, she's surely a sergeant-major angel," her brother once remarked. To "do her job and stay in her place," as her colleague recommended during her revolutionary phase, was the last thing possible; there was perhaps too much of the childhood game still to be played of going without socks in winter to shame her family. She knew, because she wrote it, that "love for our neighbor, being made of creative attention, is analogous to genius"; but as Thibon says, "she loved her neighbor with all her being, and in her devotion she often overlooked the real desires and needs of others."

But thirdly, we can see in her life story a human being so isolated, so self-deprecating, so desperate for community and affection that it is hardly imaginable. Yet her former classmates, when they came to read her writings, were "surprised to discover that she was so human." She was by no means without irony or humor but, chillingly, there is not a joke recorded in Pétrement's biography that is not against herself and her deficiencies. "It is not by chance that you have never been loved," she wrote in her notebook. In her teens she had invented an imaginary friend who would find and understand her one day; the nearest to this, perhaps, was the half-blind, elderly Father Perrin with whom she corresponded in the last two years of her life. To him she wrote:

> Nothing better enables me to measure the breadth of your charity than the fact that you bore with me for so long and with such gentleness.... It is true that you have not the same motives as I have myself...for feeling hatred and repulsion towards me. But all the same I feel that your patience with me can only spring from a supernatural generosity; and I think that except you, all those human beings for whom I have made it easy to hurt me

> through my friendship, have amused themselves by doing so.... They did not behave like this from malice, but as a result of the well-known phenomenon which makes hens rush upon one of their number if it is wounded, attacking and pecking it.

"I am a badly cut-off piece of God," she said in the hospital; and we think of Kierkegaard's "despair at willing to be oneself," of the being who feels he is God's slip of the pen and in a rage against the author will not be corrected or comforted; and even, to be harsh, of Nietzsche's "meanest of conspiracies, the conspiracy of those who suffer against those who succeed"—"in this swamp-soil of self-contempt, every poisonous weed flourishes, and all so small, so secret, so dishonest, and so sweetly rotten."

Yet her passion, her intellectual heresy, as Bercher pointed out to her, was her insistence on "purity": the great heresy of the Cathars, whom she so much admired, with their celibacy, their separateness, their belief that the material world was hell. The desire for purity is the source of all heresies, he told her: "Remember the Cathars! Man is not pure but a 'sinner.' And the sinner must stink a bit at the least." If truth were not as pure and unadulterated as her brother's mathematics she was unsatisfied: "The straight line is what I draw when I am thinking of the purely straight. Truth is what I think...when desiring the purely true." To accept and eat the Christian eucharist would have been earthly, impure. What she wanted was not of this earth: to "have her cake and eat it."

If this seems a hard indictment, it is only to say that, after all, Weil was a human being and *not* a saint. Except for those with a literal interest in canonization, her faults should be of no more importance in the end than the fact that Beethoven kept a full chamber pot under the piano or that Samuel Johnson had a compulsion to collect orange peels. For the best of her writing on the spiritual life does indeed have the quality of a straight line, and this is a fruit of, and inseparable from, her clownish, emphatic attempts to live out her knowledge. She

> wanted to be flexible to every movement of the divine will [but] could not bear the course of events or the kindness of her friends changing by one inch the position of the stakes with which her own will had marked her path of immolation.... And the way she mounted guard around her void still paid witness to a terrible preoccupation with herself.... Her *ego*, as it were, was like a word that she may perhaps have succeeded in *obliterating*, but that was still *underlined*.

This was Gustave Thibon's summing-up. Yet from her writings we see that there was not one of the pitfalls she fell into that she did not in theory know about. "We must not even become attached to detachment," she wrote; and "imitation of the solitude of God; that is the worst form of idolatry." "The pleasures of the senses," she knew, "are everything that is innocent...so long as the soul does not try to lose itself by filling up a void." Redemption is to be found "by an act of attention and consent," not by muscular efforts of the will: "the will cannot produce any good in the soul."

We seldom have the chance to see distinctly laid out the special dangers of the spiritual life, the taking of the thought for the deed, the hair's breadth separating pride and humility. Weil's life became in fact a triumph; for in some of her writing she came to achieve the intransigent lucidity she wanted, and in a manner that could not have been done by anyone able to compromise with the world and "common sense." But as a person rather than a writer we can feel sad for her, for although she knew that "there is only one fault: incapacity to feed upon light," this can never be acted on.

Her death, in those wartime years, was not much noticed—nor were her sparse published works known to many outside her own clique in France. It was during the 1950s and 1960s that her work began to appear posthumously, first in French, then in English translation. Lectures, essays, letters; in 1952 *The Need for Roots* (*L'Enracinement*), with a preface by T. S. Eliot; *Gravity and Grace* (*La Pesanteur et la grace*) in 1958. Now she began to be compared to Wittgenstein, to Bertrand Russell. I think myself that there is more of a likeness to Kierkegaard's grim struggles with truth.

Though she had felt her short life of thirty-four years to have been fumbled and crazed, in the end it hardly mattered: everything had been observed and assimilated. In a late letter from England to her mother in the States, she writes about the value of the Fool in *Lear*, the outsider so ignored that he can be a channel for truth. She had no objection, I think, to taking on the role.

Right up until her death she was filling up notebooks[2] with her final insights: on self-surrender, prayer, time, choice, suffering; on Plato, Freud, Homer; the Book of Job, the Gospels in Greek, the myths of Egypt and Greece; Descartes, Dostoevsky. A copy of George Herbert's poem "Love." "Love bade me welcome; yet my soul drew back," it begins; and ends "So I did sit and eat." But she feared to eat.

---

2. *The Notebooks*, Vols. 1 and 2 (Putnam, 1956).

5

SILENCED: NADIA

IN 1974 A SIX-YEAR-OLD girl was brought by a worried mother to the child development center at Nottingham University. Her parents were living in England as Ukrainian refugees; there were two siblings, both of them normal children who were bilingual in Ukrainian and English. But Nadia was enclosed in a bubble of silence: slow and passive, with almost no speech, she attended a school for severely subnormal children. Her early years had been disturbed by traumas and illness; the psychologist who studied her felt that she was autistic rather than simply psychiatrically disturbed.

At the time she was assessed Nadia could, rather clumsily, walk and run about, but not dress or feed herself properly. Except when tested on certain perceptual puzzles, her level of intelligence was more or less beneath assessment, as she could not understand or cooperate on most tests. Though she was happy sitting on her mother's lap, to most people, whether adults or children, she paid little attention. She was moved to a special school for autistic children.

But one thing about Nadia was special: her drawings. Lorna Selfe has compiled a book that contains some hundred reproductions of drawings produced by Nadia from the age of three onward.[1] From a

---

1. *Nadia: A Case of Extraordinary Drawing Ability in an Autistic Child* (Academic Press, 1977).

child of this kind, the existence of even one such drawing, let alone so many, raises enormously complex questions about the nature of intelligence and of artistic processes.

But is this not loading with excessive significance an abnormal child's gifted scribbles? Is it inconceivable that such a child should have special skills of hand and eye? And are the drawings really so exceptional? Selfe's achievement is that, without losing her way in jargon, she can make clear just how great a puzzle the drawings do pose, and how central are the issues they raise.

To do this she outlines Nadia's background and personality; summarizes the assessments of her abilities; describes her way of drawing and choosing subjects; compares it with what has been observed about the drawings of various types of children (normal, gifted, retarded, deaf-mute, autistic); and discusses the numerous implications, suggesting a very tentative explanation of Nadia's extraordinary gift. As we follow her exposition we are able to see that it is extraordinary, and that it leads to the central question of the book: What is actually involved in artistic representation?

It has been assumed that two interdependent factors determine the development of representation from the child's first scribble to skilled adult art: increasing intelligence, in the sense of the ability to notice, organize, and more and more successfully transfer visual observations onto a flat surface; and the work of other artists, seen in anything from comic books to masterpieces, from which the conventions for representing perspective, mass, and movement are learned. The latter factor is implicit in E.H. Gombrich's analysis of the adult artist's creation of a perceptual "code" from the work of his contemporaries[2]; the former assumption comes from looking at children's pictures and the stages they almost invariably go through.

After the stage of scribbling haphazardly for pleasure, most children

---

2. *Art and Illusion* (Pantheon, 1960).

first attempt to represent a face or figure; by four or five years old, torsos, arms, and legs are rather haphazardly in place; and after five come more details, more control of line, and simple backgrounds to figures. Attempts at perspective do not usually start before at least seven years old; and not until nine or later do most children stop drawing diagrams of what they *know* to be there and start grappling with the problems of representing what they *see*—using shading, foreshortening, the suggestion of movement and relative position. Most people do not get very far along this road; the talented eventually learn the successful techniques of lifelike realism. The very talented, later still, discard literalism, simplify, and acquire a personal style with its valuable idiosyncrasies and distortions. Such work, as we know, paradoxically has *more* life and reality in it than the photographic copy.

Looking at Nadia's drawings in relation to these norms we can more vividly see how freakish they are. The influence of other art may be there (she seldom drew from life), but only of picture books and magazines, which are utterly transformed in her copies. Far more striking is that her drawing never went through the slow stages of childish art: her earliest drawings, done at the age of three, show the same free, confident line that she used at five and six, though rather cruder. Lorna Selfe points out some of the specific achievements of the drawings—the fullness of detail, the correctness of perspective, the placing of standing where it is needed—but analysis cannot pin down the fine, flowing movement of Nadia's line, its indefinable quality of style. It is seen at its clearest when one of her drawings is next to the picture book original (reproduced in Selfe's book) or to the uninspired adult drawings the author made for Nadia to copy.

Intelligence has always been assumed to be linked with the progress of children's drawing; so much so that one intelligence test actually consists of drawing a figure and is scored on such points as eye–hand coordination, number of details used, and correct proportioning. The challenge to the rationale of such a test—that the child's drawing is directly related to his or her conceptual grasp of its subject—is shown most strikingly by the fact that Nadia's intelligence quotient, on the other tests pitifully low or unassessable, would be a brilliant 160 on this one.

This is where the crux of the problem of the drawings lies. The representation of space, perspective, and proportion must involve complex conceptualization—that is, "intelligence"; and the vast majority of children's drawings would seem to confirm that in early childhood general intelligence and "drawing intelligence" run nearly enough parallel to be considered as aspects of one process of intellectual growth. Rudolf Arnheim, after praising the cognitive achievement involved in merely drawing a chimney straight instead of diagonally against a roof, writes that "as the mind grows subtler, it becomes capable of incorporating the intricacies of perceptual appearance, thereby obtaining a richer image of reality, which suits the more differentiated thinking of the developed mind." How then did a retarded, speechless, uncomprehending child manage to grasp the complexities represented in these drawings? How, for instance, was she able to look at a crude illustration of an animal she had seldom seen in real life, retain the memory of it for a considerable period, and then correctly draw it in a *different position*?

It has been taken for granted, too, that after the scribbling stage the younger child is more concerned to make a kind of diagram of what is in front of him than to represent what he sees, and over and over again children's drawings confirm this. Gombrich has illustrated this well in his reproduction of an eleven-year-old's copy of Constable's *Wivenhoe Park*; as he says, it is "really a tidy enumeration of the principal items of the picture, particularly those that would interest a child"—and far more "childish" than the five-year-old Nadia's drawings.

Implicit, perhaps, in this (though neither Gombrich nor Arnheim would assume it) is that children use language to mediate between seeing and drawing. Nadia's muteness, therefore, also raises the question of the relation of speech to intelligence—an old question that has never had a satisfactory answer. Early psychological experiments suggested that judgments and decisions could be easily made without any verbal thinking; but introspection fell out of favor under behaviorist influence, and the question has languished. Research with deaf (and therefore dumb) children has had contradictory results. *Nadia* makes us rethink the relation of language and intelligence, and envisage a kind of rare eye–hand cognition that bypasses words but can observe, abstract, memorize, and reproduce rather like that of the brilliant but inarticulate soccer player. In theory, this is not an extraordinary idea; in practice, it has hardly ever been found to occur. Retarded children's drawings have been studied and found to be generally poorer and more stereotyped than normal children's; even deaf children's pictures tend to lag behind until they reach the age of eleven or twelve.

One final question raised by Nadia's work is that of the nature of autism—equally difficult and controversial. It is only in the past fifty-odd years that autism has been distinguished from straightforward inborn mental retardation; it is not always certain that they do not overlap, and the specific cause of the autistic syndrome—psychological damage versus organic—has been highly debatable. What distinguishes the autistic child from the severely backward one is, generally speaking, a massive avoidance of human contact,[3] a passionate insistence

---

3. In *An Anthropologist on Mars* (Knopf, 1995) Oliver Sacks describes his meeting with Temple Grandin, an extraordinary woman who was diagnosed as autistic at three years old. She has learned speech, and—with difficulty—some interaction with other human beings. But she feels happier with animals, and works as an animal biologist in Colorado; social rituals, jokes, and fictional stories she simply finds baffling. Because as a child she longed for contact yet could not bear it, she had constructed a "squeeze machine" in which she can lie and be held. Perhaps we might all like such an installation? Perhaps the interest shown in autism springs from some withdrawn but unrecognized streak in all of us? Simone Weil (see chapter 4) surely suffered from some degree of autism.

on stereotyped rituals, very little speech in spite of normal hearing, and often flashes of skill or comprehension that should be beyond the ability of subnormal children. The autistic child seems to have some complete breakdown in the sense of self and of communication with other selves, while the child who used to be labeled retarded, subnormal, or backward progresses somewhat like other children but far more slowly. Bruno Bettelheim's work in laboriously leading autistic children toward normality has revealed a great deal about the syndrome, but few have agreed with him that it is the result of a hostile environment in infancy. Autistic children, for one thing, usually have normal siblings who survive the same environment without damage.

Nadia's methods of drawing were distinctly autistic (were, because after her move to the school for autistic children she more or less stopped drawing). She seems to have seldom drawn the people around her, as normal children usually do, and seldom from life; the only life drawings included in Selfe's book are a series of detached feet and legs drawn at a time when Nadia was obsessed with watching and touching feet. She would only use ballpoint pens for her work, and simply scribbled if offered paints or crayons; she would draw on inappropriate material like newspaper, and draw over the edge onto the table if the figure was too big. A few of the pictures are distinctly bizarre, with grotesque eyes or tiny heads on skillfully drawn bodies; new sketches bulge out of existing ones turned sideways. There are no backgrounds, no scenes of things happening, such as children usually attempt, nothing representing two figures in relationship; we remember that Nadia's vocabulary consisted of a few single words but no two-word phrases.

If autism does imply potentially normal intelligence that has gone into retreat for some reason, there remains a loophole for the association of intellectual skill with drawing skill: Nadia may have channeled her "frozen" intelligence into drawing. Bettelheim quotes an autistic boy who answered a request to subtract four from ten by drawing a hexagon; he sees this kind of response as a typically autistic evasion of direct communication and believes that many of the bizarre or "stupid" actions of autistic children actually show great ingenuity toward this end. Lorna Selfe does not explore this possibility, but prefers, though very tentatively, a physiological explanation: she suggests that Nadia may have had brain damage to the speech areas of the left hemisphere of the brain, and compensated for it with overdeveloped drawing skill; she suggests that language may even block the development of such skill in normal children rather than facilitate it. It does indeed seem likely that Nadia's drawing was a kind of compensation, for after she was taught to talk a little, to work with simple numbers, and to copy letters, she stopped drawing spontaneously.

Even if the drawings were a compensation for her handicap, however, we are still left with the fact that few autistic children draw like geniuses—the Afro-Caribbean boy Stephen Wiltshire, described by Sir Hugh Casson as "possibly the best child artist in Britain" when he was eleven, being one other example. We are left with the question of what drawing talent really is. Nadia's case may be freakish, but every child talented far ahead of her contemporaries in one of the arts is an enigma. The adult artist has had years to learn to concentrate his or her energies into one channel; but why the achievement of the young Mozart or Picasso, or of any child whose talent far outruns that of contemporaries, and of his own other abilities? What is it that Nadia had *so much* of? To return to Lorna Selfe's central question: What is involved in pictorial representation?

And who, really, *was* Nadia? There is a common cliché on the lines of "Inside every fat person there is a thin one trying to get out" that could be adapted to her. Once, in later childhood, one of her horse drawings reappeared on a steamed-up window: it was like a message from someone locked away inside the slow, bewildered child.

II

PARTNERS AND MUSES

6

HOLDING THE BABY: CLEMENTINE CHURCHILL

A MEMBER OF the women's forces told Mary Soames, the youngest daughter of Winston and Clementine Churchill, how she used to look down from her office window in wartime, often after a night of heavy bombing, and see the prime minister's wife, immaculately dressed, going for a walk alone in the park behind Downing Street. The story gives us a glimpse of the isolation that attended this handsome, shrewd, hardworking woman, happy in her marriage, surrounded with people and tasks and her children. Behind her façade of cool poise and her unfailing conscientiousness, says her daughter, she was both shy and passionate, and few people were allowed to get near her. Being the support and confidante of a public man at times only emphasized the isolation.

There was nothing in her childhood to persuade Clementine Hozier that the world was to be trusted. She was six when her highly incompatible parents separated; her mother had been found dabbling in adultery, and although her father had evidently done likewise, it was enough to give him the whip hand forever after. Money—by the standards of her class and time—was kept short, and her mother, though of excellent birth, was made déclassée by the separation. Clementine and her sister were first sent to live abroad with their father, then sent to an oppressive boarding school, then kidnapped from it, more or less, by their mother and taken to live with her. Some years later the father made an abortive kidnapping effort on his own account. In the meantime life was lived in a succession of lodgings and relatives' houses, and always under the shadow of her more brilliant elder sister, their mother's favorite. When Clementine was fourteen this much-loved sister died.

It was an unusual thing for a girl of her class, however poor, to be sent to school rather than educated at home by governesses, and she not only loved it but became a suffragist and dreamed of university. This of course was out of the question; and her mother found a kind-hearted relative who helped with the expense of launching Clementine into society. By then she was beautiful, and she was twice engaged (and disengaged). When she met Churchill she was twenty-two and he ten years older; the course of true love ran conventionally smooth, though it was daring to accept an invitation to Blenheim Palace without having a personal maid. But she went, and the proposal was in the pattern of the marriage that was to follow: an early morning assignment in the rose garden; Clementine was punctual; Winston overslept.

Mary Soames justly subtitled her biography of her mother "The Biography of a Marriage,"[1] and without sentimentality it must be said that the Churchills' fifty-seven-year marriage seems to have been, for all its imperfections, the best thing that could have happened to either of them. Churchill was an egoist and a go-getter and had a vulgar streak; devotion to his fanatically loyal and scrupulous wife tempered his self-will. On her side, though clearly she was always an anxious and perfectionist woman who suffered from his vagaries, she had as well the satisfaction of knowing how much she was loved and depended on. If Churchill's ambition and extravagance had not been balanced by an irreproachable home life, might his career have been very different? Lloyd George told Churchill his wife was his

1. *Clementine Churchill: The Biography of a Marriage* (Houghton Mifflin, 1979).

"salvation." (She did not quite reciprocate the compliment: "I know he likes me, but he is a sneak...tho' he seems to recover again & again from his muddles & mistakes I am not sure his partner would; she would instead be saddled with the whole lot while Ll-G skipped off laughing.")

Churchill was seventy-one when he wrote to his wife: "I feel so tenderly towards you my darling & the more pleasant & agreeable the scenes & days, the more I wish you were here to share them & give me a kiss." When he wrote, "Do you love me? I feel so deeply interwoven with you that I follow yr movements at every turn & in all circumstances.... Do cable every few days, just to let me know all is well & that you are happy when you think of me," they had been married thirty years; she cabled back, "My darling. My thoughts are with you nearly all the time and though basking in lovely sunshine and blue seas I miss you and home terribly. Tender love. Clemmie." On their eleventh anniversary he had written, "It is a rock of comfort to have yr love & companionship at my side," and she to him, "Darling, you have been the great event in [my life]. You took me from the straitened little by-path I was treading and took me with you into the life & colour & jostle of the highway.... I have been happier every year since we started."

There are other very moving passages. But the reason that the marriage is well documented is that in fact, in spite of their affection, they were much apart. It was not only the times when Winston's career took him away; they spent many holidays apart. Clementine had too much taste to enjoy the vulgarities of the rich French Riviera set that Churchill liked ("God—the Riviera is a ghastly place," she wrote, and "I am suffocated with luxury and ennui"); and he was not to be persuaded that the beach at Frinton or museums in Paris could be enjoyed. There is the implication in Lady Soames's discreet book (almost too discreet—there is little mention of drinking, for instance) that though her mother's story is indeed the story of a marriage, and of a good one, it was a marriage that put much strain on Clementine, as much because of Churchill's demanding temperament as because of the stresses of politics. And there was no one, really, in her life except her husband.

It was of course normal for women in her position to have their children brought up by nannies; but she seems to have been a rather unusually remote mother. The young couple doted on their babies and grieved bitterly when one died; yet it is odd to read remarks like this from Clementine: "Meanwhile I have had much leisure to play with & observe the 'kittens.' You will be surprised to hear that they are getting quite fond of me. I am finding out a lot of things about them. They ask occasionally with solicitude & respect about you...." When their son Randolph, in 1942, joined a parachute unit, she was greatly upset—not, as one might expect, because of the danger to him but because it would add an extra worry to his father's life. There is something a little chilling about this.

"We soon became aware," writes Lady Soames, "that our parents' main interest and time were consumed by immensely important tasks, besides which our own demands and concerns were trivial. We never expected either of our parents to attend our school plays, prize-givings, or sports' days." Clearly she was herself the reliable and the favored daughter, though she does not say as much. Here the question of the great British nanny comes in. The elder children had a succession of them while Mary, as youngest, was lucky enough to have a long-term substitute mother just as Churchill himself had had. About the mishaps and tragedies that dogged her siblings' adult lives—drink, suicide, etc.—Soames is understandably reticent.

At the time of their wedding in 1908 Churchill already had a lifetime in miniature of adventures and successes behind him: fighting in four wars, the authorship of three books, escapades as the South African correspondent of the *Morning Post* when he was captured by the Boers and escaped, and eight years in politics, with a recent rise to Cabinet rank. And there were lifetimes of experience to come, for both of them. He was to be Home Secretary, then First Lord of the Admiralty; then after the Dardanelles disaster in the second year of the Great War—"God bless the Dardanelles," Diana Churchill at six put in her prayers, aware that the word had some ominous sense—resigned, went to the trenches for five months, then came back as Minister of Munitions. During the 1920s he held high offices; but in 1929 his ten years "in the wilderness" as a backbencher began. It was in 1939, as far as history is concerned, that his real life started. Clementine Churchill had been asked during the Thirties whether she thought he would ever be prime minister. "No, unless some great disaster were to sweep the country, and no one could wish for that," she had answered.

She was indeed always remarkably shrewd, and though Churchill seldom took anyone's advice when he really wanted to do something, her good sense must have influenced him. When it did not, and his lack of flair for understanding other people's feelings led the bull to charge into the china shop, she was usually vindicated. She never approved of the "heroic" dash to defend Antwerp during the First World War that led some of his colleagues to consider him an unstable poseur. She recognized that his support for the King during the abdication crisis would tell against him. She spotted the appalling sentence in the 1945 election broadcast just after the Nazi defeat—that Labour planning would be enforced by "some kind of Gestapo"—but he refused to delete it. And by worrying compulsively about money she kept some sort of check on Churchill's expansive gestures.

Records have survived of some of her wise counsel, because she learned to write out informal memos rather than to tackle her husband personally about problems. In the bad days of 1940, when his always unreliable behavior was deteriorating under stress, she wrote:

> My Darling,
>
> I hope you will forgive me if I tell you something I feel you ought to know.

> One of the men in your entourage (a devoted friend) has been to me & told me that there is a danger of your being generally disliked by your colleagues and subordinates because of your rough sarcastic & overbearing manner....
>
> My Darling Winston, I must confess that I have noticed a deterioration in your manner; & you are not as kind as you used to be.... I cannot bear that those who serve the Country & yourself should not love you as well as admire and respect you—
>
> Besides you won't get the best results by irascibility & rudeness. They will breed either dislike or a slave mentality. (Rebellion in War time being out of the question!)
>
> Please forgive your loving devoted & watchful
> Clemmie

Though she was the most loyal of colleagues to her husband, clearly it was not quite a question of "He for politics only, she for politics in him." Lady Soames suggests that her mother's feelings were always more with the Liberals, whom Churchill deserted in 1924. And as early as 1912, as wife of the anti-suffragette Churchill, she had written a spirited letter to *The Times* in reply to one opposing votes for women on psychological and physiological grounds. Hers appeared under the heading "Ought Not Women to Be Abolished?"

> After reading Sir Almroth Wright's able and weighty exposition of women as he knows them the question seems no longer to be "Should women have votes?" but "Ought women not to be abolished altogether?"...We learn from him that in their youth they are unbalanced, that from time to time they suffer from unreasonableness and hypersensitiveness...and...later on in life they are subject to grave and long-continued mental disorders, and, if not quite insane, many of them have to be shut up.... May we not look to Sir Almroth Wright to crown his

> many achievements by delivering mankind from the parasitic, demented, and immoral species which has infested the world for so long?

She was not a do-gooder, and of course was enclosed in the outlook of her upbringing and class, yet when she was traveling in Barbados she wrote to Winston of tin shacks, undernourishment, and disease—"And this is a sample of the British Empire upon which the Sun never sets." During the Blitz she undertook to inspect the shelters in which London housed itself at night. She was appalled and straightaway recommended stringent delousing, plenty of buckets for lavatories, and bunks large enough for human beings.

The story of the last years is, inevitably, a little sad: Churchill's infirmities and his stubborn refusal to retire for so long; the strain on his wife who, like other political wives, longed for a peaceful period out of the public eye. "One must always hope for a sudden end, before faculties decay," he had written to her in 1939, but neither of them was granted that blessing. Mentions of Clementine's needing to rest, get away, have a break, become frequent; the phrase "recharging her batteries," which occurs throughout Soames's book, becomes monotonously frequent. Clearly she did have crises of depression and anxiety that were quite different from Churchill's extroverted sulks, and she did not have his ability to drop preoccupations and relax. In 1963 she had a brief nervous breakdown and it was at this time that her eldest daughter killed herself.

It would be a pity to read Clementine Churchill's life only in terms of her husband's, and Mary Soames avoids doing that. We can read about Clementine with interest not only because she lived so close to great events but precisely because she was in many ways a fairly ordinary woman, whose devotion and conscientiousness might have happened to make her the working partner of a headmaster or backbencher rather than of Churchill. Our only chance of knowing much about the lives of non-geniuses, it seems, is when they lived in the shadow of a genius; then we do want to know about them. Perhaps the least ordinary thing Clementine Churchill did was to destroy the Graham Sutherland portrait of her husband. It makes one wonder if there was a dimension in her that Soames's biography leaves out.

POSTSCRIPT

Since the above was written in 1980, Mary Soames has published a slightly revised edition of her biography of her mother,[2] and another biography, *Clementine Churchill: The Private Life of a Public Figure* by Joan Hardwick, has come out, evidently unauthorized by the Churchill family.[3] Hardwick's account is neither hostile nor a debunking job, but it sharpens the outlines of this rather extraordinary woman's life, and the streak of tragedy that ran through it. I am not sure that I would use that easy phrase (more easily used in 1980 than now, at any rate) "a happy marriage" today, because the strains within the family clearly were intense.

For my own generation, who heard his radio broadcasts (hampered slightly by slipping dentures) at a time of great terror, Winston Churchill inevitably always stands on a pedestal. But for everyone else the aura must go, and he and the whole family be looked at as real people. Hardwick sums up the agonizingly self-effacing wife as "a person of strong independent opinions, of painful perfectionism, who frequently found her husband intolerably difficult to live with, who was not a loving mother to all her children and who was capable of doing important things independently in the world outside the home." In 1980 *The New York Review of Books*' wonderful cartoonist, David

2. Houghton Mifflin, 2002.

3. John Murray, 1997.

Levine, saw further than I did, I think: his drawing shows a haggard, haunted-looking old lady grimly nursing a swollen Winston-infant sucking on his huge cigar.

Clementine's lifelong feminism (certainly not shared by her husband) now seems even more important, as does the strangeness, for those days, of her home background: impoverished illegitimate daughter of wayward aristocrats; *déraciné* teenage years in France where she met the painters Pissarro, Sickert, and J.-E. Blanche; firm family prohibition of her unfashionable wish to go to university.

One subject in particular demands a postscript: her deliberate destruction of the Graham Sutherland portrait of her husband. In 1954 a parliamentary committee was set up to plan an eightieth-birthday present for Sir Winston. A portrait was decided upon; the fashionable James Gunn[4] was dismissed as too expensive, and Sutherland, an excellent artist though now posthumously in decline, was chosen, for a fee of 1,000 guineas. He had previously painted striking —though not particularly flattering—portraits of well-known figures such as Somerset Maugham, Lord Beaverbrook, and Sir Kenneth Clark. Sutherland was nervous about the commission; it was not long after the end of the Second World War, and his subject was probably still the most historic name in the land. The great man was friendly, and asked Sutherland shrewdly if he was to be portrayed as "the Cherub or the Bulldog." But he was a difficult sitter: restless, often on the phone or dictating letters, and prone to advise the portraitist how to achieve his effects (Churchill was a competent amateur artist himself).

Naturally enough, Sutherland went for the bulldog: it was the mask that the old man assumed for the world. He was, in fact, caught by the painter at a difficult moment: too old, really, to continue in government, survivor of two strokes and slipping toward senility,

4. Gunn, who painted a saccharine presentation portrait of my own mother, would have produced nothing of worth and nothing to offend Winston Churchill.

paranoid (or perhaps realistic) about being ousted by traitors within his own party. Had he not single-handedly saved his country from the Hun? He put on the bulldog, and Sutherland caught it excellently. Unfortunately the artist, who always worked from a realistic starting point, caught an aging man's body equally clearly—slumped shoulders, bad temper, and all. Looking at the surviving reproduction, the portrait seems to fall into two halves: the fine and light "bulldog" head, and the almost too darkly detailed lower body in its parliamentary uniform of striped serge. (The Order of the Garter robes first proposed would have been much more tactful.) The waistcoat strains open over a sagging belly, and hints at no genital bulge below. Churchill described it, among other epithets, as the picture of a constipated old man straining on the lavatory, and once one has seen that likeness it does seem apt.

First reactions to the portrait seem to have been favorable. But for Churchill it evidently acquired a positively haunting malevolence, a summing-up of everything he excluded from his idea of himself. A brief and brutal note was delivered to Sutherland's home by limousine:

> I am of the opinion that the painting, however masterly in execution, is not suitable as a Presentation from both Houses of Parliament.
>
> About the ceremony in Westminster Hall. This can go forward although it is sad there will be no portrait. They have a beautiful book which they have nearly all signed, to present to me, so that the ceremony will be complete in itself.

There was a presentation ceremony without a portrait. The gutter press jumped in: "A horrible tribute to our greatest man." Sutherland minded very much. The picture, rather than being hung in parliamentary state, was crated up and sent to Chartwell, the Churchill country home.

Churchill died eleven years later, and Clementine a further twelve years on, aged ninety-two. Quite soon after this, Sutherland received a letter from Mary Soames telling him that the Churchill portrait was "no longer in existence." Not long after it was stored at Chartwell, her mother had ordered that it be destroyed. She had told her daughter, who at the time had been aghast and made sure that the fact was kept quiet during her mother's lifetime. Sutherland returned a dignified letter, which pointed out that the painting had in fact been the property of the House of Commons, and that "for whatever reason the portrait was caused to be destroyed, it was an act of vandalism . . . rare in history." When the press was given the story there was, naturally, another furor. To reporters' questions about its financial value, he estimated it at about £100,000 (at the present day, infinitely more). A year later, in contrast, he was flown out to Bonn by the German government to see his portrait of Konrad Adenauer hung at the Adenauer Foundation. Graham Sutherland died in 1980.

What are we to make of this sad, indeed rather terrible story? We can think of an aristocracy who never doubted that they were superior to mere artists. We can think of a once heroic old man sliding into his dotage like a hypersensitive movie star. We can also remember that, at the time when Clementine Churchill caused the canvas to be slashed and the framing broken up for firewood, she had had some intolerable years nursing the old tyrant and foresaw a good many to come. She ordered the destruction, by her own account, because the picture upset Winston so. Perhaps she needed, too, to have one great, tremendous battering and slashing.

7

ECHOES: OTTOLINE MORRELL

THE LIFETIME OF Bertrand Arthur William Russell, aristocrat, mathematician, philosopher, educationalist, political writer, Nobel Prize winner, spanned nearly a century (he died in 1970, aged ninety-seven). He was orphaned early and brought up by a morally strenuous grandmother; went through intense religious doubts, and temporary conversion to Hegelianism ("I had gone out to buy a tin of tobacco... when suddenly I threw it up in the air and exclaimed: 'Great God in boots, the ontological argument is sound'"); rejected idealism altogether ("a great liberation, as if I had escaped from a hot-house on to a wind-swept headland"); and then dedicated himself to exploring the foundations of mathematics and logic. He spent ten years with Alfred North Whitehead, writing a seminal book, set by the only compositor in Cambridge able to deal with his symbols. The suspicion at the time was that intellectually he had shot his bolt; and then came the fateful meeting in 1911 with Wittgenstein, who "began as my pupil and ended as my supplanter."[1]

In spite of the biographies, it is still hard for the untrained reader to understand how it was that the "theory of classes" threw up such a

1. Bertrand Russell, *Autobiography*, Vols. 1, 2 (Little, Brown, 1967, 1968), Vol. 3 (Simon and Schuster, 1969).

contradiction for Russell that his work was held up for nearly two years, or what he and Wittgenstein meant when they said they had spent the morning discussing whether there were two things in the world or three. It is important to understand, at least, that it was his underlying need to know whether anything could be established as true that shaped his whole mind, and his sense of an unbridgeable gap between thought and feeling. He himself felt that his search had made him a "logic machine," a "spectator and not an actor," with a "mind like a search light, very bright in one direction but dark everywhere else." Those who met him were also struck by this. George Santayana saw in both Russell and his brother "a strange mixture... of great ability and great disability; prodigious capacity and brilliance here—astonishing unconsciousness and want of perception there." Virginia Woolf wrote that "this luminous vigorous mind seems to be attached to a flimsy little car, like that of a large glinting balloon." She would like though, she added, "the run of his headpiece," but might not have found it comfortable to inhabit.

The other strand in Russell's life is the story of his marriages and love affairs. His early, idealistic marriage to Alys Pearsall-Smith ran into boredom before his first philosophical work was finished, and then into hatred and misery. From this marriage he plunged abruptly and totally at the age of thirty-six into his love affair with Ottoline Morrell. In the enormous Russell archive at McMaster University in Canada—one of the most remarkable collections ever assembled around a single person—are over two thousand letters to her from Russell, covering not only the years of their affair but a lifelong friendship. In view of his later deceitfulness with his various women friends, his attachment to her seems almost pathetically intense and single-minded. Of the same age and aristocratic background as him, she did return his love, but not physically—his hands "were like the paws of a bear," she said, "no feeling in them"—and not enough to leave her husband and child. Once he had reached a dead end in this love affair and a dead end in his philosophical work, one feels Russell becoming somehow a harder, shallower, and less likable man—but he had years of puritanism to make up for. Beatrice Webb, always a surprisingly acute judge, remarked in her diary that compared to the earlier Russell, it was sad "to look on this rather frowsty, unhealthy and cynical personage."

But then she disliked Dora, Russell's second wife, whom Russell to some extent chose in order to have children. The tragicomic story of that marriage is related in the chapter following this one. The hubris of separating intellect from feelings such as rivalry, hurt, jealousy, pride, and retaliation can seldom have been so clearly demonstrated. Beatrice Webb again, many years earlier, had commented that "compromise, mitigation, mixed motive, phases of health of body and mind, qualified statements, uncertain feelings, all seem unknown to him," and that this frightened her for the future of those who loved him.

Thirty years before Russell's death, and not long after she became godmother to his third child, Ottoline Morrell died in her sixties at the hands of a quack doctor. Miranda Seymour's biography of her, *Ottoline Morrell: Life on the Grand Scale*,[2] is to some extent a partisan rehabilitation of the larger-than-life Bloomsbury character who was so much caricatured. The woman who wondered, as she looked back at her years as generous hostess at her country house, "what was wrong, why it aroused so much venom in others and why so many people turned against us," had been cruelly lampooned by former guests Aldous Huxley and D. H. Lawrence among others, as well as continuously mocked behind her back by most of the Bloomsbury set. Seymour establishes her case that Ottoline Morrell was often brave and generous and kind; the malice that pursued her Seymour attributes to the fact that, unfashionably, she held vague religious beliefs, and also was secretive about her love affairs. But can that have been quite

2. Farrar, Straus and Giroux, 1993.

enough to make so many people so merciless? It seems there must always have been something that her protégés felt to be false about her benevolence, something anxious and strained and gushing that they quickly picked up. Virginia Woolf wrote that Ottoline

> left me Monday morning to face a world from which all heart, charity, kindness and worth had vanished. How she does this, in ten minutes, between twelve and one, in the best spare bedroom, with the scent of dried roseleaves about, and a little powder falling on the floor, Heaven knows.

The patroness seems to have offended not merely by being generous but by being so with a mixture of forcefulness and sentimentality, and for this she was often unforgiven.

What was the Ottoline phenomenon really about? Surely not just the visual apparition, though that was striking enough: "so tall, so beautiful, like a giraffe," said Nijinsky; like a "marvellous female version of Disraeli," wrote Gertrude Stein. She was described more as a work of art, reflecting the fantasies of those who knew her, than as a private person: like Switzerland, they said, or the Russian ballet, or the Leaning Tower of Pisa. They look at her and go away—and write books about her, said another. The ingratitude and spite shown by so many of her literary friends—"There she sat, thickly encrusted with pearls and diamonds, crocheting a pseudo-Omega quilt and murmuring on buggery" is, of course, from Lytton Strachey—are breathtaking. Clearly she was a shy woman who constructed an elaborately decorative façade to hide behind, and naive perhaps, and silly. But if she murmured on buggery, it was because she was obliged to—she tried to persuade her young homosexual friends to take a cure with her favorite psychiatrist before resigning herself to their confidences; the pearls and diamonds were her unavoidable Cavendish-Bentinck inheritance (her family and Russell's owned most of the

Bloomsbury streets between them); the quilt she crocheted was no doubt destined for some impoverished poet. The combination of manipulation and gush, riches and vulnerability, seems to have been irresistibly attackable.

But Seymour emphasizes that Ottoline Morrell's love affair with Russell was very deeply felt: influential, and in many ways beneficial, for both. There was a deep sympathy between them that lasted as long as she lived, wrote Russell in his autobiography, emphasizing how both came from aristocratic but lonely backgrounds and had overthrown class conventions. With her in particular Russell struggled to close the gap between mind and feeling. What kind of life together they might have made is one of literary history's intriguing speculations—certainly it would not have been an idyllic one.

Both were generous, in particular financially. Russell gave away his inherited fortune—no small thing to do. (Hands up, whoever has done the same.) And both of them, essentially, were brave in their stand against class and convention; many friends turned against Russell for his pacifism in the 1914–1918 war, but Ottoline Morrell was firm in her support.

What, above all, they shared was a scarcely recognized sense of bereavement. Morrell's much-loved father died when she was four; by the time she was nineteen her mother had died too. In her diary she wrote, "It is no fun being an oddity for it makes one eternally lonely. Unfortunately, I combine being an oddity with being very proud, and that makes one aloof." Russell described a sense of loneliness even more poignantly—almost shockingly—in a well-known passage in his autobiography: "I have loved a ghost, and in loving a ghost my inmost self has itself become spectral. I have therefore buried it deeper and deeper beneath layers of cheerfulness, affection and joy of life." The ghost, surely, was the mother that in adulthood he could not remember.

Biography cannot ever quite represent the place of such feelings in a life; its nature is to fill pages, with actions and decisions and sayings.

But there are also the blank spaces that, rarely, open up and show themselves. This is not to say that Russell was not full of real energy and humor and variety; but we must believe what he himself perceived, what he felt as early as 1905 when comforting a bereaved friend—that buried griefs "burst their tombs, and wailed in the desert spaces of one's mind, from which philosophy offered no comfort whatsoever." The lifelong search for an answer to his question "Can human beings *know* anything?" could have started in the mind of a child deprived too suddenly of certainties. This was something that Ottoline, consciously or half-consciously, would have recognized.

8

FLAG BEARER: DORA RUSSELL

THERE IS A good deal of irony surrounding Dora Russell's autobiography, *The Tamarisk Tree.*[1] Irony, first of all, in the reasons for its publication: though the author has led an active and worthy life, the most decisive reason (as she acknowledges, with rather touching humility, by having his photograph on the cover with her own) must have been that she was once married for twelve years to Bertrand Russell—whose own real importance lies in work in the field of mathematical logic, which is doubtless as incomprehensible to her as to most of the rest of us. There is the same rather cruel irony in the fact that, for most readers, the lifetime of hard work and good causes, the political conferences, the humanist gatherings, the committees on birth control and sexual reform, will have less interest than the account of the marriage's curious beginning and ending. And in that story—though different people will draw different conclusions from it—lie the greatest ironies of all.

When Dora Black, as a young Fellow of Girton College, first encountered the distinguished middle-aged philosopher (in 1919 according to her account, 1916 according to his) the conversation had turned to free love, of which she was an earnest supporter. When she

1. Putnam, 1975.

answered his question about the fate of the children of such unions by announcing that they were solely the mother's concern, Russell laughed and said that whomever he had children by, it certainly wouldn't be her. Their first child was born a year or two later.

When, in the meantime, Russell had urged that their affair be legalized as soon as he was free from his first marriage, she had felt doubts about tying herself down for life, and "used to reckon how long it would be before he was 'really old' and I would have to spend my time looking after him." Twelve years after she agreed to marriage he left her for a young girl; nor—having been nursed by her once through a desperate illness—did he show much sign of being "really old" till another forty years and a couple more marriages had elapsed. Throughout the Twenties Dora was busy with sexual and birth-control reform (addressing a world congress on "Marriage and Freedom," along with George Bernard Shaw and others, with an address of welcome in Esperanto, and —as "a joyous lark"—a Russian film on abortion), and Russell was publishing *Marriage and Morals* and *The Conquest of Happiness*. By 1932, when the second of her two children by another man was born, the free, modern union with Russell was in the hands of the solicitors.

Impossible as it is, for participants and observers alike, to know the whole truth about such tangles of passion, reason, pride, and revenge, one cannot help being engaged by this hubristic tragicomedy. The fact that most people would take it for granted that a husband was justified in leaving a wife who had brought illegitimate children into the family makes Dora Russell's story seem the sadder, for by her own account her husband, impotent at the time with her, had stood by their progressive principles by all but encouraging her to have another child, while he too pursued affairs of his own. Their marriage, they had both believed, was independent of convention and too genuine to be shaken by such details as the paternity of the children. One holiday was spent in the company of the lovers of both husband and wife, as well as the children by the two fathers—undoubtedly not, as the modern cynic might think, to indulge in decadent group orgies but to demonstrate their entire freedom from competitiveness and jealousy. Theory was running ahead of practice.

Russell stated in his own autobiography that his *Marriage and Morals* of 1929 never recommended that a marriage continue once illegitimate children had arrived. Consulting, in the interests of truth, that surprisingly tedious book, I have to find in favor of Lady Russell, for he neither recommends it nor otherwise, but dodges the logical conclusion to his arguments, with many ambivalent passages about the new irrelevance of patriarchy and paternity. The philosopher's vulnerability was obviously cloaked in intellectual self-deception, and once he uncloaked things he made fast decisions. Yet Dora Russell does seem, at the least, to have been tactless—would not one demonstration of the matriarchal principle have been enough?—and obtuse, as she says, about the sensitivity of the middle-aged Russell to his younger wife's procreative triumphs; still, she did announce her belief in the superfluity of males from the start.

The author does not take her story here much beyond the ending of the marriage, though she touches on later tragedies that she suffered and survived.[2] In general she writes with admiration and affection of "Bertie," and there are nice glimpses of their life together: their nearest approach to a quarrel when, told to tie up his own parcels, he answered that he had never done so in his life and did not propose to begin now; Bertie skipping for exercise in a Chinese courtyard and suggesting that a photograph be sent home captioned "Thought in China is advancing by leaps and bounds." Even in the delirium of a severe illness, she says, he was always witty. But he spent his first two months after the divorce working on "the problem of the twenty-seven straight lines on a cubic surface." What a curious species we are.

---

2. These are described at greater length in *The Tamarisk Tree*, Vols. 2 and 3 (Virago, 1980 and 1985).

A few years after the first volume of her autobiography appeared, I was lucky enough, after a five-mile walk over the finest cliff scenery in the world, to interview Dora Russell in her home at the western tip of Britain. Our talk was mainly about education, and the "free school" that she ran when she was married to Russell.

In west Cornwall it had been a busy winter for the roof tilers; fallen slates still cracked underfoot around weather-battered cottages. The 150 mph gale that dislodged them had blown Dora Russell's sitting-room window in like a bomb blast. But she had stayed, off and on, in Carn Voel, her house near Land's End, since 1922, when she was still married to Bertrand Russell and rented the house for a summer; she wouldn't, she said, live anywhere else for the world. At that time, at eighty-six,[3] she was living there with her eldest son, who had been ill for many years, and she managed their life with only the aid of part-time home help and a once-weekly secretary.

The house overlooked a mile of green fields running down to the sea. Trim outside, it enclosed a certain degree of chaos as the household waited for the builders to arrive. Journals and papers were piled everywhere; a mass of material relating to both Dora and Bertrand Russell's lives was slowly being sorted. Dora Russell pottered amiably in an immense pair of trousers (only a woman without a shred of self-consciousness could have allowed such an unflattering photograph of herself to appear on the jacket of her book). This was the house where Wittgenstein came to stay, and Roger Fry and J. B. S. Haldane and Rabindranath Tagore. The Russells called it Carn Voel after a noble Cornish headland that takes the full force of the Atlantic gales.

Dora Russell's life had been blown apart more than once by gale-force tragedies, but she was a survivor. The separation from Russell was in 1932, and he went on to two more marriages; for her, there was the death of her lover, conflict over the custody of the children,

---

3. She died in 1986.

and eleven years of struggling to carry on the school that she and Russell had founded to provide the education they wanted for their own children and could not find anywhere else. In the late 1920s, when they ran it together, it was known—and caricatured—as the Bertrand Russell School, and many people assumed it closed down when Russell left. "Two men from the BBC came down last year to do a television piece on Bertie and when I mentioned the school they said, 'Well, that ended when Russell left it.' '*Oh, did it*?' I said." Dora Russell's voice sharpened; but it was clear that, for all her forcefulness, she was a woman quite without malice. Though she was clearsighted about Russell—"Bertie could behave *rottenly*"—she was enthusiastically involved with a committee that was arranging to have a bust of him put up in Red Lion Square in London.

Russell put it on record in his autobiography that his experience with the school disillusioned him about permissive education and, indeed, about human nature as he encountered it in small children. Dora Russell's faith in both was absolutely unshaken. "I know it can be done. It can be done by education. And every human being has got an instinctive empathy, an instinctive feeling for other organic life; that cat and I, for instance, have got a very close feeling for one another. People say, 'Oh, you're being sentimental'; but the trouble is, for the past three hundred years the whole idea has been to measure everything by an intellect from which we exclude emotion. Ever since God has been thought of as the Great Clockmaker, winding up the world as a mechanism, people have tried to organize society as a machine. But people aren't machines, you can't mechanize them—and you can't mechanize education. In my book *The Right to Be Happy* I took to pieces Christian asceticism and eighteenth-century dualism; Descartes was my enemy, and it's only now that other people are discovering that Descartes has been the enemy. Yet Bertie wrote—'The belief that metaphysics has any bearing on practical affairs is a proof of logical incapacity'! He kept philosophy completely separate from ethical and political beliefs. I've never believed they could be kept apart like that."

Most of the second volume of *The Tamarisk Tree* is taken up with the vicissitudes of the school after Russell left; but there is a last chapter (headed "Was It All Worthwhile?"—and she was in no doubt of the answer) in which she sets out her belief that we are being increasingly brutalized by an authoritarian and industrialized society. Though Bertrand abandoned the absolute faith in humanity's goodness that she retained, on this he might well have agreed. Even after the break they continued to hold many of the same beliefs; she herself was on the Committee of 100 against nuclear armament and went on five protest marches, though keeping out of the limelight for Russell's sake. But she felt they had arrived at the same point by very different routes. "I think Bertie's humanitarianism stemmed from the Christian training he acquired early from his grandmother, but mine was the reverse: compassion from empathy and maternal instinct, very earthy. It's ironical and a bit sad that Bertie and I worked for the same causes from such different motives. In *The Right to Be Happy* I wrote, 'Animals we are and animals we remain, and the path to our happiness lies through our animal nature.' T. S. Eliot said if I could think that, I wasn't fit to bring up children!"

As a lifelong, consistent feminist Dora Russell believed that women are able to feel at home in the natural world as men are not: "I think that's the whole point of us." She read to me from a preface she had just written to Sylvia Ashton Warner's *Teacher*: "It would seem as if for centuries the human race has been mishandled and misdirected by predominantly male intellectual and spiritual guidance. This observation should not be treated as a mere facet of feminism; it is not an attack on the intellect itself, but its misuse." Lady Russell's daughter Kate has written that her mother has always been her touchstone for genuine feminism because she believed in the value of women as *women*. It may indeed all look like a denigration of men; yet when

Dora Russell says, "I'm not anti-men—I love men!" we believe her; she was nothing if not innocent and open. "I believe like Alexandra Kollontai that love can be the basis of society, love between men and women"; and she broke off—"Oh, *she* was a woman, Kollontai! She was superb!" But can't women, I wonder, be just as bad as men when they want to? She burst out laughing. "Oh, of course they can be beastly, of course. Bertie used to say the true nature of women was shown up by women like Catherine the Great, who were able to do just what they pleased!"

She was not entirely specific about how her ideals were to be fed into a whole state educational system—nor quite consistent about them. Though she protested that a lower standard of literacy was unimportant, and floated off into a description of the brilliance of the illiterate medieval craftsman, she spoke with obvious regret of her granddaughter turning down an Oxford scholarship. She was not in any case totally against examinations, as long as they were not given too much importance; though at her Beacon Hill School lessons were not compulsory. In fact, since her teaching experience was with children under twelve, and the majority of these of primary age, one sensed that she was less interested altogether in secondary education. Children will pick up what they need to know, she implied, and find their own level. She was, naturally, in favor of comprehensive schools,[4] but felt that more should be done to counteract their size by teaching in small groups, more personally. "There are all these tape recorders and television sets and God knows what; we're relying all the time on the external thing, on external gadgets, until there's nothing left of what's inside the child—they all come out exactly alike, we're turning out machine-made people. Human beings are what's needed—someone to argue with, put questions to."

4. A controversial issue at the time was whether state schools should cease to be segregated into schools for the more able and the less able.

About the English "public" schools (that is, private, and expensive) she was quite definite. "I don't see that you can get anywhere in creating a new society without getting rid of them. I'm not hostile to them; they do magnificent work in their field. But there you have, in the heart of our society, a masculine hereditary tradition for generation after generation; out of those schools come men, men who expect to take the highest posts in our society; and against that I don't see how democracy, or women, are going to have any influence whatsoever." Would either she or Russell, if they had been educated in the permissive fashion, have done the intellectual work they did? She was not to be caught. "I think we would very likely have ended up as *better* people, less conceited. It took me a long time to get over feeling superior to other people after I had had a university education; it was the working-class women, when I went to talk to them about birth control, who educated me—oh yes, I learned I was not the only pebble on the beach."

Dora Russell felt that her life's work had been "quite logical really. When we started after getting the vote, we went on to looking after mothers, to see that they didn't get overburdened with children; our idea was to make children more valuable, because there were to be fewer of them. The natural thing leading on from that was educating the child. I fought for the animal side of life, if you like, for bringing up children with an understanding of their animal origin. And then I went on to conservation; upstairs I've got files and files of my press cuttings on my battles for conservation. You see, we belong *here*! I wrote a review of a book recently on man's responsibility for nature, and I said that now that we've had a look at the cold moon, and our own earth in contrast, we realize what a precious thing we have here" —she looked out at the Cornish countryside. "We should be taking care of it, and enjoying it, and *loving* it; and to me this is worth everything else in the world that anybody could invent."

9

LA STREPPONI: GIUSEPPINA VERDI

I HAD ALWAYS wanted to see Sant'Agata, Giuseppe Verdi's house a few miles from his hometown of Busseto in the Po valley. He loved it so much, loved it like the peasant he claimed he always was, the sowing and reaping, the grapes for his own wine, the building and extending, the buying of another field, and then another.

He was able to buy the farmhouse and some surrounding land in 1848, when he was thirty-five and already the maestro, with twelve performed operas behind him. Eighteen forty-eight was of course the year of revolutions, of some of Italy's bitterest struggles for independence, which Verdi so powerfully supported and incorporated into the themes of some of these operas. "Honor to all Italy," he was writing to a friend, "which at this moment is truly great":

> Do you imagine I want to occupy myself now with notes, with sounds? There is, and should be, only one kind of music pleasing to the ears of the Italians of 1848—the music of the guns!

He was drunk with joy, he wrote—though the hour had not yet quite come. At around the same time the retired soprano Giuseppina Strepponi was writing from Paris to a colleague that "all the notes in the world might go to the devil if there were room for hope that Italy could become great, united, strong and free!"

The year 2001 was the centenary of the death of the composer who became the symbol of Italy's risorgimento. Opera houses around the world were performing his work, Parma was full of tourists, and some of us were bussed out to see the birthplace and Busseto and Sant'Agata. Verdi had not ceased, and probably never will cease, to be his country's hero. Dignified, severe, hugely generous: he is *loved*. There were daily bulletins when he was dying; traffic was quietened and shutters drawn. His memorial service had every kind of grandeur, with "*Va, pensiero*" from *Nabucco* sung by a chorus of eight hundred under Toscanini's baton. "Verdi was our great unifier," it was declared,

> when the wave of his passionate music, something that the enemy could not seize, embodied the idea of the nation, which swept freely from the Alps to the sea, setting our hearts on fire.

As a sentimentalist and Italophile, an adorer of tragedy and passion rather than musically literate, I am unashamed of being among the Verdi worshipers. But Sant'Agata itself was a disappointment—overgrown by huge trees and consequently very dark, with only a few rooms left open to the public. Few mementoes there of La Strepponi, Verdi's mistress and then wife, who was often immured in the house while Verdi was away and at work. How she hated it! The solitude, the rain, the flat muddy countryside. And no children.

I had been drawn to the story of Giuseppina Strepponi's life partly because of that question of the children (so great a factor in real life and so ignored in biographies) and partly because of her link with *La Traviata*. One also need not be ashamed, I think, of preferring *Traviata* out of all the Verdian operas; the whole world has done so. And everyone knows that its heroine—truly heroic—the "Strayed One" or the "Fallen Woman," is a courtesan who sacrifices herself for love and poverty and dies of TB (so romantic in fiction, so viscous and disgusting in real life) in her lover's arms. He has returned, of course, just in time for this. "*Oh gioia*!" But you will recover, the tenor sings. She faints a little. "*Gran Dio*," she mourns, "*morir si giovane*!" To die so young, after the long night of tears. As she does; as many, many girls did.[1]

But not, in fact, Giuseppina Verdi, who died at eighty-two at Sant'Agata, stout and short of breath and praying, in her will, that she and her husband would be reunited in Heaven.

Strepponi had never been, professionally, a courtesan; but certainly she had strayed, as was almost inevitable for a young woman working on the stage. Her musician father had died early, and she had become almost the sole support of her mother and siblings. She had entered the Milan Conservatorio at fifteen and won scholarships and praise all around—"a voice of the greatest clarity, very limpid and beautiful," it was said. And more: "deep inner feeling," "all heart and temperament." By the time Verdi had sought out the *prima donna assoluta* for *Nabucco*, she had sung in Milan, Venice, Rome, Vienna, everywhere; done Donizetti, Rossini, Bellini; had been Norma, Lucia, Anna Bolena, Cenerentola, Desdemona, and a great many others now forgotten. And this over a period of only eight years; she was twenty-seven when the aspiring Verdi needed her for *Nabucco*.

The Italian opera stage in Strepponi's time was a crude place. Quantity was more the point than quality—though that was keenly understood too. Good singers could let themselves be worked like horses. Opera houses were cheap and crowded and noisy with cheers and boos. "Milton might easily have taken his idea of Pandemonium from the inside of an Italian Theatre," wrote Hazlitt from his travels—"its heat, its gorgeousness and its gloom." There was no question of treating music as something hushed and holy, of fine

1. Marie Duplessis, the model for Dumas's *Dame aux camélias*, died at twenty-three of tuberculosis.

voices as treasures to be nursed along. And yet Italy did love its native opera, screamed and shouted and quarreled over it.

That La Strepponi's voice was being worked to death was noted by music critics. Often she had to carry an indifferent performance single-handed. Over time her voice thinned, her stamina waned, she coughed so much that she had to turn toward the wings. She worked in this way because she had a mother, sisters, and a brother to support. And there was another reason for declining health: she was constantly pregnant. "All heart and temperament" she was indeed.

The story of Strepponi's children is hard to accept from our present-day point of view. She worked onstage visibly pregnant, gave birth, and handed the babies out to the orphanage or foster home. Was this so much worse than the abortions she would have had today? There were probably three children and two fathers. From her letters of the time it is clear that there was no question of her glorying in being a free spirit. "A year at this pace and perhaps I shall be no more, and all claims upon one, all conflicts, end beyond the tomb. My poor children! My poor family!" she was writing in 1841; and "I have been cruelly treated under the mantle of love.... God help me!" The next year a document was being signed by three doctors stating that she could no longer work, since she was feverish, losing weight, and liable to consumption.

Verdi had also lost children. He had married Margherita Barezzi from his home town when he was twenty-three and two children were born. In less than four years, all three had died, mother and babies, from the indistinct causes that are all we can gather from premodern times. At twenty-seven he was completely alone. It would be wrong, I think, to believe that just because such deaths were more common at the time, they were any the less grieved over. These massive blows must have schooled Verdi in that sense of the tragic that is the great Verdian strength—in those haunting premonitory motifs, the plangent calls of a single flute.

As is so well known, after his loss and after finishing the unsuccessful *Un giorno di regno*, Verdi swore never to return to music. There are varying versions of how the *Nabucco* libretto caught his eye and coaxed him back, and how into the "*Va, pensiero*" melody he poured his own grief, and his country's. He had the usual difficulties in getting the work produced, and needed Strepponi for the demanding role of Abigaille, which she had appreciated as soon as she saw it. *Nabucco* eventually was, of course, a huge success and has been ever since.

Verdi at the time was the young genius on his way up; Strepponi, the diva beginning her slide downward. Though she was able to play Abigaille finely, she was soon to be semiretired and advertising singing lessons. It seems that it was around 1848 that these two, in their thirties, already old friends, and with their tragedies behind them, began to live together. Strepponi was an excellent letter writer, and there are a number of letters that show how she cherished her maestro, feeling herself the strayed one who had been taken under his wing. She felt it keenly, though, that the Bussetans ostracized her as an immoral woman when Verdi took her to live there (they were not to marry for a further ten years). Often left at hotels or Sant'Agata—that "Vale of Yawns, if not of Tears," she said—while Verdi was busy, she wrote in their eleventh year together,

> Without you I am a body without a soul. I am different (and I think you are too) from those people who have need of frequent separations to revive their affection. I would stay with you for years, without boredom or satiety.

He alone in the world has

> never caused me sorrow! So be it as you wish; let's go back to Sant'Agata, and your will be done, as long as I have my eyes open and the strength to tell you that I love you with all my being!

But—the children? In the same year she writes to Verdi that "we shall have no children (since God, perhaps, wishes to punish me for my sins, in depriving me of any legitimate joy before I die)" and hopes that he will not produce any by other women. This sounds more as if her rapid pregnancies had left her barren than suggesting that Verdi had set his face against a family—though in fact they were still unmarried at the time of that letter, and Verdi's code might not have allowed for illegitimate children. I suspect that he may have wanted to keep the memory of his own two lost children inviolate.

Of Strepponi's children placed in foster homes, it is known that one died ("angel-makers," these fosterers were called in England) but that she kept in touch with the boy, Camillino, and arranged for his education. It has been suggested that when Verdi and Strepponi did marry it might have been for Camillino's sake, as he reached his twenty-first birthday. When he was apprenticed to a sculptor it was, in a sense, at Verdi's expense, since Strepponi no longer had any means to earn money. Could we have expected him to do more than that? And though Giuseppina was truly grateful for being "rescued" with affection and honor, could we expect her not to long for legitimate marriage? It won't do to see these happenings in a modern context.

And the other child, the daughter placed in the turnstile for abandoned infants at the Ospedale degli Innocenti and never again traced? How could she not have been thought about, wondered about, and been one of the causes of her mother's deep melancholy in later life? The couple did, in their fifties, legally adopt a second cousin of Verdi's, the child of penniless peasants who was living with her grandfather. Though she was, of course, sent away to be educated by the nuns, Giuseppina was deeply fond of her. When Maria married, Verdi provided the wedding and a house for the couple.

Lost children were not to complicate the plot of *La Traviata*, in either Dumas's *Dame aux camélias* or its dramatic adaptation. Verdi and Strepponi had been together for a few years when his interest was aroused by Dumas's story of a Parisian courtesan; it seems likely that they saw the play when it opened in Paris in 1852. In the original novel, the story ends bleakly with Violetta's death, alone. The romantic ending—Alfredo, renounced by her for the sake of his family's reputation, reaching her bedside just before she dies—may be too "soft" but is surely the making of the drama. A consumptive courtesan's life was not soft; but we need the myth. Alfredo might have, in real life, married Violetta and got rather tired of her, as did Verdi eventually with his love—but that is not the point. It is a myth, really, of rebirth and death and again rebirth. We die: but in the arms of undying love.

Some months after the play's première in Paris, Verdi's librettist Francesco Piave wrote from Sant'Agata ("it rains and rains and I fear we shall all be transformed into frogs") to say that Verdi was excited about a new project. This must have been *Traviata*. Verdi was writing that he had a contemporary subject now, one that some might have avoided because of morality or "a thousand other silly scruples." He was held up, as usual, over the choice of a soprano and was "in an infernal bad temper," Piave said—the great man, it must be admitted, was often irascible. As a matter of fact, it was partly poor casting that made this most loved of operas a failure at first. Verdi revised it, and when put on again it was a huge success. "Indescribable enthusiasm!" "An unexampled triumph!"

Partly we love *Traviata* just because it is contemporary for the time of its writing, not encumbered by those huge Verdian historical themes and casts that are so confusing. Though we think of it perhaps as supremely romantic, it appeared at a time when there was a move toward realism in France: Millet and Courbet painting peasants, Flaubert and Balzac breaking new ground in realistic fiction. The demimonde itself—not actually too pretty a place—was being examined in a way that was never permitted in English novels. Verdi doesn't sanitize Violetta: when she first veers toward falling in love with Alfredo, she is given an aria—a declaration of self-hate—in praise of pleasure as all that she is fit for. She falls in love with Alfredo not because of youth or good looks, but because, out of all the guests crowding her party, only he notices that she is ill and needs care. The self-contempt of the "fallen" woman, her gratitude for the touch of almost maternal care, were surely learned by Verdi from Giuseppina—this shows up indeed in her letters. And when at the end Violetta sings of the pain of *morir si giovane*, he perhaps thought of his first wife.

So—two people with great losses behind them meet and love and stay together. But, of course, just as Sant'Agata was darker and gloomier than I had expected, the romance is not quite perfect. *Oh Dio*! How I wish it were! There was no promiscuity or divorce, but later—there was another woman. Verdi and Giuseppina were legally married and approaching old age when she heard rumors about an affair with Teresa Stolz, a younger German soprano who had sung for him in *Aida*. She was distraught: it must have been what she had always feared. It even reached the newspapers in a degrading way worthy of the twenty-first century ("Stolz, this Temptress Eve, directed too many covetous glances toward the Author of *Ernani*, who, in a moment of desire, fell at the feet of the God of Love," and so on). For some years, Giuseppina (like Clementine Churchill) had been noting in her diary her husband's increasing irritability both with herself and with the servants, in terms that will sound far from unfamiliar to most people: it was not what she actually said, he would complain, it was the way she said it. Noble, brilliant men really should not have such extremely commonplace feet of clay.

To a friend she wrote that by now she could hardly believe in anything or anyone:

> I have suffered so many and such cruel disillusionments that I am disgusted with life. You will say that everyone has suffered disenchantments, but that means that others, stronger than I am, have kept alive some hope and some trace of faith in the

> future. I, on the other hand, now laugh, when someone says that they love me. Even my religious convictions have disappeared and I hardly believe in God when I look at the marvels of creation!

Giuseppina, however, did gain some counsel and support from the Church; she had always remained devout, while Verdi was a staunch freethinker. She acquired a certain dignity, which she needed: the frequent presence of Stolz constituted almost a kind of ménage à trois. She was expected to maintain, and did maintain, a courtesy toward the younger woman. There remained, of course, the depressive, self-hating streak that had always been a part of her, and that surely brought thoughts of her lost children. Of her son, Camillino, it is only known that he became a medical student and died at the age of twenty-five.

It would be nice to believe that Verdi's passion for his large Germanic soprano faded away, but he was still writing love letters to her after La Strepponi's death, when he was eighty-seven. Still, he never left his wife, and she could stand legitimately beside Italy's great man. Perhaps there were good moments as well as bad: at sixty-seven she was writing to him that she "still loved him like mad," sometimes with a kind of love fever unknown to doctors. While she was aging and dwindling, he went on to his last great operas. They worked together for the people of their district, making charitable disbursements, endowing hospitals and schools, and, at one time of great local poverty, running a soup kitchen from Sant'Agata. When floods wrecked the Po valley, Verdi organized a benefit concert for the homeless. The soprano was La Stolz.

Verdi was seventy-three when *Otello* was staged to huge success, and *Falstaff* came six years later. Giuseppina Verdi, once the incomparable Strepponi, was present at these triumphs; earlier, after the tumultuous reception of *Otello*, she, with Verdi and the librettist

Arrigo Boito, had been physically lifted in their carriage by enthusiasts, and music was played under the hotel windows all night.

During Giuseppina's last illness at Sant'Agata, Verdi was at her bedside. Her will asked that he keep with him the gold bracelet, given to her in Naples, inscribed "To my dear Peppina." During the few years remaining to him before the great memorial crowds filled the streets of Milan, he was supported by friends, among them La Stolz. Oh, how she spoils the story of the strayed one!

10

FAMISHMENT: STOSSLOVA, ABBA

THAT WAS A love story, even though imperfect. But love (let's call it "love") can also flourish in the imagination, hold on with the grasp of an infant, in spite of little contact with its object.

Reading the passionate letters of two elderly men, the composer Leos Janacek and the writer Luigi Pirandello, to two much younger women, one is led to wonder whether relationships quite like this would be possible today—even assuming that telephones and faxes did not exist and letters were still written. The 1920s were not so extremely long ago, not a period of fans and fainting fits and cabriolets. But we are accustomed now to think of inconsolable yearning at least as a more feminine than masculine habit, and a rather neurotic and undesirable one at that. If an eminent sixtyish man today fell hopelessly for a girl forty years younger, would he reveal it in letters? Would she be flattered, embarrassed, brisk, amused...? We won't, in the telephone age, have much chance to find out in any case; letters like those of Janacek and Pirandello must be, along with Kafka's to Felice Bauer, some of the last to document how it is to live for, and feed off, the image of someone *absent.*[1]

---

1. See *Intimate Letters: Leos Janacek to Kamila Stosslova*, edited and translated by John Tyrrell (Princeton University Press, 1994), and *Pirandello's Love Letters to Marta Abba*, edited and translated by Benito Ortolani (Princeton University Press, 1994).

Though the personalities of the composer and the writer come across in their respective letters as very different, both were distinguished men at the time of the correspondences, both habitually addressed by the women they were writing to as "Maestro." Pirandello was fifty-eight when his letters to the twenty-four-year-old actress Marta Abba started in 1926; Janacek sixty-three when in 1917 he sent roses to twenty-six-year-old Kamila Stosslova with the message: "You look on the world with such kindness that one wants to do only good and pleasant things for you in return. You will not believe how glad I am that I have met you. Happy you! All the more painfully I feel my own desolation and bitter fate."

Both men were deeply lonely. Pirandello's wife had been hospitalized for mental illness for years and he had fallen out with his children. Janacek had lost both his children and was tied to an openly unhappy marriage. On a solitary visit to a spa town near his home in Brno he had seen Kamila Stosslova sitting on the grass and, to put it simply, picked her up. But this was not a pickup as we know it. He was afterward introduced to her husband and children, polite compliments and invitations were exchanged, and in fact for the next ten years, no less, the mainly epistolary relationship remained very proper.

Invitations to concerts and proposals for visits were extended to the young couple but were mostly refused; much was made of commissions for antique carpets and food parcels, for Stosslova's husband was something of a wheeler-dealer. Zdenka Janacek wrote in her memoirs that Mrs. Stosslova's letters to her at this time were friendly and those to her husband "irreproachable." "I thought she was quite nice," she said after the couple's first visit, "young, cheerful, one could have a really good talk with her, she was always laughing.... One thing was certain was that they brought action and laughter into our quiet sadness." Stosslova was uneducated—"Her letters were full of spelling mistakes. In music she was totally ignorant, knowing almost nothing about composers. She called Leo's pieces 'those notes of yours,' and hadn't heard of Wagner.... She was completely unimpressed by my husband's fame, and also by his person." Zdenka Janacek went along with the friendship, she said, when she saw how desperately her husband wanted it.

Janacek's letters to Stosslova were making it clear how he did indeed cling to contact with her—he needed it as "the dry weather needs the rain, the dawn needs the sun." With her, *die ferne Geliebte*, he could entrust "my thoughts, my longings, to reveal my internal life —and to know that it's as safe in your mind as if it were hidden in mine." A few letters from her, artless and unpunctuated, are included in John Tyrrell's collection of the correspondence; at times she mentions boredom, and a husband constantly away traveling. "Dear Maestro," her letters begin; "Dear Mrs. Kamila" his. But if it were not for her, he says, he would not want to live. Meanwhile his opera *Jenufa* had its première, *Katya Kabanova* and the *Glagolitic Mass* were composed, and a biography of Janacek by Max Brod (Kafka's close friend) was published.

It was in April 1927, nearly ten years after the first meeting, that the relationship between Janacek and Stosslova took a decisive turn during a brief visit by Janacek to the couple's home in Pisek. But first consider those ten years in the light of present-day assumptions about the speed of consummations and changes. Janacek's letters suggest that he was not an unsensual man—even when the relationship was officially just friendship, Stosslova sometimes sounds like something wholesome he would like to eat—yet for all that time he nourished himself on her image. That she existed and scrawled a kindly letter from time to time was enough. He seems to have seen something in her instantly—simplicity, cheerfulness, warmth—that he needed like a missing vitamin.

"I do so like happy people," he had written in 1918; for himself, he was "isolated, shut in on myself," drugged with work. In 1924 he was still drawing on a brief stay in Pisek:

> And believe me, Kamila, there were no more beautiful days for me in my life than those few spent in your company.... You were like an open window: one could see through it all just as it was. I had nothing to hide, it was peaceful and so pleasant in my soul. I saw you in your household, always natural in your behaviour, not artificial, with slippers and even bare feet; some sort of secret flame always shone and one warmed oneself up with it. Not with starchiness, affectation. No-one looked for a speck of dust on the furniture.

Though otherwise well edited, Tyrrell's collection, like Benito Ortolani's of Pirandello's letters to Marta Abba, suffers from the lack of a biographical introduction that would give some idea of its subject's earlier life, so we do not learn from it why Janacek's marriage was joyless—it was always so, he says in later letters—or how his two children died. Studying the photographs, in which Kamila Stosslova looks attractive or ridiculous according to 1920s hat styles, the couple look much of a pair—stout and twinkling. Perhaps he saw in her an earlier and happier twin of himself that he needed to recapture.

The way in which her existence ignited his creativity was not simply lovelorn or possessive. He wrote in 1921 that it was in fact her youthful affection for her husband that gave him the spark for *Katya Kabanova*. Prior to this she had sent thank-you presents to him and his wife after a visit; his was a silver pen, and he sat down to write an opera with it. "And Katya, you know, that was you beside me.... That's why there's so much emotional heat in these works. So much heat that if it caught both of us, there'd be just ashes left of us."

Over these years of platonic inspiration Stosslova herself, at home with children and housework, had perhaps changed. It is not surprising that, if marriage grew boring, the unfailing adoration from a man she now realized was eminent made its impression. When Janacek made a brief visit to her home in 1927, something momentous happened—perhaps an avowal, or a kiss. "Never in my life have I experienced such an intermingling of myself with you. We walked along not even close to one another and yet there was no gap between us." From here on the letters become even more ardent; about two thirds of those selected by Tyrrell are from the last fifteen months of the relationship. Janacek went on to explain more about his feelings to his wife, and wrote to Kamila that he felt things drawing toward a decision. She wrote back to him that

> I've not longed for anything else my life just went by without love and joy. But I always went along with the thought that that's the way it had to be. Now I think that God was testing you and me and when he saw that we've been good and that we deserve it he has granted us this joy in life.

Janacek's composing continued to flourish. He called his latest quartet—"our quartet"—*Intimate Letters*. "And Kamila, it will be beautiful, strange, unrestrained, inspired, a composition beyond all the usual conventions! Together I think that we'll triumph!" "Oh, it's a work as if carved out of living flesh. I think that I won't write a more profound and a truer one. So I end."

He did not plan to end. He was planning to bring Stosslova to his country cottage for the visit he had waited so long for. But meanwhile her mother was dying, and when he wrote to her plaintively she turned on him: "Who's suffering more than me but what can I do?... You're at home all year long without me so why carry on so?" He did persuade her to come to the country with one of her children, some days after her mother's death. What happened is not of course recorded in the letters; but within a week Janacek fell ill with pneumonia, and within another few days was dead.

It is not necessarily an enviable fate to be a famous man's *ferne Geliebte*. What the double bereavement must have been like for Kamila

Stosslova we can only imagine. She was excluded by widow and biographers, and herself died only seven years later, at forty-three. Her husband had to go to court to claim Janacek's legacy of royalties from *Katya Kabanova*, and the letters had a long way to go before they reached publication.

Was she ever a real person to Janacek, or someone who had to glow from afar in order to bring out his music? Did the old man die of the shock of having his dreams come true? He had written that she could be drawn on continually, never used up; but in ordinary living there is a lot of using up. He had said earlier that they had a private world between them, "but what's beautiful in it, these desires, wishes, the *Tva* [you] and all, all just made up! I told Zdenka [his wife] that this imaginary world is as necessary for me as air and water." And he was triumphant that "now it's known how love helps a composer to make his work dazzle." But is it?

The imaginary world and the real world, the intricacies of illusion, were always central themes in the plays and stories of Luigi Pirandello, a more demanding and tortured man than Janacek. A madwoman mistaking a bundle of rags for a baby is just as happy as if it really were one, he writes to his love Marta Abba—apropos the photograph of her on his desk. He does not suggest that he is inventing *her* out of a bundle of rags, but perhaps Abba felt he was, for his letters are monotonously plaintive and her replies—none actually included in Benito Ortolani's edition—evidently brisk. She too addresses him as "Maestro" and, the editor notes, uses the formal *Lei* for *you*, rather than the informal *tu* (the *Tva* that Janacek uses is the equivalent of the Italian *tu*).

The two had met when Pirandello was fifty-eight and Abba a little-known actress of twenty-four auditioning for the company he was forming. She was taken on by the maestro, and traveled with the company for three years. This relationship too, it is clear, was a platonic one. The notion of a muse has a different twist here: rather than glowing from afar, she had to be present to be molded by Pirandello in the roles he created for her. "It is excruciating to see my drama interpreted by others," he wrote. "You were Fulvia for me, you were Ersilia, you were Signora Frola, you were the Stepdaughter, you were Silia Gala, you were Evelina Morli.... *They are all dead; and I am dead with them.*"

It must have seemed a great piece of luck for a young actress. Pirandello was very famous and very prolific. But the fact that after three years she left the company to take on other roles (thus initiating this correspondence) suggests she may have come to find it stifling. Pirandello scarcely separates her from himself: all his dreams are for their mutual triumph. "Now, in our case, the *true truth* is this: that I am your true father, and that you are my creature, my creature, my creature, in which all my spirit lives with the very power of my creation, so much so that it *has become your thing and you are all my life.*" "*My* Marta," he begins every letter. His appeals for her affection are monotonously desperate; but he has never understood her at all, she evidently says in one of her replies. And he makes it clear that he does not want her for discussion of the plays, that when he did discuss one of them with her it interfered with the writing. She must just be there, and embody the roles he invents for her.

Apart from the recurring plaints of love and loneliness, much of what Pirandello talks about in his letters to Abba is not of great interest except to historians of Italian theater. There were peaks in these late years of his career—he was in fact awarded the Nobel Prize in 1934—but also troughs. Plays unexpectedly flopped; because of the Depression, cinema contracts failed to come through (his comments on the new "talkies" are scandalized). Money seems to have been a recurring problem, though the notes make it clear that it need not have been; and there were embittered family quarrels. There is a paranoid feeling in Pirandello's repeated statements that his native land cares nothing for him or his work, and a grandiose one in his plans for a great future. For a time he had hopes of support from Mussolini, though it would be wrong to conclude that he was a paid-up Fascist—theater was all that concerned him. When he found that the Duce had no intention of setting up the network of theaters that he had hoped for, Pirandello returned to his view that Mussolini was "rough and coarse human material, made to command mediocre and vulgar people with disdain"—though unfortunately needed by Italy for the moment.

Pirandello alludes continually in the letters to suicide and death. His last letter to Marta Abba, in December 1936, ends with a sense of "horrible loneliness, like an abyss of despair." He was seventy. Six days later, pneumonia had finished him off, as it did Janacek. Marta Abba lived to be eighty-eight; she married a rich American named Severance A. Millikin, divorced, and made a late comeback to the Italian stage for a time. Two years before her death, she gave a reading from a wheelchair from Pirandello's letters at Princeton, to which she had just donated them. Perhaps she read this letter, which uniquely reveals how creativity can be invested in the image of one sole person:

> What not only matters but is also absolutely necessary for me this moment is to think that I'm writing for you.... I follow this image of you, in the situations in which I placed it, and little by little it finds for me the words and creates for me the scenes, and carries me ahead.... Without being aware of it, from so far away, perhaps not thinking even a little bit about me, taken by other thoughts, other preoccupations, you are doing my work.... Ah, my Marta, I absolutely must think that you are the same for me in order to continue to work as I am working. If for one moment I feel certain that you have already detached yourself from me...then everything dies inside me. I feel my soul and my breath falling apart; every light goes out in my brain, and

> my hand falls on the paper, motionless as a stone. Help me, help me.... Do not abandon me; think that not only I would die, but also your work.... The one who dictates inside is you; without you, my hand becomes a stone.

That such intense investment is fostered by absence, and less compatible with day-to-day life, is suggested by *Significant Others*, a collection of essays on "creative partnerships"—close alliances, whether temporary or permanent, heterosexual or homosexual, between partners who are both working in the arts.[2] The outcomes of these are mixed. At the best, these artists and writers could say, as did Robert Rauschenberg of his alliance with Jasper Johns, that "we gave each other permission." And "there was that business of triggering energies," Johns said. At the worst is André Malraux saying to Clara Malraux: "Better to be my wife than a second-rate writer." The talented Clara did cling to him as sole "significant other" long after they separated, but Isabelle de Courtivron, who wrote this chapter, considers that the angry tenacity prevented her from achieving as much as she should have.

There are characters, like Henry Miller and Anaïs Nin, who did each other good but—fortunately no doubt for them—were much too self-absorbed to ascribe dominance to someone else. One cannot imagine either of them saying, "The one who dictates inside is you." More temperately, Nin wrote to Miller that "you gave me reality and I gave you introspection, but we have to keep ourselves balanced against each other." And there are couples who, like Sonia and Robert Delaunay, managed by dividing the artistic field, easel painting for him and applied arts for her. "One made one thing and one made the other," she said. She also said that she chose to play second fiddle:

---

2. *Significant Others: Creativity and Intimate Partnership*, edited by Whitney Chadwick and Isabelle de Courtivron (Thames and Hudson, 1993).

"Robert had brilliance, the flair of genius. As for myself, I lived in greater depth"—which sounds like a justifiable claim to first-fiddling. Several of the women partners here are seen using forced strategies to define the boundary of their art against their partnerships.

Two asymmetrical couples from Bloomsbury are discussed. Though one cannot agree with Louise deSalvo that Virginia Woolf and Vita Sackville-West's affair "became the most significant and long-lasting in each of their lives," Sackville-West certainly was for a time a muse to Woolf. Woolf wrote *Orlando* specifically for her, one of the lightest and most easily written of her books. The editors of *Significant Others* bring in the transatlantic phrase "mothering the mind"; such long-term mothering was surely provided by austere Leonard Woolf and his cups of hot milk. Woolf did, incidentally, write in her diary that if her father were still alive she could have written nothing; a significant other can be damning. Of Vanessa Bell and Duncan Grant, Lisa Tickner points out how Bell's art flowered during her first years with Grant. It also declined thereafter; and the deep sadness picked up by the portraits and photos of Bell suggest that the price paid for the odd alliance may have been heavy. Overall, these shifting, difficult, hard-working companionships are as various as those of Janacek and Pirandello are similar.

11

SHELTERING: OLIVE SCHREINER

OLIVE SCHREINER WAS very anxious about the fate of her letters to her devoted friend Havelock Ellis. As she said, "All beauty & sacredness of human fellowship passes if the words you carelessly pour out to your friends are to be violated & given to the vulgar herd to gnaw on." The 607 letters between the two of them that make up *My Other Self: The Letters of Olive Schreiner and Havelock Ellis, 1884–1920*[1] are the remains of what its editor estimates were many thousands. Schreiner destroyed a huge number herself later in her life, and insisted that Ellis do the same. Moreover, in some of those that do survive, pages are torn or missing at what often seems to be a crucial point. All the more cheers for Olive Schreiner and for her preservation of some privacy: since even the letters collected in this volume can make one feel a crass intruder on the deeply personal, it is a relief to know that what she really wanted hidden is gone for good. (Besides, ten thousand letters would have been tough for both reader and reviewer.)

It is not that the correspondence is a steamily sexual one, though the "sex question," like the "woman question," was a crucial theme for both correspondents. Far more disturbing to us liberated readers is a pervasive tinge of yearning sentimental baby talk. The fact is that

1. Edited by Yaffa Claire Draznin (Peter Lang, 1992).

these two talented and deeply lonely people, having been deprived of an ordinary childhood, found each other and mothered each other—preferably by post, as they ran into difficulties when they were actually together. But we have to be brave about this and overcome contemporary squeamishness; Schreiner and Ellis, trembling pioneers both, taught themselves to overcome squeamishness about topics—"free love," birth control, homosexuality, perversion, women's suffrage—that to them were forbidden.

Schreiner was the older by five years and today is probably the better known, though her writing output was small compared to Ellis's. When the correspondence began she was twenty-nine, and had come to England from South Africa a few years earlier with a manuscript, *The Story of an African Farm*. She found a publisher eventually, and when the book came out it was a striking success. The story of young people growing up in the remote South African countryside, it reads a little creakily now, but what struck the readers of the 1880s was its bold feminism. Not only does its heroine, Lyndall, choose to live with a man without marriage, but she puts the woman's case with great eloquence. She is talking here to a boy of her age:

> "It is not what is done to us, but what is made of us," she said at last, "that wrongs us.... We all enter the world little plastic beings, with so much natural force, perhaps, but for the rest—blank; and the world tells us what we are to be, and shapes us by the ends it sets before us. To you it says—*Work*! and to us it says—*Seem*! To you it says—As you approximate to man's highest ideal of God, as your arm is strong and your knowledge great, and the power to labour is with you, so you shall gain all that human heart desires. To us it says—Strength shall not help you, nor knowledge, nor labour. You shall gain what men gain, but by other means. And so the world makes men and women."

(Lyndall, of course, dies young for her boldness, as women authors' heroines often do.)

Schreiner wrote the book in her early twenties, when she was governess to a family out in the karoo, the South African bush. Ninth child of a feckless missionary and a singularly unaffectionate mother, by the age of fifteen she had already left home to be shuffled between various families, doing governessing and other jobs. When she came to England on borrowed money she left behind some scandal or love affair about which little is known, and there was apparently another during her early days in England. Her aim in coming over had been to train as a doctor or nurse, but apart from the fact that she was asthmatic—more and more severely so in England—she was so agonizingly hypersensitive that she dropped out of training almost at once.

So when Havelock Ellis, a medical student of twenty-five, wrote to her in 1884, Schreiner was a single woman of nearly thirty who had "knocked about a bit." Ellis had read and liked *The Story of an African Farm*, and wrote to say so. His letter is in fact a little patronizing, though certainly not because the author was a woman, for she had written under the rather pathetic name of Ralph Iron (Ellis, a more unambivalent feminist, was later to chide her for taking the name). But what particularly moved him, he wrote, was that he too had lived out in isolated, beautiful country like the African karoo.

How this came about is an odd story. Ellis grew up the only boy in a family of four sisters and a dominating mother. His father was a sailor and away at sea most of the time. He grew up solemn, bookish, and self-contained. When he was sixteen his father took him on a sea voyage with him for his health and quite casually, it seems, decided to drop him in Australia because the climate might suit him. With no friends or relatives there, the boy managed to get by for four years on ill-paid jobs. The closest human contact he had in those years, he recalled, was when a girl said to him, "Ain't the moon lovely!," from which he fled in embarrassment. But in his last year there, when he was sole teacher in a tiny outback school that he shared with mice, he had some kind of revelation, coming out of the utter solitude, that the universe was good and right. Soon afterward he realized that he wanted to be a doctor, and left for England.

So both Schreiner and Ellis had had a similar experience of beauty and terror in the wilderness. Both had lacked ordinary mothering and had had to grow up too soon. Both were extremely literate and intelligent and concerned with the issues of the age, particularly the issues of sex—how men and women should live with them and with each other. They were confronting these rather than shrinking away; Ellis is now known for his dozen or so books with titles like *The Erotic Rights of Women* and *Sexual Inversion*, though he wrote on many other topics—poetry, drama, biography.

When they met after some weeks of correspondence, both must have felt that a soul mate had been found, truly an "other self." They told each other everything, including, on Ellis's side, his sexual feelings for his sister; he followed this with "I never even dreamed that I could ever meet anyone like you.... It is a marvel to me that two people who had never known each other, of different nationalities, living in different continents, could ever have had so much in common, in big things and little things." Schreiner wrote that "the dream, the faith that I should find some one just like myself was with me all through my childhood." Her appalling asthmatic ill health, exacerbated by the drugs of the time, became of great concern to Ellis as an aspiring doctor, which was just the comfort she needed—

> I feel so weak & I feel so tired, love. Put your arms round me. Yes, I know you do & it helps me so. I am unwell & I have such pain in my body. I feel so weak as if I wanted someone to stroke my hair. Oh I haven't anywhere to go to. I must have a place somewhere if it is only one tiny little room & no one shall turn

> me out. My comfort, my boy, you do let me rest my head against you. Please write to me.

Because Schreiner had a neurotic habit of moving from lodging to lodging, letters were her lifeline, and they wrote every day. She sewed his letters into little booklets like amulets. "My other-self, the little word I write to you & the word you write to me every day just makes life livable." It is like, and yet so unlike, the yearnings of Janacek and Pirandello. This was mutual.

It was, as she said, "no figure of speech when I say you are my other self." She was "not clear as to where you begin and I end." Ellis felt this infantlike loss of boundaries even more deeply and dizzily: "I sometimes feel as if you were living inside me & the Olive at St Leonards were only an unsubstantial shadow"; and "I'd like to be a part of your body that was always closest to you. I wish I was a little tiny thing that you could graft into you somewhere...." But if one is not in fact an infant, such radical loosenings of the self, such creepings into another, are frightening. Why, after all, did they not marry, or—since they both deeply distrusted conventional marriage—form a forward-looking late-Victorian free union? They were afraid; also, when they went on vacation together, Schreiner must have discovered that Ellis was effectively impotent. She did not draw away from him for the next two years or so—they were comrades, brother and sister, mother and child, two halves of one soul, both female, both male—but eventually there come hints of a changed relationship, Ellis claiming hurt and confusion, Schreiner exasperation and guilt. She makes the strange statement, from someone who has written a letter a day for over two years, that "I *need* you greatly in my life, but we seem to have so little to *say* to each other."

What they *had* been saying to each other and had now at last exhausted was not an exchange of news and views. Yaffa Claire Draznin, the editor of the correspondence, argues that in letters to anybody else Schreiner appears brisk and trenchant, and that it was Ellis's attitude that forced her to seem so plaintively fragile; Schreiner herself in one letter makes much the same point. All the same, the reliving of lost childhoods that is discernible in the first two years of the correspondence must have been something they both wanted. Schreiner's husband, in the biography of her he wrote after her death, relates a pitiful story: that she had said the greatest bliss of her life had been when once, when she was twelve, her mother had read one of her stories and hugged her. The reader feels that it was the waif-Schreiner, even more than the writer-Schreiner or the feminist-Schreiner or the fighter-Schreiner, who needed to be understood and loved.

But she moved on. Though Draznin's editing is careful, even to the point of telling us who Percy Bysshe Shelley was and where Genoa is, it is rather skimpy on biographical backing. When Schreiner left England in 1886 to spend two years in Europe, it has to be inferred that it was not only in the endless quest for health but because she was in a state of confusion over another man, the psychologist Karl Pearson—though she denied this. In Italy she was happier on the whole; then in 1889 she decided to go back to South Africa. Here in the clearer, dryer air she became better both physically and mentally. She wrote to Ellis in 1890 that for the first time in her life she felt now that she *could* marry: "It's very curious but I could now. It wouldn't impinge on my individuality too much. No one could reach me now. You know what I mean." And in 1894, reader, she did. Her husband was a South African politician, some years younger than herself, who took her name; the partnership seems to have been moderately successful, at least at first. She lost a daughter at one day old, and thereafter had miscarriages; what this must have meant to her cannot be known from the surviving letters. Nor do we learn from them anything about her strong views on South African politics, her disillusionment with Cecil Rhodes, and her opposition to the Jameson Raid and to the Boer War. There were many stories and articles, two posthumous novels, and in 1911 the book *Woman and Labour*, but nothing ever as popular as *The Story of an African Farm*. *My Other Self* should really be read with biographies of the two correspondents at hand.

Ellis also married, discovered his wife to be a lesbian, and used the material for another sexological volume. There were no children; his wife eventually became psychotic enough to have to be institutionalized. (She was perhaps rather like Olive Schreiner, in having a shell of tough intellect but deep inner confusions and despairs.) When Schreiner was in England in 1916 she visited her in the hospital. Ellis had further affectionate friendships with women, and became highly respected as a prolific and pioneering writer. The absence here of most of the later letters between Ellis and Schreiner gives the impression that it was a relationship that tailed off in disappointment, but in fact they went on writing sporadically up until Schreiner's death in 1920. The love affair that had been so deeply felt remained a lifelong friendship.

III

SEERS

12

SCALLYWAG & CO.: BLAVATSKY AND BESANT

HELENA PETROVNA BLAVATSKY, the founder of Theosophy, kept in her New York apartment in the 1870s a stuffed baboon with a copy of *The Origin of Species* under its arm, along with a platonically infatuated American colonel, a golden Buddha statue, and many piles of esoteric books. The baboon represented the science and materialism that were creeping up on the late nineteenth century and that Blavatsky and many others felt to be threatening and arid. At the end of *Madame Blavatsky's Baboon*, his survey of a century of cults and gurus, sincerity and fraudulence, hopes and disappointments, Peter Washington detects the faint sound of Blavatsky's baboon having the last laugh.[1]

Washington packages his subject as the rise of the Western guru; in fact, charisma, faith, leader and follower have never been absent from religion or history. In the period when Theosophy was founded, though, conditions were right for a really grand outburst. Washington outlines the background: the slow bombshell of Darwinism, the undermining of Christianity by biblical scholarship, decades of growing interest in the underpinnings of psychology, the beginnings of psychical research.

---

1. *Madame Blavatsky's Baboon: A History of the Mystics, Mediums, and Misfits Who Brought Spiritualism to America* (Schocken, 1995).

Blavatsky was an odd figure to step into the gap, though Theosophy waxed and prospered and became very influential. Nor was she really a *Western* guru. Daughter of eccentric Russian aristocrats (her mother, who died when Helena was five, was an important feminist writer of the early nineteenth century), she grew up shuttling between Odessa, Astrakhan, Tiflis, and St. Petersburg as her military father's career dictated. She was a wild child before the wild child was invented, passionate and uncontrollable, happiest riding cossack horses bareback. She was undoubtedly touched with some kind of psychic gift that caused odd things to happen in her wake. From time to time the local priest had to be called in to exorcise her. She sleepwalked, talked to invisible companions, and spun fantastical fairy tales that were prototypes for some of her accounts of her life. Growing up among the florid kitchen superstitions of the house serfs, she also read widely in occultism and could not have been unaware of the proliferating hermetic and cabalistic literature then becoming popular.[2]

As a motherless and lonely child whose adored father paid her little attention, Helena von Hahn convinced herself that she was under the special protection of exotic Eastern gurus who were grooming her for some great future task—and indeed she managed, more or less, to make this come true. But at seventeen, on hearing that her father had remarried, she married a middle-aged friend of the family and almost immediately ran away from him. Thereafter her own account of her world travels in search of esoteric wisdom has to be taken with a grain or two of salt. It is doubtful whether she could have got into Tibet, as she claimed, but certainly she roamed Turkey, Greece, Egypt, and Europe. She may have learned conjuring, may have taken drugs; she definitely frequented spiritualist groups and set up her own circle, complete with fraudulent apparatus, in Cairo.

Though Helena liked to claim, as a baggy old lady, that she was a

2. See Marion Meade, *Madame Blavatsky: The Woman Behind the Myth* (Putnam, 1980).

virgin, during her travels she became the common-law wife of an opera singer and had a son. He died, as children so often then did, at a few years old; she is said to have declared that at that moment she stopped believing in a God. Her companion, Metrovitch, was drowned in a shipwreck in which she nearly died herself.

Life had been rough with her. She swore like a trooper, smoked hand-rolled cigarettes continually, and, as she became stouter and stouter, was less and less the very image of a spiritual leader. "A sort of old Irish peasant woman, with an air of humour, and audacious power," Yeats called her, as he did the rounds of occult groups; G. K. Chesterton called her "a coarse, witty, vigorous, scandalous old scallywag."

She was in her forties when she washed up in New York. Her platonic military flatmate, Colonel Olcott, had been drawn to her by her psychic tricks—part genuine, perhaps, part conjuring. She was from time to time to call her followers to heel by staging a "miracle." Together they founded the Theosophical Society, acquired Indian connections, produced a journal, set up London premises, and attracted respectable, aspiring members. Blavatsky wrote Theosophical texts, astrally dictated to her, she said, by Tibetan masters. They told tales of universal electricity (Fohat) and a secret language (Senzar), the seven Dhyan-Chohans and seven sub-races, the Grand White Brotherhood and the Lords of Karma, the Hyperboreans, Lemurians, and Atlanteans. Most Theosophists did not read this part, but were attracted by the society's benign general aims of uniting religions and promoting brotherhood. Who could find fault with that?

Annie Besant, Blavatsky's unlikely successor to the leadership of the Theosophical Society, was right at the other end of the fraudulence spectrum from Blavatsky—scrupulous and idealistic, though sometimes short on humor and imagination. She would not have had the audacity to write an explanation of the universe, nor to claim to be under mystic instruction from Tibet, but, having inherited Theosophy, she also did not have the audacity to challenge any of its eccentricities.

When a Theosophist described his astral trips to Mars or was pursued by the police for molesting boys, she turned a blind eye, and in her own way was blurring fact and fantasy as Blavatsky did. Like Blavatsky, too, she suffered from the loneliness of the long-distance guru.

The scope of Besant's life is as extraordinary, in its way, as Blavatsky's. At sixteen, she was a passionate Christian who flagellated herself and begged Christ in her prayers to "kiss me with the kisses of His mouth; for thy love is better than wine"; at twenty-eight, she was notorious as a leader of militant atheism, and was to have her children forcibly removed from her because of her pernicious influence. At thirty-six, she was converted to socialism and went out in support of a strike of women workers. At forty-one, as a member of the powerful London School Board, she introduced free lunches and medical treatment for the first time in elementary schools. And then, at forty-two, she was converted for life to a "religion" hastily patched together by a psychic Russian aristocrat on the basis of occult messages from Tibetan gurus in the Himalaya. At sixty-six, after many years in India spreading the Theosophical gospel, she took up the cause of Indian independence and later presided over the Indian National Congress in Calcutta.

At the start, her marriage at eighteen to an austere young clergyman had been an obvious choice; for a girl passionate to do good and achieve something, being a vicar's wife offered almost a career. "She could not be the bride of Heaven, and therefore became the wife of Mr Frank Besant," her friend the editor W. T. Stead was to say. "He was hardly an adequate substitute." The marriage seems to have been doomed from the start, though a son and daughter were born. She doubts, in her autobiography, whether she was ever cut out to be a docile helpmeet.

She proceeded to take the most shocking course open to a clergyman's wife: she lost her Christian faith. As it was for Charles Darwin, the final straw seems to have been the sight of her young daughter suffering agonizing illness. Having worked through the tenets of Christianity point by point, she made an appointment to discuss them with the theologian Edward Pusey. He was outraged by her blasphemy: "It is not your duty to ascertain the truth." But this was something she was never to believe.

As she refused now to attend Holy Communion, her husband presented her with a choice: conform or leave. She left, permitted by law to keep one of her children with her, as well as a tiny sum of money. Like Helena Blavatsky in New York—though so much younger and less traveled—she was now outside society's conventions and had to choose a new direction. She chose a kind of anti-church: the National Secular Society, the home of Freethought. Besant espoused this cause passionately, writing, traveling, and lecturing. In her totally different way she acquired, like Blavatsky, charisma. She was our martyr, wrote an admirer:

> She faced a hostile world on behalf of liberty and truth. We young men, who had the passion of these things in our souls, responded readily to the passion with which she pleaded for them. We were carried away. Mrs. Besant's portrait was for sale at the close of the lecture and I still have the copy which I bought at the time. Its colours are now faded, but the image of this young prophetess of religious and political progress as she appeared on her first lecturing tour is still fresh in my mind.

As she was to say of herself, by now "all orthodox society turned up at me its respectable nose"—and there was worse. Her husband gained custody of their second child on the grounds that the girl would be "outcast in this life and damned in the next" if she were to stay with her mother. Besant was not to see her children again until many years later.

But she worked on doggedly, moving from Freethought toward

radical politics. In the 1880s unemployment was high and people were hungry. She fought in the "Bloody Sunday" demonstration in London's Trafalgar Square, in which 130 marchers were injured and two killed in battles with the police. In the history of the labor movement it has not been forgotten, nor has the "match-girls' strike" that Besant supported, mounted by young women working in dangerous conditions for a pittance. By this time she had probably seen more of the way the poor lived than any other woman of her class in the country. "Oh, those trudges through the lanes and alleys round Bethnal Green Junction late at night, when our day's work was over," she wrote, "children lying about on shavings, rags, anything; famine looking out of baby faces, out of women's eyes, out of the tremulous hands of men."

She was still, nevertheless, deeply unhappy: the questions that Christianity had once answered for her still remained. She was reading a good deal around the then current topics of spiritualism, clairvoyance, thought transference. Then she was given to review Blavatsky's (almost) unreadable *The Secret Doctrine*. "I am immersed in Madame Blavatsky!" she quipped. "If I perish in the attempt to review her, you must write on my tomb, 'She has gone to investigate the Secret Doctrine at first hand.'" But in spite of its length and its obscurity, Besant was to find here the light, the answers to her questions. She made an appointment to visit Blavatsky at the London headquarters of the Theosophical Society. "From Storm to Peace" she headed this chapter of her autobiography:

> "My dear Mrs Besant, I have so long wished to see you," and I was standing with my hand in her firm grip, and looking for the first time in this life straight into the eyes of "H. P. B." I was conscious of a sudden leaping forth of my heart—was it recognition?—and then, I am ashamed to say, a fierce rebellion, a fierce withdrawal, as of some wild animal when it feels a mastering

> hand.... She talked of travels, of various countries, easy brilliant talk, her eyes veiled, her exquisitely moulded fingers rolling cigarettes incessantly.... We rose to go, and for a moment the veil lifted, and two brilliant, piercing eyes met mine, and with a yearning throb in the voice: "Oh, my dear Mrs Besant, if you would only come among us!" I felt a well-nigh uncontrollable desire to bend down and kiss her, under the compulsion of that yearning voice, those compelling eyes, but with a flash of the old unbending pride and an inward jeer at my own folly, I said a commonplace polite goodbye....

And so the two extraordinary—and extraordinarily different—women met. Besant was to stay with, and eventually lead, the Theosophists until her death in 1933; it was a genuine example of conversion, as described with such intensity by William James in *The Varieties of Religious Experience*—the "shifting of men's centers of personal energy within them and the lighting up of new crises of emotion" (and the Jameses knew much of this, in both its benign and malign forms). Annie's loving but slightly cynical friend George Bernard Shaw, somewhat appalled by the turn of events, believed that the key to it was her strong histrionic streak:

> She was successively a Puseyite Evangelical, an Atheist Bible-smasher, a Darwinian secularist, a Fabian Socialist, a Strike Leader, and finally a Theosophist, exactly as Mrs. Siddons was a Lady Macbeth, Lady Randolph, Beatrice, Rosalind, and Volumnia. She "saw herself" as a priestess above all. That was how Theosophy held her to the end.

Theosophy was extraordinarily successful because it filled a gap in the late nineteenth century that is now very apparent to us. Christianity was ostensibly still strong but its foundations had been shaken by

Darwinism, and the more intelligent knew it. At the same time, it was an age when spiritualistic phenomena were flourishing and catching the attention of serious investigators. When the Society for Psychical Research was founded in 1882, it was headed not by nonentities but by Cambridge philosophers. Freud had not yet arrived, but there was a feeling that psychology contained many mysteries; James's *Principles of Psychology*, published in 1890, devoted full chapters to hypnotism, the stream of thought, and the consciousness of self. And the scraps of Buddhist and Hindu thought that were incorporated into Theosophy were exciting at a time when knowledge of comparative religions was confined to a handful of scholars. Along with these, a revival of occult traditions going back to Neoplatonism, Gnosticism, alchemy, and Rosicrucianism was under way.

A new and exotic "religion" was needed, and Theosophy had something for everybody. It managed to coexist with the "higher thought" generally—Fabianism, the Ethical Church, spiritualism, and Theosophy rubbed shoulders, and Annie Besant was not the only one to dabble in them severally. Edith Lees, Havelock Ellis's wife, left in her novel *Attainment* a semifictional account of a cooperative she ran in the early 1900s. Her characters include a poet, an anarchist, a botanist, and a Theosophist who is a "developed soul." Vegetarian food is served, a book on ethics lies open on a table, and on the walls are pictures of Madame Blavatsky, Queen Victoria, Goethe, and Walt Whitman. "We have tried to assimilate all the newer ideas of the day," says one of the members.

In 1883 Besant moved into the society's London headquarters, and from then on worked tirelessly for the cause. When she returned from a visit to the United States in 1891, she found that Blavatsky, who had long been ailing, had at last died. She took over the society's European branches; then a couple of years later, when she first visited Ceylon, India became her base. The Theosophists' beneficent works in India cannot be overestimated: they involved not only the founding of schools and colleges but a restoration of Indian self-confidence by Westerners who treated the color bar with contempt, and encouraged Indians to respect their religions and literary heritage. Both Nehru and Gandhi spoke of Besant's influence with admiration.

As early as 1902 she had been writing that "India is not ruled for the prospering of the people, but rather for the profit of her conquerors, and her sons are being treated as a conquered race." She had encouraged Indian national consciousness, attacked caste and child marriage, and worked effectively for Indian education. It was inevitable, with her restless need to build new empires, that she should move on to active political work. As she put it in the familiar Besantine "thrilling voice": "Liberty was being strangled to death, and I, as one of her old soldiers, could not stand aside. I joined the political campaign not to lead, but to take risks." She did take risks, and she also led. When she started her campaign she was in her sixties. Interned during the First World War for a time on the grounds that she was acting "in a manner prejudicial to the public safety," her finest hour was as president of the Indian National Congress in 1917.

As Theosophy had prospered and spread, two important cults diverged from its main stream. In 1913 the German branch, led by Rudolf Steiner, broke away from the parent body and renamed itself Anthroposophy. (Kafka reports in his diary, deadpan, a visit to Steiner: he tells Steiner of his passion for writing, his dead-end insurance job, his attraction to Theosophy; Steiner nods, sniffs, his nose runs, he works his handkerchief "deep into his nose, one finger in each nostril." End of anecdote.) Anthroposophy survives today remarkably successfully, in England and on the Continent, running schools, colleges, nursing homes, shops, training courses, and homes for the handicapped. In *Madame Blavatsky's Baboon* Washington traces its history through the building of the great Goetheanum in Switzerland, its burning down and Steiner's death of heartbreak, up to its present-day efficiency.

The other offshoot, the Krishnamurti branch, is less Germanically worthy and more extraordinary. Washington recapitulates the story as told in the books of Lady Emily Lutyens and her daughter Mary, both deeply involved in the events, to the dismay of her husband, the architect Edward Lutyens. Krishnamurti, son of an Indian Theosophist hanger-on, had been picked up on a Madras beach by the evil genius of the society, the shady pedophile Charles Leadbetter, who claimed the child had an especially spiritual aura. Krishnamurti was certainly beautiful, as a child, as an adult, and even as a very old man—which was perhaps his bad luck. Under Annie Besant's leadership, the Theosophists adopted him and decided he was to be the new World Leader predicted by Theosophical theory. The boy was dressed by London tailors, coached (unsuccessfully) for Oxford, and fostered to manhood in a bewildering mixture of adulation and racial snubs. He had the courage to throw off the whole Theosophical fantasy in adulthood and, being trained only for gurudom, went freelance. (Though I have been surprised by quite intelligent people's affection for his books and lectures, I had always thought of Krishnamurti as gentle, sad, and virtuous, and was sorry to read of a recent update on his life—a book accusing him of a long affair with a married woman who befriended him, and of his ordering her to have abortions.)

The other main cultist stream followed through by Washington (as well as those of many, many mini-gurus) is the life and times of Greek-Armenian Georgei Gurdjieff, born near the Russian–Turkish border and, like Blavatsky, only a Western guru perforce, since he had to flee the Russian Revolution. Like Blavatsky, too, he was outrageous, jokey, and disconcerting, leaving his followers suspended between adoration and shock. He looked and sounded rather like Hercule Poirot (could Agatha Christie have heard of him?), but for little gray cells substituted planetary forces, sevenfold rays, and the three bodies of man. Chiefly, though, he was a direct teacher, by talks and examples, of the disciples he gathered around him; anyone who knows the encounter-type groups of the Seventies or has read about brainwashing techniques will recognize the instinctive skills he used to draw and hold people. Reading about Gurdjieff and his communities, if you are intrigued by that sort of thing, can become addictive, and evidently so can writing about them—there are a number of books by intelligent followers, and the movement has been extensively documented by James Webb in *The Harmonious Circle: The Lives and Works of G. I. Gurdjieff, P. D. Ouspensky and Their Followers.*[3]

Washington also traces the career of Ouspensky, a clever and melancholy Russian disciple of Gurdjieff who adopted Gurdjieff's system but broke away from him personally because he disliked his morals (Gurdjieff had several children by followers, and there must be dark-eyed descendants of the magus in France now). Ouspensky was an original and a scholar; before he ever met Gurdjieff he had experimented with two techniques now fashionable: "lucid" dreaming and the expansion of consciousness by drugs. He led an earnest and secretive group of mind improvers in England for many years; after his death it became the School of Economic Science, which advertised meditation classes in the London Underground. The update on the SES, according to Washington, is its amalgamation with the Maharishi (*the* Maharishi, of Transcendental Meditation), the opening of its own schools in England and abroad, and the development of a repressive fringe group "exposed" by articles in the London *Evening Standard* in the Eighties.

It is easy to have fun with the ridiculous aspects of gurus and cults —too easy. But if one assumes that they cover a spectrum, from the positively sinister at one end to the established religions at the other, it is worth asking what it is that makes a guru, and what it is that makes a disciple. A common denominator of discipleship seems to be the wish to find, as Casaubon of *Middlemarch* wished, a Key to All

3. Putnam, 1980.

Mythologies—a scheme, a pattern or patterns, that makes everything fit together. It is a far from unreasonable wish. The disciple wants, too, that the Key should be embodied in a Teacher. The Teacher has the plan and the words and has done the thinking, and need only be followed implicitly. And if the Key and the Teacher involve Secrecy, it is much the better. That the Key should simply be: be aware, be collected, think clearly, behave generously, is too ordinary. This is not to say that there have not been underground or secret traditions drawn on by the gurus—Gnosticism, cabalism, alchemy, Rosicrucianism, and the rest—and that they have a great deal of fascination; but where there is good sense quoted here from the cults, it is usually reducible to simple, difficult precepts.

What on earth, then, does the guru want? "Fame, riches, and the love of women," the goals that Freud ascribed to artists? To change the world, or to acquire ninety-seven Rolls-Royces? Assuming a spectrum again, from fraudulence to sincerity, it would seem that most of these gurus—Annie Besant entirely excepted—wanted some mixture of the two. Some of them did not even claim to be gurus. Rudolf Steiner was a quiet and earnest leader who did not aim to annex lives or hold crowds spellbound; Ouspensky led a serious movement without demanding star status; Krishnamurti never ceased saying that right living came from personal decision rather than from a teacher. Very little fraudulence there; but the trouble is that such people attract blind devotion, whether they want it or not. Gurdjieff (who was certainly not simon-pure) based his teaching on waking up and taking control of life—but his charismatic and capricious personality made him absolute dictator to his groups. He was, incidentally, the only really modern guru, in spite of his occultism, in that what he offered was not simple salvation, but a *self*, that twentieth-century grail. Ignore your "personality," he taught, and find your real self. His most famous follower (though not for long), Katherine Mansfield, wrote when she joined his community shortly before her death from tuberculosis,

"The question is always: *Who am I?* . . . If I were allowed one single cry to God, that cry would be: *I want to be* REAL." (Even Christ, though, did not say, "Come unto me, and I shall make you real.") Gurdjieff could almost be seen as a kind of exotic anti-Freud, constructing his psychology out of some of the same materials; news of a subconscious self had reached as far as the town of Kars in Kurdistan, where Gurdjieff grew up reading everything he could lay his hands on. Both men, even, had been hypnotists and given that up. What Freud, but not Gurdjieff, cracked, though, was the problem of "transference," which dogged Gurdjieff in the form of sheeplike followers.

On the fraudulence spectrum, Blavatsky herself could be put pretty near the guilty end, having invented her Tibetan masters transmitting global commands, and being thenceforth bound to the production of missives out of the air at appropriate moments. The handwriting on them was suspiciously like her own. Richard Hodgson of the Society for Psychical Research, who was sent to investigate her claims, concluded in his report that she was "neither the mouthpiece of hidden seers, nor a mere vulgar adventuress; we think that she has achieved a title to permanent remembrance as one of the most accomplished, ingenious, and interesting imposters in history." He was so puzzled by the pointlessness of her frauds that he concluded she must be spying for Russia, which is unlikely. And yet, if all she needed was to keep afloat financially, there must have been easier ways to do so than by founding a new religion—giving Russian lessons, for instance, or being a cleaning lady. Some of what she proclaimed she probably believed, and, where she knew she told lies, she was able to convince herself that, in a way, they were truth. At other times she knew they were not, and felt surrounded by dupes, which was lonely.

In spite of their extraordinary careers, both the outrageous Blavatsky and the fastidious Besant harbored an underlying sadness. Both had lost children, the most terrible of experiences (Annie's could only join her when they came of age), and had no personally supportive partner. Blavatsky always missed Russia and her family there. In old age she retreated into herself—ill, playing endless games of solitaire, hurt despite herself by press ridicule. Besant kept melancholy at bay by compulsive work, and lapsed if she was deprived of it.

The good and bad effects of cults seem to be unpredictable. How is it that Steiner's Anthroposophy has become so far-reaching and beneficent, while the enormously influential parent group, Theosophy, has dwindled? Anthroposophy's particular success, its work with the mentally handicapped, is directly linked with the belief in karma and reincarnation that was picked up from Eastern sources by Blavatsky: for if handicapped people are souls going through a particular kind of incarnation, it is easier to treat them honorably than if they are just nature's mistakes. Theosophy itself seems to have done no harm (except perhaps to the unfortunate Krishnamurti), but in its early days it could not have been expected that its best achievement would be its schools in India and Ceylon (there is an Olcott Street in the center of Colombo) and perhaps a restoration to Westernized Indians of pride in their religious heritage. Gurdjieff's and Ouspensky's movements had their suicides and breakdowns, but also a large number of people claiming to have benefited greatly. Only those who hold that believing anything without rational backing is intrinsically wrong, or who are sure they can distinguish second-rate spiritual experience from the real thing, can take an austere view of the Western guru.

13

IS IT REAL?: RUTH

MORTON SCHATZMAN IS perhaps best known as the author of *Soul Murder*, a groundbreaking study of the most famous of nineteenth-century madmen, Judge Daniel Schreber.[1] While his contemporary subject, "Ruth,"[2] is not as extraordinary as Schreber and, indeed, not in the strict sense mad, his account of her ability to hallucinate has interesting implications. (Was Enid Blyton hallucinating when she watched her stories of Little Noddy and Mr. Plod unfold in her mind's eye?[3]) Ruth's story is very much of the 1970s, but might well be followed up by inquisitive psychologists.

Schatzman, an American psychiatrist working at the Arbours Crisis Centre in London, had a very distressed American girl referred to him. She had recently become anxious, claustrophobic, sleepless, and suicidal, and had also come to hate sexual relations with her husband and to hallucinate him as looking like her father. In view of her life story this was not surprising: the father, who had been away in prison for much of her childhood, had raped her when she was ten, and as a

---

1. Random House, 1973.

2. *The Story of Ruth* (Putnam, 1980).

3. See chapter 15.

result she had been put in a children's home for seven years. There had been many other traumatic childhood experiences.

In her sessions with Schatzman she revealed that she was hallucinating her father more and more vividly and more often—though she showed no signs of any psychotic delusions that the hallucinations were real, and in all other ways her symptoms were simply those of anxiety neurosis or mild "nervous breakdown." Schatzman chose to treat her in an unorthodox fashion, which he says led to a successful recovery: he encouraged her to practice hallucinating deliberately, to control her visions and vary them and act out dialogues with them, to consider hallucinating as an imaginative skill rather than a symptom of madness. One would suspect several influences at work in this choice of treatment: the arguments of R. D. Laing (guiding spirit of the Arbours Association) that "mad" experiences can be valuable; the Gestalt therapy of Fritz Perls, in which the patient is encouraged to act out histrionically the personages of his dreams and fantasies; and the "dream therapy" of a Malaysian tribe, the Senoi, that has been much discussed (and somewhat discredited)—the Senoi are said to train their children to control their dreams and turn them to good account, redreaming a nightmare, for instance, until it has a successful ending. (This latter is reminiscent of Henry James's account in *A Small Boy and Others* of a "dream-adventure," an "immense hallucination," in which he turned the tables in his dream on enemies who were trying to break into his room by bursting open the door himself and scattering them.)

Schatzman encouraged Ruth to practice hallucinating friends, relatives, her children; then himself, then her "self"—that is, she would hallucinate another Ruth across the room and act out a dialogue with her in order to gain insight into her troubles. She hallucinated her husband making love to her and reported it to be very satisfactory. As the psychoanalysand eagerly produces dreams and fantasies for the analyst, Ruth produced more and more lively hallucinations for her psychiatrist. She was persuaded to project the hallucination of her father onto her own body, so that when Schatzman interrogated "him" she gave a convincing impersonation of a violent and brutal man. She remained sane, and became, on the whole, less anxious, less plagued by involuntary hallucinations, and less bitter about her father.

Schatzman was obviously hoping for paranormal psychic manifestations while she was in these states of semi-trance. He plants a series of come-ons: Would the hallucination leave physical traces of itself behind? If Ruth hallucinated someone turning on the light, would she be able to read by it? If she hallucinated a conversation and left the tape recorder running, would there be anything on the tape? If she hallucinated Schatzman and asked him questions, would "his" answers be correct? "No" was the answer in each case; any reasonably gifted medium could summon up more clairvoyance than this, and the story —even though Schatzman uses the word "apparition" persistently for the hallucinations—is not of particular value to parapsychology.

The next stage of Schatzman's experiments with Ruth was age regression: having her hallucinate (or rather imagine) herself back to the age of fifteen, ten, five, a year. This remarkable ability had been demonstrated before under deep hypnosis, given exceptionally good hypnotic subjects (there is actually a Stanford Hypnosis Susceptibility Scale to assess this). An adult Japanese, for instance, who had spoken no Japanese since early childhood, is said to have been taken back under hypnosis to the age of three and to have spoken Japanese fluently; when he was awake he could not understand his own speech on the tape. In the nineteenth century Pierre Janet cured a girl of hysterical blindness by taking her back to a trauma at the age of six. Ruth, too, produced vivid and in some cases verifiable memories of her childhood; but she differed importantly from the other cases that have been described by being her own hypnotist. She claimed not to be able to remember these trances afterward, and to be very exhausted by them.

The third stage of the experiments consisted of psychological and physiological tests, at the Maudsley Hospital and the University of Bristol, administered to Ruth both in her normal state and when she was hallucinating. Various tests of the adult Ruth and the "child" Ruth showed the childish responses, and the handwriting, to be quite consistent with the age she was enacting—as has been found in other experiments with hypnotic age regression. Perhaps most interesting were the physical tests. Electroencephalograms were taken while Ruth deliberately "saw" one of her hallucinations against a lighted screen. There were some ambiguous results at first; but Schatzman declares that, at one point, the pattern of electrical activity from her brain indicated that she was not seeing the light—the hallucination had blocked it out and inhibited the visual response. Noise was fed into her ears through earphones; when she hallucinated someone switching it off, the brain's response to sound disappeared. Schatzman does not make it clear, however, whether such effects have been obtained before.

How much in this case history is sensational or new? There is, first, the question of credibility. Schatzman's style tells heavily against him here. That neither Ruth nor her husband comes across as a real person may be ascribed to a simple lack of literary skill; but when Schatzman describes Ruth as having a dream in which she tells him that her anger "is like a great big ball of fire. If it starts to roll, I don't think I could stop it," asks her husband, "Could you love me when I'm full of hate and anger?" and has Schatzman tell her, "You mustn't keep your feelings from being released. Feel the anger. Don't suppress it any longer," credibility sags to the point of collapse. So it does when Ruth, asked to hallucinate Schatzman writing a note to her, declares that it reads: "Hello, Ruth. This note is to you. Our research is going to interest many people all over the world. Sincerely, Morty Schatzman." Embellishment there certainly is, but since on previous evidence all that he relates *could* be true, let us take the story at face value nevertheless.

Hallucinations, first of all, are not as rare as is supposed, nor different in kind from a whole spectrum of dreams, fantasies, and images; although they are most likely to occur when people are delirious, drugged, fasting, or exhausted, they quite soon start appearing to sane people if they are kept in total darkness. Even ordinary mental imagery is a much more vivid affair for some people than others. Francis Galton, investigating it in the 1880s, interrogated friends and acquaintances of great respectability and turned up cases like the authoress who explained that "when I think of the word Beast, it has a face something like a gurgoyle. The word Green also has a gurgoyle face, with the addition of big teeth. The word Blue blinks and looks silly, and turns to the right"; the statesman who found his speeches annoyingly interrupted by hallucinations of his scribbled manuscript, which he had to stop and decipher; the clergyman who automatically saw a series of pictures whenever he closed his eyes—for instance, a crossbow, flight of arrows, falling stars, snowstorm, rectory, fishpond, bed of red tulips, and so on.[4] (The clergyman was sometimes able, with difficulty, to control and direct the images, as Ruth did; but this is unusual.)

Hypnogogic imagery—visions just before falling asleep—are especially common; a study at the University of Sheffield found that nearly half of a group of students had experienced them. Galton knew "no less than five editors of very influential newspapers" who had these night visions—a result of the anxieties of journalism, perhaps? Another distinct variant is eidetic imagery; "eidetikers"—usually children, for the ability fades in adulthood—are able to image things to themselves in photographic detail, sometimes long after they first saw them. (Ruth, who reported that she always won the "Pelmanism" game as a child because she had a photographic memory of the cards, qualified as an adult "eidetiker" when she was tested; when regressed to childhood

4. *Enquiries into Human Faculty and Its Development* (Macmillan, 1883).

in her trance states, she had the ability to an even more striking degree.) There is one detailed case on record of a hypertrophied visual imagination: in *The Mind of a Mnemonist*, published in the 1920s, the Russian psychologist A. R. Luria investigated a professional "memory man." The mnemonist's hallucinatory visual recall enabled him to earn a living by extraordinary feats of memory, but disqualified him for ordinary work. All in all one must agree with Galton that there is a "continuity between all the forms of visualization, beginning with an almost total absence of it, and ending with complete hallucination"; and that most people could visualize much more vividly if they had not been taught in childhood to discredit these experiences.

Nevertheless, realistic hallucinations appearing all over the place are, of course, well out of the ordinary. A study at the University of Sheffield, for instance, found that only fourteen out of the seventy-two student participants reported having had a "real" hallucination. Even in schizophrenia, auditory hallucinations ("voices") are commoner than visual ones, and when the latter appear they are taken for real. Schreber, for instance, the brilliantly mad German judge whom Schatzman has written about, described black bears, small yellow men, two suns simultaneously in the sky, people changing heads, a magic building growing out of the earth; and they were real, he insists in his story—God arranged them by special miracles. Ruth apparently was never confused about the reality status of her visions, only frightened, upset, and isolated from others by them.

More relevant to her case than schizophrenia are the hysterical phenomena so often reported in the nineteenth century and now so rare. Hysterical patients in those days would have, for instance, paralysis or anesthesia in just one part of the body, would go easily into hypnotic trances, or have total amnesia about some of their experiences—they were liable, in other words, to dissociate or repress parts of their experience very thoroughly. Nowadays we perhaps express a sense of dissociation less graphically and naively. Hallucinations, which imply a blocking out of the actual world in order to attend to the inner world, were part of the nineteenth-century pattern: in Josef Breuer's celebrated case history of Anna O., for example, he describes his patient falling into a *condition seconde* every evening, in which she believed she was still living in the previous year, before her father died. She thought herself to be in the bedroom she had had then, and would walk toward the door when she wanted the window, for instance. Though she "knew" her dress was green, she complained of seeing it as blue; it transpired that on exactly the same day of the previous year she had been sewing a blue nightshirt for her father. Yet she was quite unlike Schreber in that she knew she was ill, and could communicate what was happening.

We also have to consider, apropos of Ruth's trances and impersonations, how normal and deeply rooted is our tendency to dramatize our inner life (even to Schatzman dramatization comes naturally: as he ponders Ruth's case he is "haunted by a skeptical inner voice," "hears a whimsical voice whisper," and so on). We take for granted the extraordinariness of a play or novel that presents us with a whole world of people whom we discuss as if they were real; but the fact that Hamlet did not exist before Shakespeare crystallized a part of himself into the character is really as odd as anything reported here. Writers have reported over and over again that at times their work seems as if "given" from somewhere else; actors and actresses find themselves inventing a whole human being out of the pages of a script. If our ordinary fantasies could be instantly scripted, acted, and transposed to a television screen they would, no doubt, be amazing.

The phenomenon of mediumship (which, like hysteria, was more prominent in the nineteenth century) is an instance of this ability to project imaginary personae. Though mediums *can* acquire information clairvoyantly, the "Red Indian" and Egyptian priestesses whom they claim as their "controls" are patently projections of themselves. In the 1930s Whately Carrington, of the Society for Psychical Research, carried out a psychological test very like one of Ruth's on the highly reputable medium Mrs. Leonard. Mrs. Leonard claimed that her communications in trance came via "Feda," a Red Indian girl who had died in childbirth. Carrington gave both Mrs. Leonard and "Feda" word-association tests and found that the reaction times and word associations of the two were almost polar opposites; "Feda," he believed, was a secondary personality of Mrs. Leonard's based on her own repressions. And then, finally, there are the physiological tests that showed Ruth to be responding to what she was hallucinating rather than what she was actually "seeing": there are precedents for this too. Experimental subjects have been trained by biofeedback, for instance, to influence the alpha rhythms that appear on their EEG tracings; and Luria reports that his mnemonist could increase the temperature of his right hand, and lower that of his left, by imagining they were placed on a hot stove and a piece of ice respectively.

Nothing in this story, then, is beyond belief—whether or not we are "haunted by skeptical inner voices" ourselves. What is extremely unusual, if it is true, is that such a powerful and dissociated imagination should appear in this century and in a sane (though very traumatized) person. Clearly Ruth's skill in hallucinating developed fast in order to please her psychiatrist; it is also very relevant that there was a family tradition of "seeing things" that provided an encouraging context, like the cultural context of a shaman or medicine man. In particular, her alcoholic father, whom she both loved and hated, had had hallucinations when he was drunk, so that by hallucinating *him* during her breakdown she was doubly identifying with him. Whether Schatzman's novel form of therapy would always be safe and advisable is dubious; but it is certainly time, after nearly a century of neglect, that we investigate these byways of the imagination again.

14

BENIGN SPELLS: WITCHES

THE WORD "WITCH" still carries a tremendous charge, at least to those brought up on fairy tale and myth, who half remember the stony gaze of Medusa; and the Graeae "by the shore of the freezing sea, nodding upon a white log of drift-wood, beneath the cold white winter moon"; and mothers who turn out to be stepmothers, grandmothers who are wolves in disguise, godmothers who bestow a curse when they are not invited to the party. These witches are always women (the magician figure is different altogether) and often they *seem* beautiful—the cannibal witch in *Hansel and Gretel* lives in a house made of delicious sweets—beautiful enough to entice you into their power. In my dreams of witches in childhood you were safe as long as you pretended to be fooled by them. The word "wicked" automatically goes with this witch; there are fairy godmothers, of course, and benign fairies, but in comparison they are rather wishy-washy figures. Whether the *frisson* is there for someone nourished only on TV and comics I don't know; I suspect it is, even if faintly. Since even before the organized persecution of the witch-hunts, there has always been this image of a dangerously powerful woman, either a beautiful "Belle Dame sans Merci" or a hideous hag. When Papageno in *The Magic Flute* is tricked into uncovering the false Papagena, it is the archetypal witch hag he finds.

It may be a psychoanalytic cliché that the image arises from the fact that we start our lives in the hands of a powerful woman who sometimes frustrates us, and that (for men) she tempts and frustrates again in adulthood; but I think it is true. In old, durable myths the powerful good/bad woman, instead of being split into wicked witch and fairy godmother, is more realistically worshiped as a giver of both pleasure and pain—as Kali in India, or the very temperamental Greek goddesses, or (as the modern witches studied by T. M. Luhrmann maintain[1]) a fertility goddess behind all religions, such as the German Holda, still extant when Grimm was researching. Holda brings fertility to women and farmers, but can turn into a hag with huge teeth when she is angry.

Though we are still wary of the witch, the traditional European trappings—pointed hat, cauldron, and so on—have become Disneyfied, Halloweenized, and have lost meaning. To Shakespeare's audiences the witches of *Macbeth* were terrifying, but I have never seen a performance where there was not a suppressed giggle; and who can forget the hag stirring her cauldron in *Il Trovatore* while the Marx Brothers zip up and down the backdrops in *A Night at the Opera*? To be frightening the witch dresses up differently now—as Alex Forrest in *Fatal Attraction*, perhaps.

The modern London witches studied by Luhrmann do not wear pointed hats with stars on them, and strongly dissociate themselves from the wickedness stereotype. Though the dangerous and the holy, the curser and the blesser, are inevitably linked, white magic is at pains to distinguish itself from black.

Sex and secrets and the breaking of taboos must be somewhere on the occult scene, though the youngsters you see on the London Underground draped with chains and their black leather jackets daubed over

1. *Persuasions of the Witch's Craft: Ritual Magic in Contemporary England* (Harvard University Press, 1989).

with swastikas and death's heads are probably sweet kids really. Luhrmann does mention a type of antisocial occultism linked with pop music, but believes it to be mainly harmless (though she was called in to advise on a murder associated with it). The influence of horror movies on some of these teenagers must be considerable, though we know little about it. But Luhrmann (she is an American anthropologist, and a fellow of an English university) understandably wanted to carry out her research among a nicer class of people. The groups she mingled with, though they certainly believed they could raise psychic energy to influence the material world, claimed chiefly to see their work as spiritually healing.

In spite of their genuinely serious aims, this is somewhat at odds with the rationale of witchcraft as described by anthropologists and historians. From E. E. Evans-Pritchard's study of the Azande onward, anthropologists have tended to see witchcraft beliefs as a way of apportioning blame for the bad things that happen, even if the witches themselves (unlike sorcerers) are unaware of causing harm. From the historian's point of view, there have been two distinct kinds of magic: village *maleficium* like that described by anthropologists, and high ritual magic based on the early "sciences"—cabalism, astrology, alchemy, and Neoplatonic philosophy. Both, to the Church, became anathema, conflated with heresy and Satanism and all things evil. Shaw's pious Saint Joan, for instance, is burned as a witch for a confusion of reasons—because she magically wins battles, because she wears men's clothing, because she claims God and his angels speak directly to her. Magic would seem to involve both a sense of having power within and of being threatened by power without; but particularly the latter, as worldwide beliefs in the evil eye show.

The coven Luhrmann attended was concerned with fostering power within, with the magus tradition of conjuring up force. Luhrmann's own quest, in living with witches for over a year, was psychological and epistemological: she wanted to know what enables people—in this case, mostly educated middle-class city dwellers—to adopt beliefs and practices that run counter to those of their society. Whether the practices "work" or not, she says, is irrelevant (which is somewhat disingenuous, for if she had observed spells affecting the external world—and she did—there would be no great puzzle about why practitioners stuck to their beliefs). She calls her method psychological anthropology; and the fact that, unlike most anthropologists, she could really participate in the group and speak its language makes her book highly accessible to the ordinary reader, far removed from boring kinship diagrams of a tribe in some jungly spot we are never likely to visit. The center of her whole enterprise, she says, is the nature of rationality and irrationality: no small subject.

It is surprising that the people Luhrmann mixed with trusted her so completely, for secrecy is the essence of magical practice. They were friendly, and by no means isolates, apart from their shared worldview. She did tell them about her project, she says, but they tended to forget. She joined fully in their activities and did no note-taking on the spot, though there are a few interesting taped conversations. She scanned occult publications, went to festivals and conferences, attended workshops and various transitory groups, and was lucky enough to be accepted by an old, established, and dedicated coven.

The British occult scene, she found, is itself jungly. A rough map would show it at one end joining the whole New Age or Aquarian territory that includes alternative medicine, vegetarianism and veganism, dreamy music, and groups of a generally "mind-expanding" nature; at the other end it links with old magical traditions, revived in the 1880s, via Rosicrucianism and Freemasonry, in the Hermetic Order of the Golden Dawn (to which Yeats belonged), and again in the 1940s and 1950s by Gerald Gardner. Gardner, who claimed to have been initiated by an older witch representing a long line, wrote rituals and organized covens led by high priestesses.

All kinds of rival subgroups now proliferate, alike in being woman-centered and worshiping the ancient Goddess figure—Diana, Hecate, Holda, Isis, Cerridwen. The writings of the eccentric historian Margaret Murray, postulating an old fertility religion hiding behind Christianity over the centuries, have been crucially influential, as has the spread of knowledge about folklore and shamanism and Renaissance magic.

In the United States the witchcraft jungle is even more tangled, and more a part of feminism; a good account of it is given in Margot Adler's *Drawing Down the Moon.*[2] (Being English, I find London witches much superior to American ones, who say things like, "This is what I consider my task to be, to bust my ass to achieve my Godhood," and "I relate to the Goddess every day, in one way or another. I have a little chitchat with Mommy.")

What do witches do? At the time of the spring equinox, Luhrmann went to a terraced house in a London suburb, with a black robe she had made to specification. After meditating, she was blindfolded and led into a specially prepared room, candlelit and smoky with incense, where there were twenty other hooded and gowned members:

> The suspense and mystery, the months of solitary study on the course, the drama of the smoky blackness, had worked their effect: I was awed and elated.

The ritual, aimed in a general way at raising spirituality, dedicated the temple, then led the participants to the level of another "plane," and took them on an imaginary journey to the Goddess, before returning them to north London. "Controlled visualization"—focusing intently on imaginary journeys, meetings, symbols—was the backbone of the procedure in this and the other groups. Luhrmann also attended outdoor gatherings where the rituals—these are created by participants

2. Viking, 1979.

from a medley of magical and mythical sources—were chanted around a bonfire. She attended dream interpretation sessions, read the books popular with magical groups (by Tolkien, Ursula Le Guin, C. S. Lewis), learned to divine with the tarot, did a study course on the cabala.

Although (like everybody else) her witches did not function on the basis of a scrupulously worked-out philosophy, she is able to give a rough sketch of their underlying worldview. Matter and mind, to start with, are essentially one, and everything is indivisibly interconnected. "Individual objects are not fixed but fluctuating, constantly responding to their surroundings, bundles of relationships, rather than settled points." Which sounds pretty reasonable, and (rash though it is for a nonscientist to say it) in agreement with the extraordinary world of quantum physics, in which each particle influences the others, probability supersedes conventional causality, and the observing scientist will "create" either wave or particle, position or momentum. Magic goes on to propose that

> if all the universe co-exists in delicate balance, minor variations should produce substantial change. Like a lever, a small magical spell can shift the world.

A spell is not an ordinary wish, but a wish fired off by a deliberately directed surge of psychological energy—the existence of such energy being a crucial assumption.

The magical thesis assumes also that the world is not random but a pattern of meaningful correspondences, the linchpin of which are symbols. Drawn from a whole range of sources in this eclectic magic, symbols radiate connections in all directions—one of them might represent an emotion, an astrological concept, a god or goddess, a physical element, a number—and carry some kind of energy of their own, as do the cross, the holy water, the saint's relic, for the Christian.

Behind these patterns a purposeful force is envisaged, whether it is personalized or seen as the living, animate planet.

Luhrmann goes on to describe the kind of people who choose to take up magic. Sociologists, she says, have assumed that they must be marginalized or deprived; she did not find this to be so. In one group she describes there were teachers, secretaries, actors and actresses, librarians, a nurse, an electrician, a lawyer. The mentally unstable did seem to be attracted to the groups, but tended to drop out or be edged out (and even within London the status and standards of groups varied). If there is a typical magician personality, she sees it as someone imaginative, self-absorbed, emotionally intense, and concerned with issues of power and control. Some participants had had religious upbringings and had subsequently tried out a number of fringe cults. A rather high proportion worked specifically with computers. Luhrmann suggests that those drawn to the "symbol-rich rule-governed" computer world might be ripe for magic; also that they have learned to live in a rather isolated, jargon-ridden group. One would imagine too that the symbols of the computer world are arid, and the lack of human response in the work depressing: many members of the magical groups openly enjoyed magic as a return to childhood, and felt that they had rediscovered something that had once been very precious to them.

Magic, as Luhrmann says, "re-enchants the world." She herself felt this. "I never have and do not now 'believe' in magic," she emphasizes; but as a child,

> I lived in the world my books carved out for me.... By the time I was ten I had developed a secret fictional character, a child with a silver circlet, and before I slept each night I told myself stories in which he was the central actor and in which novels and television became the basis for his scripts. The nightly stories became almost sacred inner worlds.... These [London] witches

> were recreating a childhood world, enchanting adulthood, and their involvement offered me a means to come to intellectual terms with my past.

Joining a coven changes people in ways that sound rather enjoyable. (If any members were damaged or even just disappointed, Luhrmann does not mention them.) Imagination expands, dreams become more intense and filled with high imagery. Luhrmann had these experiences herself:

> Magicians are not simply learning a language with which to communicate with each other; they are learning (or possibly relearning) ways of experiencing. These experiences become important in persuading magicians of the validity of their theory and its practice.

Away from the group, a magician complained, "everything gets so dull and uninspired." Joining an emotionally close group is itself therapeutic; and women, in particular, seem to find the Goddess-centered practice a source of confidence.

Besides making sense of the world, magical imagery can be a way of managing irrational feelings, Luhrmann says, particularly where participants are taught to immerse themselves in, and survive, the "dark side" of the Goddess. "Therapy seems to work when someone externalizes, or labels, some internal feeling and then is able to transform it, though how and why that happens seems quite unclear"; and many of the people she talked to claimed they practiced magic chiefly for personal enrichment. In this therapy, she says, the promised reward is not only a meaningful world, but implicit power to influence it where it seems uncontrollable. Death and darkness and threat and fear are dramatized, and a bargain struck with them.

Obviously the price to be paid is the giving up of "consensus rationality," and Luhrmann devotes much of the book to analyzing how people involved in magic become able to see it as valid. They remember "successful" spells and forget others. Spells, anyway, are vaguely defined—a ritual to do with water might produce either floods of tears or burst pipes: a fertility spell for Mary might home in on Joan standing next to her. The symbols of astrology and the tarot are complex enough to be interpreted in many ways, as oracles always are. Coincidence is ruled out in favor of connection of some kind; as a W. C. Fields character said when asked whether he was playing a game of chance, "Not the way I play it." As among the Azande, therefore, while a particular practitioner or ritual may be said to fail, the system itself is not discredited.

The very view of reality that prevailed among the people Luhrmann talked to takes her into deep epistemological waters. To the practitioners of magic, subjective and objective are not sharply distinguished, and an inner event like a vision or fantasy will be described in literal terms. As Wendy Doniger O'Flaherty says in *Dreams, Illusions and Other Realities*,[3] describing the traditional Indian view of reality:

> For Rudra to think of something is for him both to make it exist and to find that it has always existed as part of him. These two kinds of creation—making and finding—are the same, for in both cases the mind—or the Godhead—imposes its idea on the spirit/matter dough of reality, cutting it up as with a cookie-cutter, now into stars, now into hearts, now into elephants, now into swans.

The word "plane" was found useful by the magicians; things could happen on a different plane, which was not clearly distinguishable from other planes. The people Luhrmann met felt no need to commit

3. University of Chicago Press, 1984.

themselves to "an ordinary truth-status assertion" about magic; they were happy to play with fact and fantasy simultaneously. Everything, they argued, was in some sense relative anyway; different explanations, different philosophies could coexist.

Much depended on a particular use of language. It was not only that by the use of a specific terminology the user of magic, like the psychoanalyst or priest or literary critic, comes to fit the world into a new scheme ("becoming a specialist often makes an activity seem sensible," as Luhrmann says). Words themselves, within magic, have a status beyond that of a mere signifier; that is the essence of a spell. There are many examples in anthropological literature of the power that resides in a name. There is also what Malinowski called the "coefficient of weirdness," the use of vague language to arouse awe—something with which we are familiar in most professional fields.

In general, those who learned to practice magic were confirmed in their theory chiefly by what they felt and experienced. Then their way of perceiving things altered. The witch or magician

> acquired new ways of identifying events as significant, of drawing connections between events, with new, complex knowledge in which events could be put into context. At the same time his involvement embraced rich phenomenological experience which he found deeply important, experience labelled and understood within the practice but not outside. Hard to abstract, hard to verbalize, these dynamic experiences became part of the business of engaging in magic, and they made the magic real for its participants, because they gave content to its ideas.

In sum, as Luhrmann says, "imaginative language significantly increases the capacity to learn about and accept new and unusual ways of interpreting the world." What she ignores here is that the magical way of thinking is not new, but very much the way we first thought as children. Also, in spite of her sternness with the rationalizations used to justify magic, she rather too often identifies it with imagination, ignoring, for instance, the person who finds a Beckett play more imaginative—more imaginative for this particular time—than an astrological reading. Conventional science also draws on another version of imagination.

The choice of magic as a way of life rather than, for instance, the accepted mythology of Christianity or Judaism does not seem to be fully explained by this preference for the imaginative over mass culture. The issue of power is one that Luhrmann says only a little about. In their talk about life enhancement her informants, too, seem to have played it down. It is something that most people at some level have conflicting feelings about; Piaget's early studies of young children show clearly how they grope with feelings of magical power and shattering disappointment. When things go wrong even older children fear that it is somehow their fault. The psychoanalyst and parapsychologist Jules Eisenbud has suggested that the paucity of experimental findings within parapsychology is due to unconscious reluctance to dabble in this childhood sense of omnipotence, which is both fascinating and frightening.

Luhrmann's witches had evidently come to some terms with the wish for, and fear of, a magical power; but perhaps preferred not to talk about it. Luhrmann says she felt they were slightly horrified, yet secretly pleased, by the popular conception of wicked witches. Religion would have told them—which is why it has been hostile to witchcraft—to subordinate their own power to God's.

Psychoanalysis, on the other hand, would have no hesitation in classifying their beliefs solely as a regression to the childhood sense of omnipotence. Such a dismissal is complicated by the evidence that paranormal phenomena can happen; rarely, and generally in a climate of sympathetic belief, but indicating, in William James's words, "the presence, in the midst of all the humbug, of really supernormal knowledge." The florid phenomena of the séance rooms of his time, however, like the hysterias that Freud and Charcot saw, have altered in our time, as we have absorbed the concept of projection, of relocating "spirits" in dissociated parts of our own minds. Anthropologists themselves keep to a strict objectivity about the magic claims of the societies they study, though, as C. R. Hallpike says in *Foundations of Primitive Thought*,[4] it may be simplistic to assume that they can all be explained by "pre-operational" thinking (and a surprising number of anthropologists are Catholics, as if to go armed with their own magical system). Meanwhile respectable medicine extends the concept of mind over matter, from attributing nausea or a headache to stress to proposing a possible psychological factor in almost every serious illness.

The fact is that we live in an epistemological hodgepodge, a transitional time in which we have the wearisome responsibility for tacking together our own individual belief systems. Witches and old-fashioned rationalists have the easy time. Other people have to go through their own process of sorting: prayer in, spells out; psychosomatic backache in, hexing out; dream interpretation in, astrology out; meditation in, acupuncture out. In a pinch, Hamlet's "more things" comes into service. Theologians—Luhrmann quotes a number of views—are engaged in the same struggle. Some argue that dogma is literally true, some that it is a working hypothesis, some that emotional rather than literal truth is the only criterion, some that religious language is in a category of its own. Luhrmann's inquiry into the nature of rationality and irrationality lands us in the center of the hodgepodge.

Bare rationality as envisaged by philosophers and anthropologists actually plays a rather small role in life; we use it for buying groceries and mending a faucet and to some extent in our jobs, as the Azande use it for agriculture and building huts; if we have been extensively

4. Oxford University Press, 1979.

educated we have it as a tool that we can also bring out when reading poetry or having a love affair to see if it fits the case. Irrationality, going directly counter to it, or confusing one kind of truth with another, is also not as widespread as is assumed; what we need is a concept of *arationality*, as Luhrmann's discussion implicitly suggests.

She introduces the concept of "knowing of," as opposed to "knowing that" or "knowing how"—surely as common as the two latter, and only downgraded because less easily expressed. "Belief," too, covers a variety of states of mind. The philosopher H. H. Price has written cautiously of "half-belief," which he distinguishes from mild belief and suspension of disbelief; but there is also double and triple belief, when several are held simultaneously. Probably only a few of those who read newspaper horoscopes would swear they "believed" them, but a favorable one might brighten a whole day. Multiple beliefs in particular cluster about traumatic events. Of a number of people I interviewed recently on the subject of death, over half proved to have referred in some way to arationality; indeed, everyone who has undergone bereavement or disaster knows the state of mind in which belief that it has happened and belief that it has not simply coexist. And of course there are the states of mind in which plays and films and novels are "believed."

All this is very obvious, but as Luhrmann says it has not been much explored by anthropologists, even where they rather reluctantly report that an informant states one day that the dead turn into butterflies and the next day that they haunt the village to steal pumpkins. The London witches' adoption of beliefs that are rejected in theory by the rest of us raises this question of how, in a society of mass communications, we map out the contours of our belief, invest our stock of faith now here and now there.

It also raises the question of a need not only for imaginative experience, as Luhrmann suggests, but for a specifically symbolic way of expression. We dream and write poetry in symbols, they feel resonant and satisfying, and they are our primary way of thinking. As Susanne Langer says,

> Whatever purpose magical practice may serve, its direct motivation is the desire to symbolize great conceptions. It is the overt action in which a rich and savage imagination automatically ends.... Its central aim is to symbolize a Presence, to aid in the formulation of a religious universe.... It is part and parcel of that greater phenomenon, *ritual.*

We are deprived of ritual, though it springs up in primitive forms like the structure of office coffee breaks. There are Catholics who will surmount serious obstacles to attend their Tridentine mass. Freud, as he wrote magic and religion out of psychology, had a secret love affair with his collection of archaic statues, and brought back scriptural symbolism in another shape.

Western witchcraft, whose traditional goals have been somewhat preempted by telephones and fertilizers and antibiotics, seems for its practitioners to work as an unusually dramatic way of putting symbol and meaning and color back into the confused post-Christian world. Like Einstein, we find it hard to believe that God plays dice, and as Luhrmann says,

> People strive for order. They find it difficult really to accept the existence of coincidence, if only because there is a creative pleasure in drawing connections between events, in making interpretations.

Whether it is heroic, or just foolhardy, or actually inaccurate, to see life as utterly random, few people consistently do it.

Luhrmann's account of life among the witches may for most readers be chiefly intriguing for its descriptions of this "enclave of the

Azande on the Hornsey Rise" and of Luhrmann's own reactions (including the hallucination of five druids coming through her bedroom window). But her underlying aim is to question the way anthropologists and other scholars approach the beliefs of societies and individuals—though we nonanthropologists may feel that we do not need to be told that people are "fuzzy" rather than logical, that irony and contradiction and ambiguity and paradox are not the prerogative of magicians justifying their ways. As the powerful rationalist Niels Bohr said about the horseshoe over his door: no, he didn't believe it brought luck, but he understood it worked even for people who didn't believe.

Anthropology, Luhrmann says, is at bottom psychological, concerned with why people choose to do this or that, in particular why they practice the "irrational" arts of ritual and magic and religion. It is an ethological psychology, people observed in their natural habitat rather than in the experimental laboratory. So what we need is

> ethnographies that describe the cognitive impact of cultural experience in its natural setting, rich, detailed accounts that are sensitive to psychological theories and philosophical problems but which are neither experimentally based nor speculatively abstract.

Scholarly debates about the goals of magic in nondeveloped societies have been too narrow; in London or in Africa, feeling and belief constantly influence each other, and a sensitive, serious anthropology, Luhrmann argues, needs to study the complexities and contradictions of how this happens. Her own book raises questions about the way we think, believe, imagine, know, in a most fascinating way.

IV

EXOTICS

15

SOPPISTS AND SAPPHISTS: BRAZIL AND BLYTON

THE WORLD OF English popular books for girls nowadays looks truly exotic—even more so, I do believe, than that of witches or Russian mystics. (I exclude, of course, popular books for teenage girls from the past twenty years or so, which face up to drugs, parental divorce, and blow-job techniques.) The books discussed by Mary Cadogan and Patricia Craig in *You're a Brick, Angela!: The Girls' Story, 1839–1985*[1] are in general not the classics, still (just) read by children and adults—*Alice in Wonderland* and *Through the Looking Glass*, C.S. Lewis's Narnia tales, Tolkien's Hobbits, or the wonderful turn-of-the-century books by Edith Nesbit: *The Railway Children*, *The Amulet*, *The Magic City*. Those were and remain superior fare, and may they live forever.

The period covered by Cadogan and Craig's solid history starts about a century and a half ago: from the pious *Fairchild Family*, the gentle tales of Mrs. Gaskell and Charlotte M. Yonge and the transatlantic sentimentalities of *Pollyanna* and *Anne of Green Gables*, through the first "New Woman" phase of the *Girls' Own Paper* and the Girl Guide and Camp Fire Girl, the rise and fall of the great jolly-hockey-sticks age, the unclassifiable anarchies of Just William and

1. Gollancz, 1986.

Just Jane, the millgirls and skivvies of the *Girls' Friend*, to the ponies and ballet shoes and camps by Lake Windermere of the interwar middle class and onward. Cadogan and Craig's viewpoint is briskly feminist and their critical stance moderately astringent—"there is nearly always something flaccid and sentimental about the books which have been described as well-loved," they state—but they combine a light touch over the absurdity of much of their material (only losing their cool over dreadful *Pollyanna*) with a modest engagement with its social and psychological implications. Without jargon, they cope with the problem of finding the right criteria for evaluating popular and ephemeral literature; not only have they obviously read their way through *all* of Elinor Brent-Dyer, Dorita Fairlie Bruce, Winifred Darch, Angela Brazil, and the rest, but they can demonstrate with enthusiasm why Bruce's *Dimsie Among the Prefects* is better in its way than Darch's *Heather at the High School.*

For it is the English boarding-school genre that is, for sheer and lovely ridiculousness, the jewel in the crown of ephemeral girlie lit.[2] "Schoolgirls—dear things!—are the same the world over," wrote Angela Brazil. They are not; but it seems that from Brazil's first appearance on the scene—surprisingly, as early as 1906—a world came into being that in some ways remained remarkably stereotyped for fifty years. L. T. Meade's Lavender House girls, in 1886, were still given "a mother-kiss and murmured blessing" at bedtime by their headmistress, but this would have gone down badly in 1923 with the Anti-Soppist League at Dimsie's school (founded "to protect against—against a lot of silly rot"; Rule III being that "every member must solemnly promise not to kiss anyone at all during the term, unless absolutely obliged to"). The Anti-Soppists' reactions to the *Anne of Green Gables* style—"do you think amethysts can be the souls of

2. Yes, I read them up to the age of twelve—along with Dickens, Robert Louis Stevenson, and Rider Haggard. But *never* Angela Brazil—now, of course, out of print.

good violets?"—defy conjecture. It was with the passing of soppism and the arrival of the Edwardian New Woman at the turn of the century that sport for girls, like bloomers and bicycles, arrived and "a pile of new books, a chest-expander and a hockey stick" became the symbols of girlish liberation and the new schoolgirl fiction. Cadogan and Craig make it clear that for Angela Brazil, deprived of hockey sticks and chest expanders during her own Victorian schooldays, sport really was revolutionary and the start of a new "rosy, racy, healthy, hearty, well-grown set of twentieth-century school-girls." She herself was revolutionary in adopting, more or less, the vocabulary and viewpoint of her characters rather than those of an outside adult narrator. Family relationships, overt moralizing, and piety were out, as well as almost all of the world outside the school boundaries.

Banished as old-fashioned and Victorian, soppism, however, did creep in again by the back door. Friendships in the Fifth continually "flamed to red heat"; soul reached out to soul and auras mingled. Lesbia Ferrars of Brazil's *Loyal to the School* was not the only one loved by her chum Regina "much as a boy would, for her pretty hair, her dainty movements, and the general Celtic glamour that hung about her"; Regina "behaved, indeed, more like a youth in love than an ordinary schoolgirl chum." Tush. In the next generation, the slightly more sophisticated successors of Angela Brazil, the games mistress was more likely to be a love object:

> "Coo!" Joy murmured. "Isn't she a treat? She looked jolly before, but in her gymmy she beats herself into fits!"
>
> "You see so much *more* of her," Jen remarked truthfully. "And when she's as topping as that, the more you see the better!"

When marriage and that sort of rot did appear on the scene in these later stories, however, it came with a bang:

> Dimsie awoke from her dream, and turned a radiant face to her friend. "I'm marrying my mate," she answered simply, but with a world of joy and content behind the ordinary words.

Elsie Oxenham's Jen, who found the games mistress so topping, has two husbands and four children within a comparatively short time, and another of the Abbey girls manages two sets of twins in ten months.

The 1920s saw the founding of the comic papers *School Friend* and *Schoolgirl's Own* as offshoots of Northcliffe's twopenny papers for boys. Cadogan and Craig give them their seal of approval: gripping, well written and constructed, they say, and founded on an impeccable moral code that excluded smoking, swearing, and even, at one time, the word "rotten." But there was more than moral impeccability at Cliff House. There was, of course, Bessie Bunter and her weekly "Extrax from the Clif Howse Ensyklopedier"; Tess Everton, one of a long fictional line of Irish madcaps ("shure, an' phwat is so curious darlint?...it's agrayin' with ye entoirely I am"); bounderess Augusta Anstruther-Browne, who used face powder and went out in fast cars, but came a terrible cropper; tiresomely popular Babs Redfern; dusky Naomer from Nakara, prone to exclaiming "bekas—what ze diggings—oo gorjus!"; and best of the bunch, Jemima Carstairs, incarnation of a stock figure of the period that deserves at least a doctoral study, the "intelligent ass" concealing a razor-sharp brain behind an inane exterior. "Funny little tangles this old brain puddle of mine gets into at times" was likely to indicate that Eton-cropped, cane-carrying Jemima was about to screw in her monocle and solve an international jewel robbery.

More colorful than the world of the early Angela Brazil books, perhaps, and yet in many ways not substantially different. The code of the school story consistently hinges on two principles, conformity and "honor." A masculine, Eton-and-Harrow conception of honor—

the honor of the regiment or the cricket side—seems to have come in (and womanly docility gone out) with the hockey stick and gym slip. "Owning up" is virtue, "sneaking" the major sin; plots revolve around misunderstandings and variations on the theme. Conformity —"it just isn't done in the Lower Fifth, you know"—is as important and takes a variety of forms: chauvinism ("'you may call it British prejudice but I can't stand foreigners,' Dulcie remarked with a gusty sigh"); culture-hatred (Madge Minden, who "cricket bat in her hand, and carrying batting gloves, was strolling down the passage whistling a César Franck Sonata," is a rare bird); snobbery ("everybody likes Mabel, but somehow she is a little different from other people. You see, her grandfather is Bishop of Holcombe and her uncle is Lord Ribchester"). Even the anti-snobbery element is loaded ("we must be frightfully careful not to let her feel that it's queer for her mother to keep a second-hand shop").

Style, plots, and props stay much the same too; the distinctive feature of school-story prose being the number of verbs used instead of "say." Characters "burst out," "retort," "groan," "declare," "taunt," "sigh," "mock," "explode," and "grimace" their words, but seldom actually say them. Variations on the plots—loyalty versus sneaking, "mad" escapades, rescues—appear and reappear, orphans and cripples survive in pockets, while girl sleuths, pony heroines, and Girl Guides have their own special genres. Two archetypal figures are the outcast (for mistaken reasons of course, and reinstated into the group at the end), and the madcap or tomboy, who varies from just "irrepressible" to actually claiming to be a boy, like Enid Blyton's Henry (Henrietta) and George (Georgina). "A girl is as good as a boy any day" is a frequent refrain, implicit or explicit.

What kind of person invents this world, in which most of the themes of drama and fiction can be found in grotesque, diminished form; and why? If a biography of Angela Brazil, its guiding star, had to be written (which is debatable), it should justify itself by suggesting some answers. Unfortunately there seems to have been a scarcity of material available for Gillian Freeman's *The Schoolgirl Ethic: The Life and Work of Angela Brazil*[3]: Brazil's publishers had preserved no correspondence, files were destroyed in the bombing of Coventry (where she lived from the age of forty-two on), and twenty years' worth of personal letters were thrown away only six months before Freeman advertised for material—an event probably more dramatic than the sum total of the authoress's own life. Nor is there anything as revealing about Angela Brazil's method of work as the account of Enid Blyton's imaginative processes that was elicited by an enterprising psychologist. Crucial details about output, sales, and income are left vague, and padding out the flimsy facts with parallel extracts from the books is sometimes confusing.

A picture does emerge, however, of the creator of the flaming passions at St. Cyprian's, the dorm feasts and nature rambles and secret societies: a stately lady inclined toward flowing mauve chiffon, the doyenne, with her brother and sister, of Coventry society ("the holy trinity," a friend recalls); giver of scrumptious parties for "poor little forlorn children who...don't find this planet a very bright place" (catering by the Geisha Café, a "rendezvous highly thought of by Coventry residents"); generous on her own terms, and with pliant recipients, but ruthless toward any signs of independence, devoted to Cornish piskies and cream cakes, ultraconservative, steely, sentimental—a nice, ordinary provincial lady, in fact.

This is enough to explain the Cathedral Committee work, the Coventry Natural History Society and the YWCA, the traveling, the entertaining, the literary causeries and openings of bazaars, but not the fifty books, the total bibliography of 142 items. What remains unaccounted for and turns a nice, provincial lady into a sacred monster, in Angela Brazil's case as in Enid Blyton's, is the gift of the supergab,

3. Allen Lane, 1976.

the unstoppable flux of words and fantasies. It requires three things for full operation: unshakable self-confidence, an absolute capacity for suspending disbelief, and a total lack of irony or humor. Any suspicion of the value of the product, any true scrutiny of fact, any capacity for holding more than one point of view (which would permit irony), and the whole edifice is in danger. Really bad art is a fascinating special case for any critical or aesthetic theory, because it is produced by just the same processes of imaginative absorption as real art, and yet arrives at an opposite place: where art tries to get as near as possible to the truth of a thing (a character or an action or an object), anti-artists or fantasists seem positively obliged to repudiate it with a fainter substitute.

A certain exceptionally developed capacity for self-admiration seems essentially to be involved, which defies the envisaging of character or action outside the writer's own personality, and from time to time produces personages who are easily detectable as enlarged and gratifying versions of the writer. Such is the Lavender Lady of *For the School Colours* ("on internal evidence" decidedly Miss Brazil, Gillian Freeman says):

> It was Easter time when the Lavender Lady first rose upon the horizon of Lyngates. She came with the dog violets and the ground ivy and the meadow orchises, and several other lovely purple things....
>
> When Avelyn first saw her she was sitting in the flowery little garden raised above the road. She wore a soft lavender dress and an old lace fichu, and she had dark eyes and eyebrows, and cheeks as pink as the China roses, and fluffy grey-white hair that gleamed like a dove's wing as the sun shone on it. She looked such a picture as she sat there, all unconscious of spectators, against a background of golden wallflowers and violet aubrietias, that Avelyn was obliged just to stand still and gaze.

> For a whole week Avelyn, terribly in love, lived in a mystic world in which the Lavender Lady, robed in the glory of the purple night and stars, was as the central sun, and she herself revolved like a planet round her orbit. The family could not understand why she insisted upon choosing heliotrope for her new dress.

Irresistible, these self-appreciations. And not only to the girls who responded to the hockey captains and new girls and madcaps lurking in Miss Brazil's matronly breast—as we see from the following, a tribute from a local poet who was granted the honor of visiting the authoress:

> *At the head of the grand staircase She received me.*
> *Angela . . .*
> *We talked of pods and the sycamore tree*
> *Roof tops and vista of old Coventree,*
> *Away o'er the Green to three precious spires,*
> *"Sermons in stone" to match high desires.*
> *Beneath the crystal chandelier, Angela . . .*
> *Clear cut as the diamond glass above,*
> *Queen of literature and art's own love.*

The United States undoubtedly has had its own versions of the schoolgirl story. Is the Enid Blyton phenomenon of books for younger children purely a British one? Noddy, Big Ears, Mr. Plod et al. are still big business—books, T-shirts, toys, and, I am sorry to say, videos watched by my grandchildren. Critical scrutiny of a tattered copy of *Noddy at the Seaside*, appreciated in its day by *their* parents, reveals absolutely no forgotten charisma: no suspense, humor, or poetry, and little scope for psychological or sociological analysis. Noddy and his friends clearly belong to the world of toadstool salt-and-pepper sets, bearded garden gnomes, crinolined telephone covers and warbling doorbells, matchbox holders made like rustic cabins, and tiny shaggy dogs in knitted coats and hair ribbons. They are as harmless as a soggy rusk and as appetizing as tepid Ovaltine with skin on top, and they prove nothing except that babes have no more discrimination than adults. They must have passed through a few million children as cleanly as a dose of salts, leaving no trace behind. The Enid Blyton story has only two points of interest. One belongs to the commercial story of publishing in this century, the other to psychology: What trick of mind was it that hitched an extremely commonplace mentality to compulsive fantasizing and iron determination to produce a one-woman fiction factory? Childish fiction written out of a lifelong obsession, say, with animals or ships or soldiers would be more comprehensible, for these have roots in the imagination; but what are the roots of the Blyton pixies and bunnies and teddies?

Barbara Stoney's biography of Blyton,[4] even-toned and tactful though it is, suggests that the creatures represented a childhood that ended traumatically when her father left home to live in sin when Enid was thirteen (when, in her thirties, she consulted a gynecologist about her failure to conceive, she was told she had the undeveloped uterus of a thirteen-year-old). The exact circumstances of her early life she kept deliberately vague, even to her own children; on leaving school she had made a complete break with her mother and brothers, and was absent from her mother's funeral thirty-five years later. But the Toyland Tales and Sunny Stories must have been devitalized substitutes for memories of a real childhood that was both denied and preserved. In the last years before her death at seventy-one, Noddy, Big Ears, and the rest had deserted her—through some kind of early senility she had become too confused to write or even to answer her letters—but the real memories seem to have returned: she talked of going home to Mother and Father.

---

4. *Enid Blyton* (Hodder and Stoughton, 1974).

The suburban home she left at nineteen was respectable enough apart from the absence of a father. She had been a compulsive reader and scribbler there and collected a few hundred rejection slips; the quick rise to popularity began as soon as she started specializing in writing for children. As a young teacher in 1923 she was already earning £300 a year from her part-time writing—at the time, Stoney points out, the price of a small house. At twenty-seven she married her publisher; the couple settled in a London flat—a "quiet residential area, which contains a good class of people who keep themselves to themselves," she described it in a letter. Something—perhaps the Little Folk?—was missing in Chelsea, however, and they moved to leafy Beckenham, Kent:

> If, in the New Year, you come across a funny little house peeping at you from behind a chestnut tree, look at the name on the gate. If it's called "Elfin House" you'll know it's mine.

So she wrote in her column for children in *Teacher's World*; adding that children were to tap with the Peter Pan knocker four times, adults twice, and the Little Folk from the woods seven times.

Though Little Bunny—Enid's nickname for herself—was now pushing thirty, at Elfin Cottage she enjoyed playing rounders (US baseball), making snowmen, and collecting conkers (US chestnuts). She had a secret belief, she wrote in another of her columns,

> that fairies and elves, brownies and gnomes have visited the house and left some of their flower-loving, sunshiny personalities behind. It's such a happy, cheerful, elfish little house, the right place for poetry and fairy stories, dreams and laughter....

For fairy stories it was the right place—a regular cottage industry, you might say; so were the later and larger houses. Although the biggest

Blyton explosion seems to have come after the Second World War, by 1939 she had published seventy-three books, as well as magazine articles, weekly children's pages, poems, and other oddments. When she herself privately published a book of "letters" from her fox terrier Bobs, ten thousand copies were ordered from the house in the first few days. About a hundred letters a week were answered in longhand in the early years, and the number grew; a special postal delivery was laid on. Charities sponsored, or even mentioned, by Enid Blyton prospered. During the wartime paper shortage it was rumored that one of her publishers had been allotted the paper for an edition of 150,000 of one of her books.

And so, during the 1950s and 1960s, it went on, now with television and plays, the formation of a limited company, translations—Blyton coming third in the most-translated stakes after Lenin and Simenon. A curious trio. Nineteen fifty-five, a record year, has thirty-seven published titles recorded in Stoney's bibliography. Yet it seems that the text (if that is the right word) of all the books really was written by the author herself and not by a team of ghostwriters, as was inevitably rumored. She was highly perturbed by the rumors and a young librarian who had made some incautious statements was pursued by legal action. Her fluency was genuine and extraordinary: "I began it on Monday," she wrote of a book, "and finished it this afternoon (Friday). It is 60,000 words long and flowed like its title."

Among the successes were a few setbacks. A divorce and a remarriage unobtrusively took place. She never succeeded in writing for adults: a novel and a play were rejected. In the 1950s an appropriately ridiculous storm in a teacup blew up, and the nation divided over little Noddy. Librarians had started to ban Blyton books because they were too numerous and popular—clean-limbed middle-class stories like Arthur Ransome's *Swallows and Amazons* presumably being neglected. But supporters rallied when Noddy was subjected to right-wing criticism in the magazine *Encounter*: not only was he described there as "the most egocentric, joyless, snivelling and pious anti-hero in the history of British fiction" but—surely the unkindest cut of all—as an unintentional parody of welfare-state man.

It is a little too easy, really, to mock the Blyton saga and to discern some less sunny qualities in the author than the bland tales suggest. Her daughter, Imogen Smallwood, has written an ambivalent account of a mother who was more often entertaining child fans to tea and making good copy out of her sweet little daughters than actually mothering them.[5] The woman was, in a nutshell, a tiresome, insecure, Thatcheresque queen of kitsch. What is more interesting, in view of her astonishing fluency, is her description of how she did her writing. When the psychologist Peter McKellar was doing research into hypnagogic and imaginative imagery, he had the brilliant idea of writing to Enid Blyton on the subject. Her replies, quoted by Barbara Stoney in full, are clear and detailed:

> I shut my eyes, for a few minutes, with my portable typewriter on my knee—I make my mind a blank and wait—and then, as clearly as I would see real children, my characters stand before me in my mind's eye. I see them in detail—hair, eyes, feet, clothes, expression—and I always know their Christian names but never their their surnames.... As I look at them the characters take on movement and life—they talk and laugh (I hear them) and perhaps I see that one of them has a dog, or a parrot, and I think—"Ah—that's good. That will liven up the story...." The first sentence comes straight into my mind, I don't have to think of it—I don't have to think of anything.

Without counting, she reported, she was able to bring each book, almost to a word, to the right length. They wrote themselves. This

5. *A Childhood at Green Hedges* (Methuen, 1989).

dissociated talent fits well with the personality we meet in the biography: prone to cut herself off from whatever was inconvenient, and in her own personal utterances, judging from the leaden extracts from her diaries, somewhat impoverished. But when Toyland took over,

> I don't know what anyone is going to say or do. I don't know what is going to happen. I am in the happy position of being able to write a story and read it for the first time, at one and the same moment.... Sometimes a character makes a joke, a really funny one, that makes me laugh as I type it on my paper—and I think, "Well, I couldn't have thought of that myself in a hundred years!" And then I think, "Well, who *did* think of it then?"[6]

Who did? It is a question writers do sometimes ask themselves, as psychotics ask it about their voices, psychic investigators about messages "from the other side," and psychologists about the oddities of split personality or hypnotic feats. That feeling of "otherness" can take any number of forms, and one salutary lesson from these letters of Enid Blyton's is that inspiration, like dreaming, will stand for no damned nonsense about good taste. Assuming that this kind of experience is as valid as the experiencer feels it to be, then if Blake and Rilke took down their writings straight from the angel's mouth, so in her own way did little Noddy's creator.

6. Peter McKellar, *Imagination and Thinking* (Basic Books, 1957).

16

DOWN TO WORK: PROSTITUTES

GOODBYE TO FANTASY: this is going to be nasty.

Prostitution is not going to disappear for a long time, says one of the six women who tells her story in *Prostitutes: Our Life*,[1] so it is time people accepted prostitutes. "They could at least be ready to look them in the face and acknowledge them," she says; and so say the other five, and the heads of the prostitutes' collectives who have contributed chapters, and the male journalist who edited the book. Fair play, both legally and socially, is what they ask for, for working women who have simply struck a private bargain with another individual. How could one disagree? But the looking in the face, the sorting out of disgust, sympathy, blame, envy, are horribly difficult. The book's spokespeople are clear where the blame lies (in male-dominated society), and what the remedy is (much larger welfare allowances for single women with children); the women who tape-recorded their stories seem more muddled and more honest.

The two deeply emotive things involved are money and bodily integrity. Prostitution is one of those things, like payment for psychotherapy or breach of promise, where the money involved seems to become meaningless, both too much and too little. Getting paid, for

---

1. Edited by Claude Jaget (Falling Wall Press, 1980).

fifteen minutes of passivity, what it takes hours of book reviewing or concrete mixing to earn, is obviously ridiculously too much. For losing social acceptance, sexual choice, and physical safety it is obviously ridiculously too little. Putting up with strangers' disgusting bodies is what nurses happily do for low pay; but then, there is no question of monotonously dealing in just what seems most private, fruitful, of their own.

It really isn't simple:

> We worked on vaseline. That means we smeared ourselves with loads of vaseline and then afterwards got the sperm out. I only had time to wash after every four or five clients. While the guy was washing I'd go to the top of the banisters and shout, "Coming down." The boss downstairs, she'd answer, "Coming up." And the next client would be getting ready to come up while the other one was still washing.

The six stories recounted in this one book are of course too few to explain the whole scene (there are no male prostitutes among them, no casual part-timers, no choosy and successful call girls) but are vividly informative. This is what I have learned from them. First, how it all starts: usually little by little, not difficult to imagine. "Each time I realized that it was really impossible to stop. Yet it wasn't because I didn't want to. I did, from the start." Only one out of the six set out with any deliberation; the pattern described is from casual jobs to bar hostessing or "doing a favour" to plain prostitution. Money and habit are crucial: "There's no mystery—if it weren't for the money, then I'd rather be doing any job than this one." Even if Margaret Valentino and Mavis Johnson of the English Collective of Prostitutes are right that better pay for women is the heart of the matter, it is unlikely that there will never be anyone willing to earn even more and finding the bargain worthwhile: "I tried taking a job . . . clocking in at eight in the morning, going out to lunch, one month off in the summer, waiting all week for Sunday to come—I tried it and I couldn't do it."

How they feel about the job when they start: usually they hate it and cherish plans for getting out. "You make light of it, you try to condition yourself to it inside, and yet the first time it really is horrible. At the last moment, you desperately want to run away; but you can't any more." Dennis Potter, in his television series *Pennies from Heaven*, very clearly got across a sense of drastic change in the girl once she had gone on the game—shocking not in a moralistic sense, but because she had acquired a kind of new, brittle façade that obliterated her as much as the clothes and makeup did. A split takes place. This is described in a similar way by most of the women here. Just as society splits them off, as "bad," from the rest, they themselves make a very strict demarcation between what is for hire and what is not. Kissing is taboo; the head is inviolate. It is not in fact the body, a whole body, that is involved at all:

> To me, being a [bar] hostess is even more revolting than being a pro.... You really have to let yourself be fooled around with to get a man to order one more bottle; whereas as a prostitute there are hardly any caresses, there's hardly any touching.

One or two of the stories, in fact, suggest a move toward prostitution because in a way it provides *more* autonomy over the body than mutual sex. Again, not simple.

Sexual pleasure is more or less mutilated by the demands of the job. The attempt to keep men as lovers or friends separate from men as clients is made as strenuously as the demarcation of body zones, but is difficult: "It's very hard for me to have a normal relationship with them, everything's out of sync. For example, if I go out with a man and flirt with him, and at the end of the evening he makes it clear that he wants me, it gets my back up. . . . A client doesn't matter one bit." Social life is determined by the work: "I stopped going out with men from the moment I did my first client; and yet before, I liked going out, I liked going to nightclubs—I loved dancing, for instance." A quotation used as a chapter heading—"It's Over So Fast"—could not be more untrue: for the pro it is never over, because it profoundly determines attitudes. "I saw men's penises, all kinds of pricks—big, small, long, bent, thick, hairy. They were all the same to me. It became a complete non-event, it left me utterly indifferent."

Because money is the raison d'être it acquires extra significance, extra mystique: "You 'live' through money and what you can buy with it, in the same way those other people live through their shop or their profession"; and it is addictive: "When you're used to earning a lot of money, it's hard to be satisfied with 2,500 francs a month, and even harder to be satisfied with a secretary's wage. Money's a drug." But pros—those who remain in the work at any rate—do not seem to organize money well: muddled, recurrent debts that are never quite cleared appear in the stories. Nevertheless, though the job may be started at a time of financial desperation, the money becomes a small symbol of power among humiliations and powerlessness. The question of pimps comes in here: an area of confusion in the contributors' stories, partly because a pimp can mean anything from a property dealer to a husband, partly (says the editor, Claude Jaget) because it is the part of their lives that prostitutes least want to talk about. When they do, they give little support to the popular conception of the oppressor from whom helpless victims should be freed. He may be the lover they take pride in financing and cherishing; another part of the life-style where there is a chance to choose rather than be chosen: "Some of us, if we have the money, prefer and are proud to support friends or lovers, men or women, rather than send them out to a factory or a hospital job and get them back destroyed after a day's work. We consider this *our* business." In the Potter script the man is the weak partner, the girl the stronger one, whose affection for him makes sense out of the life she had adopted. What the women quoted in Jaget's book are angry about seems not to be exploitation, but the fact that any men who live with them are liable to prosecution for pimping.

Ideals: just as some parts of the body are inviolate, some parts of life are separated sharply off from the rest. Several of the women describe the simplest kind of roses-round-the-door daydreams—home, husband, children. Children, by these accounts, are almost sacred: "My own dream is for my daughter to get married in white and be a virgin.... After all I've gone through, that would make up for it all, it would be ideal." The two founders of the English Collective of Prostitutes claim in their chapter that most women go into prostitution to support their children—"Generation after generation, we've made sure that the younger ones get a better deal." But it seems that the children may have to be brought up in foster homes, and perhaps theirs isn't the most enviable situation. One of the women describes her son's reactions of severe shock on discovering when he was thirteen what his mother's job was.

Rewards: quite apart from money, from the tangle of things that make it hard to go back to straight life, there is a suggestion that a kind of glamour and camaraderie in the life can be appealing. "I like this street world, this night life.... When you know it, it's extremely lively, it's exciting, it's a fascinating world. There's a kind of freedom you don't find anywhere else." The "freedom" aspect of the life is crucial: the bodily freedom is given up in exchange for a freedom—theoretically—from employers, conventions, clock-watching, penny-pinching. Yet there are dangers: the work invites real risk of attack and even of murder. A proportion of the clients go to prostitutes not for simple sex but to vent their hatred of women: "Once she got there she found herself faced with four of them.... They went at her from all sides, they did every conceivable thing to her." Prostitutes, in an even more fundamental way than Jews or blacks, are pelted with society's projections; occasionally projections of goodness (there was an inane remark by Malcolm Muggeridge, a media star of the Seventies, about some quality—holiness? spirituality?—shared only by nuns and prostitutes) but usually, of course, of badness: "The ones that ask me to defecate in their mouths, they're the ones who turn on me afterwards and say, 'You're disgusting, agreeing to that, you're a slut, I don't know how you can do such filthy things.'"

The idea of safe, legal, and well-regulated brothels, however, is anathema to all the contributors. It denies the precious area of freedom:

> "The following ladies to the salon," she'd say. When I heard that I'd freeze up inside.... It was the man who'd chosen me, who'd had me, I was the thing he'd literally bought. He'd judged me like he'd judge cattle at a fairground, and that's revolting, it's sickening.... When you're on the street...you feel less like their property, and also you can always refuse.

Out in the open there is the illusion that it is the woman who does the choosing. The super-efficient German version of the brothel—the Eros Center complete with bars, swimming pool, and sauna—is no more popular. The women have to line up and proposition semi-naked. If such centers multiplied, one contributor predicts, they would become "hooker supermarkets," with compulsory competition for the most pornographic getup.

Solutions, then? I can't feel at all clear about them on the basis of Jaget's book alone. It should be explained first what the legal situation is, for those who are as ignorant as I was before reading it. (Though it is the British setup that is described here, the women whose stories are recorded were in fact French, and the book was inspired by the "strike" of French prostitutes against their working conditions in 1975, when they organized a sit-in a church in Lyons. But the catch-22 to be described seems to be much the same in both countries.) The schizoid aspect of the lifestyle and of society's attitude toward it are reflected in legislation. Briefly, while prostitution is not illegal, any action which leads to its practice is; in other words, it is legal to be a prostitute but impossible to operate as one without breaking the law. A prostitute cannot, legally, solicit or advertise. A restaurant or bar cannot "harbor" her; a landlord cannot knowingly rent premises to her. It is hard to see where or how she can carry on her "legal" trade. The result of the system is to put a great deal of power into the hands of the police and to open very wide the door to corruption. Nearly all the women quoted in the book express deep bitterness against the police and the system that empowers them. Their demand—presented by Baroness Joan Vickers to the House of Lords in 1977—is for the abolition of all laws relating to prostitution.

But, yet again, it is not simple. Do I personally want to rent my spare room to a prostitute? No, not as long as I can get any other tenant. But this "legal" trade—and we would be even deeper into hypocrisy if we tried to make it go away by a total ban—has to be carried on somewhere, and the women say with one voice that they don't want official premises. Some giant effort of honesty and rationality seems to be needed—but the problem is so fantasy-ridden. John Updike's story "Transaction" shows the prostitution bargain from the side of the male partner: his confusion about her blank availability and boredom, his attempts both to reach her as a real person and to use her in his imaginative life. The man going to a prostitute hires a fantasy as much as part of a body; the women know this:

> We're often the only chance men get to sleep with their fantasy.... Their sexuality is quite different from women's. On the one hand, they can really make love with a woman, and it'll take an hour, two hours, the whole night, and they'll have a real relationship with this woman.... But they've got their own desires, and now and then they need to let go, they need a safety

> valve. Then, a woman has to understand, take it with a smile. And it's really hard.

One thing that can only make it all worse is to scapegoat men's sexuality for the fact that the women who trade with them get scapegoated in *their* turn. Now that it is fashionable to assess everything from music to mental illness for its biological value to the species, the purported usefulness, for perpetuating ourselves, of an assertive male sexuality complementing a more conservative female one is too obvious for comment. Remarkably, some of the women represented here, like the one quoted above, manage not to scapegoat men. In any case, if male heterosexual prostitutes were only more feasible, women might certainly try them.

And where it is a question of sorting out the roles of victim and aggressor there are, again, utter confusions. The most shocking chapter in the book is the one told by a girl who specializes in sadomasochism. At nine years old she was raped by her stepfather and was dumb for a year afterward. At eighteen, she left the children's home where she had lived and bought a butcher's knife and stabbed the man in the genitals. She spent five years of a nine years' sentence in prison. She is the only woman in the book who admits to getting a sexual kick out of her work. She starts: "When they want you to stick pins in their penises, the blood really gushes out"—I'll censor the rest. How can one restrict one's pity to only one of the partners in this transaction? Each is necessary to the other.

17

INNOCENT, UNSTOPPABLE: MARIE STOPES

If through a mist of awful fears
Your mind in anguish gropes
Dry up your panic-stricken tears
And fly to Marie Stopes.

NOEL COWARD MET Marie Stopes on board a transatlantic liner in 1922, and they got on like a house on fire. It would make an excellent opening for a game of consequences: what he said is the above (and more in the same vein); what she said, writing to her husband, was that

> he is a dear.... He thinks you tremendously handsome... and he is hoping to use his power of laughter to help in social progress.... He told the people at my table that I am one of the greatest living intellects.... I have read two of his plays—one very good and one very bad—I told him it was "putrid" and he took it ever so nicely.... I think he was sent by Providence to reopen my interest in my dear old love the drama.

And the consequence (to borrow a gambit from the game) was that "the world laughed"—or rather that part of the world which reads either of the two excellent biographies of this preposterous woman today will be highly entertained.[1] Another ironic consequence of Marie Stopes's existence is that, preposterous or not, the sacred monster did a great deal of good.

The letter in which she describes the transatlantic encounter is typical Stopes in every line: the prodigious lack of humor (what a naughty Noel to tell her he planned to forward social progress with his plays!), the vanity, the confidence in her own opinions that assured her no one could mind having his play called putrid, and the egotism that assimilated everything to her own purposes—young Mr. Coward had been sent, obviously, to revive her own dramatic skills (she wrote several unperformed plays, but Ellen Terry advised her that the public would prefer "a little bit of fluff" and Bernard Shaw was heartless enough to use the words "irrelevant twaddle"). No doubt she lectured Mr. Coward on the need for hygienic birth control, and no doubt—for the corrupter of the nation's morals remained remarkably naive—it did not cross her mind that he was not the ideal recipient for her advice.

Marie Stopes was forty-two at this time and a household name, even a notorious one. The notoriety had arisen from her authorship of two books that had hit England like bombshells, *Married Love* and *Wise Parenthood* (*Radiant Motherhood* was more calmly received). Touted around for three years among publishers who refused to touch it, *Married Love* when finally published in 1918 sold two thousand copies within the first fortnight of publication and had run through six editions before the end of a year. Couched in jeweled prose—"The half swooning sense of flux which overtakes the spirit in that eternal moment at the apex of rapture sweeps into its flaming tides the whole essence of the man and woman"—it was written by a virgin, and (reputedly, at least) shocked the country to the core. Its argument, that women were capable of sexual pleasure and should be given a

---

1. June Rose, *Marie Stopes and the Sexual Revolution* (Faber and Faber, 1992); Ruth Hall, *Passionate Crusader: The Life of Marie Stopes* (Harcourt Brace Jovanovich, 1977).

chance by their husbands to experience it, was not the sole cause of offense: among the jewels there was quite a lot of down-to-earth information not all previously compiled in book form ("You certainly get in a *lot* of important points—menstruation, positions, ejaculation without penetration, birth control, insemination etc," enthused a supporter).

Wise Parenthood, much of it devoted to the eugenic benefits to civilization of the cervical cap, went so far as to state that sexual enjoyment—only within marriage—was "of supreme value" quite apart from the procreation of children. A reviewer wrote that the novelist Arnold Bennett's introduction to "her filthy book is a disgrace to him and to his profession." At the Lambeth Conference the Church passed a resolution against any teaching that "encourages married people in the deliberate cultivation of sexual union as an end in itself." Free copies sent to Queen Mary and Queen Alexandra remained unacknowledged; and even Lloyd George, a much more obviously suitable recipient, would not jeopardize his career by backing the Stopes propaganda for birth control. Noel Coward may have been tickled to death by the Stopes phenomenon—but for the public, once the press had had its way, rubber goods, Stopes, and animal lust were inextricably associated. Even at dinner parties she was inclined to bring out pessaries and Dutch caps from her handbag and explain their uses.

The origin of the phenomenon—the chaste lady scientist who became, in her own eyes, "a kind of priest and prophet mixed," who wanted to replace Christianity by a new religion based on Christ's wholesome love of sex, who loved lilies because they "reveal to the delighted eyes of mankind not merely the outer vestibules of sex but their very organs," and who at fifty-eight was outraged when asked to write on "Facing the Forties" because, she said, scientific diagnosis put her age at twenty-six—the origin lay, conventionally enough, in her curious childhood. It was an unhappy one and its elements reappeared in reverse and parody in Marie Stopes's adult career. The family was "intellectual": her parents met at a scientific meeting, and her father was a distinguished amateur paleontologist and archaeologist (Marie was to become the first woman paleobotanist). Her mother, thirty-nine on her marriage, was a Shakespearean scholar and the first woman in Scotland to complete a university course of study. She believed, as intellectual ladies did, in Rational Dress (no corsets), permitted no smoking in her presence, and was a passionate suffragette. She also had a Calvinistic horror of the flesh. On her death an old friend wrote to Marie that "it is a long sad story—your mother's married life and yours and Winnie's girlhood... if ever there was a born old maid your mother was that woman—she should never have married." A quotation from a letter to her husband on his deathbed is scarcely credible—"the sensual look has passed away from your face that so pained me," she wrote, "and you seem to have regained the chastened expression of your youth, which made me trust you."

For her father, a gentle man given to childish jokes and unwise financial speculations, Marie naturally felt much more affection. He had, it seemed, begged his wife to "put from you the teachings of your splendid brain" and find some affection for him, but in vain, and the marriage became an overtly unhappy one. In this household the two children were kept secluded, Marie being taught by her mother until she went to school at twelve; a picture of the little girls shows two small replicas of their mother, but with expressions of blank distress rather than her dour self-satisfaction.

From her mother Marie must have got her passion for emotional chastity, which for years combined oddly with revolt against the taboos of physical chastity; from the relationship with her father her undaunted belief in an ideal partnership and also her penchant for marrying ineffectual, overgrown schoolboys. Under the self-centered megalomania that grew with the years she carried from her childhood a burden of insecurity; and there is something about the gush and gabble of her writing that suggests an underlying emotional incapacity that only disappeared when she was involved in practical battles.

Like so many of her generation, she directed the moral force of her pious upbringing into quite different channels in her adult life. She got firsts in botany and geology, and became one of the first woman Ph.D.s; she went down coal mines to study fossils, led a party of male scientists across a remote part of Japan, trekked with a rucksack to the Arctic Circle. And, of course, she found herself patronized by men: "For too long men have been accustomed to look upon woman's views and in particular on her intellectual opinions, as being something demanding, at the most, a bland humouring beneath the kindest smiles," she said.

She fell in love, first, with a diminutive, married, middle-aged Japanese professor. She was much taken at the time with the idea that a kiss was as binding as a marriage vow—logical enough in view of the fact that she had never heard of any other consummation to marriage—and once the deed was done considered herself irrevocably committed. Something could be arranged about his wife. Marie Stopes was a pretty woman and the professor, too, felt "mysteriously electrified till the minutest points," he wrote, at the very thought of her. She managed to get a grant to study in Japan; but Professor Fujii cooled and disappeared, leaving Marie a hurt and angry woman at twenty-eight.

Nor was she much luckier in her two marriages. She was the kind of forceful woman who attracts weak men, and on her part she was not one for scrutinizing the genuineness of her own feelings with much interest. Though she scarcely knew her first husband when they married in 1911, she broke the news to her sister with "except that he has a stupid little nose he seems absolutely perfect! I couldn't have made him better myself"—more the description of a new cushion cover than a new husband. Anyway, he had the essential qualification that he had never kissed another woman.

The nonconsummation of Marie Stopes's first marriage, the fact that she did not, at thirty-one, realize for at least a year that there was anything unusual about her state, the marriage's eventual dissolution, and her writing of *Married Love* to enlighten other innocent wives is a tragicomic story. But there is something exceptional, even for those far-off days, about her extreme ignorance. She was a scientist, had worked as a lone woman among men for years, and by the standards of the time was almost a middle-aged bride; there must have been many younger and more sheltered girls who went chastely but not in utter ignorance into marriage, even then. Mrs. Stopes's upbringing had certainly left its mark; but the story also suggests an egotistic absorption in her own preconceptions that was typical of Marie Stopes—and perhaps an isolation, an absence of ordinary gossipy friendship with other women.

Such was the background to *Married Love* and its historic consequences. After the annulment of this first marriage, she met Humphrey Roe, a fellow contraceptor who was engaged to a clergyman's daughter named Ethel, detached him briskly from her, and married him in May 1918. Rapturous at first ("I wish I were with you.... I'd pull your hair and tickle you and behave altogether like a wild pussy kitten"), the marriage declined with Roe's sexual stamina. It is clear from letters from the couple's doctor that the apex of rapture and its flaming tides were not easily achieved; Humphrey Roe, in fact, had "problems," and after a few years Tiger Humphlekins began to be more and more of a nuisance to his Wood Nymph, and he died banished to a seedy bed-sitting room. His position was already foreshadowed when he wrote during the engagement, "You could have captured anyone you wanted. Yet little me has won this great prize." There is, it seems, a curious inverse ratio between writing about sex and actual experience of it: not only Marie Stopes, but Annie Besant, Havelock Ellis, Edward Carpenter, even, it seems, Freud with his six children, all had cramped or odd sex lives.

Roe, however, was useful to his wife in the early days in other ways than by giving her a child: with his money and personal support he helped her open the Mothers' Clinic for Constructive Birth Control in a working-class area of London. Contraceptive advice was given free, the clinic and its staff of midwives being paid for out of the couple's own pockets. Although it was never as besieged with clients as Marie Stopes liked to claim, it undoubtedly—taken together with the books and the constant flow of Stopes publicity—did much to alleviate ignorance and distress. Part of the enormous archive of Stopes papers that she bequeathed to the British Library consists of letters from an army of correspondents, all of whom received personal answers. "When I first saw you at a meeting about 25 years ago you looked to me like a beautiful Goddess, preaching a sermon of hope to a girl like myself 25 and allready a mother of 5.... My gratitude goes out to you. I might easily have been the mother of 12," runs a typical letter. At the height of her fame Stopes was receiving about a thousand letters a week, from overburdened mothers and from sexually unhappy people of all kinds.

A paradox is thus involved in the attempt to sum up the good and the bad achieved in such a lifetime. Lacking all the virtues we currently admire—honesty, imagination, generosity, and even common sense—in her private life Marie Stopes hardly brought sunshine to those associated with her. She very deliberately detached engaged men from their fiancées because it suited her, and despised and discarded two rather pathetic husbands; having brought her son up in skirts (trousers might injure the growing genitals) she quarreled irrevocably with him when he married a shortsighted girl ("the awful curse will carry on and I have the horror of our line being so contaminated"); she brought in a series of adopted "brothers" for him and discarded them when they did not come up to specification. One failed to get his alphabet right, two did not "bloom so as to be a credit to us," one wet his knickers. All were sent back.

She was anti-Semitic, right wing, and more concerned in her campaigning to breed the "C3" strain—the underclass—out of the population than to ameliorate its lot. And Stopes not only offended against political correctness, she offended grossly against literature, by writing, and sometimes publishing, many dreadful novel and poems. Bernard Shaw, who called her Dottisima—a felicitous mix of "doctor" and "dotty"—did tell her they wouldn't do. Altogether a ridiculous and really rather dreadful woman—who in her public work did much good, although she was not quite the lone pioneer she claimed to be. And when we read her assertion in 1942 to Prime Minister Clement Attlee that "the whole peace of the world depends on my work being available and rightly presented to the backward peoples," do we now laugh or not?

In 1935 a group of Americans listed *Married Love*, along with Einstein and Freud, as among the twenty-five most influential books of the half-century. Her biographer June Rose quotes the young Naomi Mitchison sending a copy to her husband at the front during the First World War: "Read this before we meet again"; and she might also have remembered Harold Nicolson to his absconding wife: "The book is wonderful: it goes into every detail.... I am appalled at my own ignorance." Her message, after all—"I do not believe that the normal man's sex needs are stronger than the normal woman's"—was far from mad, and was wrung from hard experience. And God's personal message to the bishops has certainly reached its target, as they rush to recommend the God-given, healthy, wholesome joys of sexual union.

The biographies of her also throw light on a particular aspect of social attitudes. While there was certainly considerable support from progressives for the birth-control campaign, we also read of a symposium published in 1920 in which various contributors deplored the unnaturalness of contraception; of an official medical discussion in 1921 expressing similar views; of the prosecution and conviction in 1923 of the authors of a too graphically illustrated birth-control pamphlet.

Now the 1920s was the decade in which I was conceived—indeed I see that in the month of my birth Marie Stopes was in court attending a libel action in which the prosecuting counsel described her as "an author who has devoted a considerable amount of time and study to the arresting and interesting proposition of how to achieve sexual satisfaction while at the same time avoiding the attending inconvenience of having children." Few of my contemporaries from the respectable middle-class university circles my parents belonged to have more than one or two siblings, and indeed I remember my mother's attitude toward those university families where there were a lot of children: they were liable to go in for eccentricities like nude bathing and Greek for girls. Only the poor and the aristocratic (like the Mitfords) casually *bred*. The check pessary or some such thing must have been as accepted, therefore, though less visibly so, as the silver cruet on the mahogany dining table: an interesting sidelight on the time lag between public and private attitudes.

18

EADIE OR EDDIE?: PATRICK WHITE

TO BE A WOMAN and yet not a woman is about as singular and isolated a condition as can be imagined. Patrick White's *The Twyborn Affair*[1] is about a transvestite who changes gender, to and fro, three times. Eadie Twyborn, who lives inside the body of Eddie, has a definite place alongside other excluded women.

The difficult novels of Patrick White, born in Australia in 1912 and awarded the Nobel Prize for literature in 1972, have now shifted somewhat below the literary horizon. Without exception they are about outsiderdom, great feats of loneliness and endurance. I think many critics are frightened of Patrick White. Who can blame them? I quail myself at the task of conveying why I believe this turgid, crotchety, tortuous, racked, oblique writer is nevertheless great—and a Nobel Prize winner. I looked for inspiration at the eulogies on the book jackets. "Epic" recurs, and "monumental"; comparisons are made with the Alps, a cathedral, the Book of Genesis, even Everest; "greatness," "power," "scope" are evoked. The blurb for *The Twyborn Affair* goes right over the top with "irresistible sweep of a symphonic poem" and more. The most honest reaction comes from the critic who says a Patrick White novel defies review. It defies reading sometimes, too;

---

1. Viking, 1980.

intelligent people have said to me that they know the books may be important, but they can never get beyond the first few pages.

Those who do admire White's greatness have to get through a thicket of stylistic idiosyncrasies, be alert to meanings only obliquely indicated, accept the level of intensity the author demands; there is a relentlessness about White. You submit or drop out. The little mediocrities and compromises that relax both novelist and reader have no place in his books; when he writes badly, as sometimes he does in *The Twyborn Affair*, it is because he concentrates his style to the point of self-parody—to the detriment of the affection and humor and variety that season his intensities.

The Twyborn Affair is White's thirteenth book. He was entirely committed to being an Australian writer and all his books are concerned, tenderly or savagely, with his homeland; but in fact he was educated in England and only went back to Australia to live in 1948. So he is an outsider; and his characters are outsiders, outlaws, afflicted, and linked by their affliction. If there is a guiding theme in White's novels, it comes in a phrase in *Voss*: knowledge, says Laura Trevelyan there, "only comes of death by torture in the country of the mind." Perhaps the most powerful and accessible of White's books, *Voss* is the story of an attempt to cross the Australian continent in the 1840s, based on the life of the explorer Ludwig Leichhardt. But it is a mythical journey. White can balance reality and fantasy so that we accept their unity: deserts blossom into phantasmagorias; Voss's inexorable death is paralleled by Laura's torture "in the country of the mind." At his best White can effortlessly create myth from a thread of realistic narrative.

White's subject is illumination: a radiant structure behind the grotesque material rubble, which can—by some—be glimpsed; but it is only the outcasts who have endured a death of this kind to whom the glimpse is allowed. The rest, the rabble, are comfortable, rather cruel: casual, busy crucifiers. Those who can see—the burnt ones (title of one of the books)—tacitly recognize one another; in a sense they are the structure that informs or redeems the indifferent mass. In *Riders in the Chariot*, for instance, he follows the linked histories of a Jewish refugee, an impoverished truck driver's wife, an "abo" artist, and an eccentric spinster. Dubbo, the aboriginal, paints a celestial chariot carried by four winged creatures; White makes it clear that his four rejects are the charioteers. He quotes from Blake as epigraph: "The prophets Isaiah and Ezekiel dined with me, and I asked them how they dared so roundly to assert that God spoke to them.... Isaiah answer'd: '... my senses discover'd the infinite in everything....'"

It sounds pretentious; but the visionary element in White's novels is inseparable from a tough irony and a microscopically close, sometimes savage attention to physical minutiae. The coarser the texture of the physical—of bodies especially—the more likely it is to be illuminated by flashes of meaning and power. To quote from *Voss* again:

> He added at once, louder and brisker than before: "Topp has dared to raise a subject that has often occupied my mind: our inherent mediocrity as a people. I am confident that the mediocrity of which he speaks is not a final and irrevocable state; rather is it a creative source of endless variety and subtlety. The blowfly on its bed of offal is but a variation of the rainbow. Common forms are continually breaking into brilliant shapes. If we will explore them."
>
> So they talked, while through the doorway, in the garden, the fine seed of moonlight continued to fall and the moist soil to suck it up.

His *The Tree of Man*, for instance, is a long, patient story of Australian peasants in the outback, of dry landscapes and poor smallholdings; yet in the great bush fires and floods of the continent there is again the mythical and elemental quality. But as White's charity toward the physical grew smaller in his later books, his obsessive repulsions got stronger. These later books are darker; the bed of offal more visible than the rainbow; the earthy, ironic vein of tenderness thinning out. In the earlier *The Tree of Man*, for instance, an old man is being badgered by a callow evangelist selling instant salvation; the old man coughs and spits; there is an illumination:

> He pointed with his stick at the gob of spittle.
>
> "That is God," he said.
>
> As it lay glittering intensely and personally on the ground.
>
> The young man frowned. You met all kinds....
>
> After he had gone and the tracts were flapping and plapping in the undergrowth, and the black dog had smelled one with the tip of his dry nose, the old man continued to stare at the jewel of spittle. A great tenderness of understanding rose in his chest. Even the most obscure, the most sickening incidents of his life were clear. In that light.

In *The Twyborn Affair* excreta are smeared about gratuitously. A man masturbates and feels "the trickle of his own cooling sperm. A single gob, on reaching his kneecap, struck him cold, disgusting him..." (and us). A woman crushes fleas, and "that," she said with some satisfaction, "is the creamiest flea I've ever squashed" (inaccurate as well as gratuitous; fleas do not squash creamily but crisply into a blood spot).

The protest against the physical—"But to the girdle do the gods inherit,/Beneath is all the fiend's"—is central to *The Twyborn Affair*'s special preoccupation, the experience of gender. Eddie/Eadie Twyborn is twice-born, has two lives, as a man and as a woman, though (s)he is barred from belonging securely to either. In *The Vivisector* White has a character write of a homosexual: "He has understood through what he calls his 'Infirmity' (which I am told is also known as 'The Third Sex').... I believe the afflicted to be united in the same purpose." Not a true hermaphrodite but a transvestite homosexual man, we see Eddie/Eadie first as Eudoxia—Doxy—Vatatzes, the lovely concubine of a fierce old Greek from Smyrna. This first incarnation is set in the pre-1914 Côte d'Azur: olive trees, warm sea winds, English tearooms, a faded pink villa with marigolds in the garden. Angelos and his E. stroll arm in arm on the terrace, play Ravel together. She loves, after a fashion, her "old monster." In a shabby pension he has a heart attack. It is a pity, at this point, to have to reveal the twist of the plot, for the reader's shock is in Angelos's dying words: "I have had from you, dear boy, the only happiness I've ever known." Until this point we had accepted E. for what she seemed to be, the lovely Mme. Vatatzes.

In the second of *The Twyborn Affair*'s three sections Eddie Twyborn takes up life as a man. There has been the Great War in the meantime, and a Distinguished Service Order for courage—just "despair running in the right direction"—and, going back to his homeland, he throws himself forcibly into masculinity: working as a jackeroo in the bleached outback of Bogong, New South Wales, acquiring blistered hands and a leathery neck and a slouch. He even lets himself be drawn into fathering a child with his employer's wife. But this embodiment is no more durable than the first. His cover is sprung when the queer-bashing farm foreman pitches himself into his bed. He moves on.

Then the third and last attempt to construct a passable self: an outré and dreadful petrification, this. There is a loosening of realism here, a jolt toward the fantastic. It is London in the 1920s, and E. has become Eadith Trist, madam of Mayfair's most elegant brothel. She is imposing, heavily *maquillée*; the male body hair meticulously removed with wax and honey by an Arab girl. She is abbess, headmistress, a neuter among "the moaning and sighing of whores as the leftovers among their pseudo-lovers, the prickling pursy or smooth sinewy male animals, ground between their thighs or squelched against their buttocks.... It seemed as though the bawd alone must fail to drown in this loveless social orgasm." She is *triste*; and arranges trysts, unattainable for herself, between aristocrats and her stable of handpicked and disciplined whores. One of these milords she loves, as she loved Angelos. He would marry her, but she has no way of telling him who she is.

White said that *The Twyborn Affair* was his only semiautobiographical book, the nearest he has come to examining his own homosexuality. It becomes, at times, too much of a case history, too near the clinical; where White might have brought off a sense of the universal in bisexuality, he remains too much bound to Eddie/Eadith's muddled personal pain. His burnt ones, so often, have those glimpses that transcend their afflictions; E. remains a somewhat passive figure, molded helplessly by chance circumstance. And there is something clinical in the recurring gusts of repulsion. White is always obsessed by mouths, but here the omnivorous vagina dentata dominates: mouths gaping, smeared with paint, flecked with crumbs, bubbling with saliva.

> But the eyes: if only they had been less daunting; and the ferocious mouths. All the veils had been raised to allow the parrot-ladies to fall upon *le goûter*, the black, the white, the beige gloves unbuttoned, folded back like superfluous skins for the ivory-skeletal or white-upholstered claws to fork unencumbered at confectioner's custard, whipped cream, chocolate pyramids, and chestnut worm-casts.

Behind E. the androgyne, White places the figures of his loved and feared parents in their Australian suburb: Judge Twyborn and his raddled, alcoholic wife Eadie, who loves terriers and other women, in that order. But here as elsewhere he allows marriage a certain solemnity, contrasting it with the chancy horrors of sex; E.'s tragedy is to be outcast from marriage. The climax, less crudely melodramatic than it sounds, is the meeting of E. and the widowed Eadie in a London church during an air raid. "Are you my son Eddie?" the mother scribbles on a prayer book. "No, but I am your daughter Eadith." There is a reconciliation of mother and daughter, of sister and sister, perhaps of one merged person, wife of the father judge that E. loves so much. But then E. must be killed in a raid, one hand blown off, "a detached hand lying in a stream of blood."

Yes, horribly clogged with crude Freudian sexual symbolism. But a summary of White's plot gives no idea of the intricacy and density of his style; and I have quite failed to suggest his humor—it is unquotable, because it is not "humorous," not added on in little detachable units. Nor, even in these later books, is all darkness. "Common forms are continually breaking into brilliant shapes." Even toward sex there is one passage in *The Twyborn Affair* where White extends his mercy. An Australian soldier is talking to E.:

> "I'll tell you something," the captain said, "I've never told it to anyone before—somethun funny that happened to me.... I went over to a farm that was still of a piece under cover of the next ridge. Always take a squint at what they're up to on the land. Got a place of me own at Bungendore. Well, I was pokin' round this poor sort of farm. God, it stank! of pig shit, like most of these Frog farms do. When I saw a bloody woman's face lookin' out of the winder at me. So I went in to apologize. We stood there sizing each other up.... And we started takin' off our bloody clothes.... I don't mind saying I was tremblin' all over from what we'd been through up the line. But I mounted, and she let me in. An' then this funny thing happened. It was not like I was just fuckin' a Frog woman with greased thighs.... Just joggun along like it was early mornun, the worst of the frost just about over. As you doze in the saddle. The light as warm and soft and yeller as the wool on a sheep's back...."

> The captain spat on the estaminet floor.
>
> "You'll think me a funny sort of joker. But that's how it was as I fucked this Frog. And more. Wait till I tell yer." If he could; he'd begun to look so uneasy. "It was like as if a pair of open wings was spreading round the pair of us.... An' don't think I'm religious!" The captain had followed him as far as the door. "Because I believe in nothun!"... "NOTHUN!" he screamed.

This is the White who "discovers the infinite in everything," White the visionary and critic-defying. Over marriages, and over such lovers, as E.'s journal says, despite all "the Holy Ghost presides.... Sometimes the Holy Ghost is a woman, but whether He, She, or It, always there, holding the disintegrating structure together (or so we hope in our agnostic hearts) and will not, must not, withdraw."

V

REINVENTORS

19

SATAN LAUGHED: ISAK DINESEN

IN 1931, WHEN she had lost her lover, husband, home, income, and health, Karen Blixen—she tells us in *Out of Africa*—went out to look for a sign to tell her the meaning of the losses, of all that had gone so wrong.

> It seemed to me that I must have, in some way, got out of the normal course of human existence, into a maelstrom where I ought never to have been.... All this could not be, I thought, just a coincidence of circumstances, what people call a run of bad luck, but there must be some central principle within it. If I could find it, it would save me.

She went outside on her African estate. A white cock strutted onto the path; at the same moment, from the other side, a chameleon ran onto it. The chameleon, frightened, stood its ground opposite the cock and darted out its tongue in defiance. The cock bit the tongue out.

> The powers to which I had cried had stood on my dignity more than I had done myself, and what other answer could they then give?... Great powers had laughed to me, with an echo from the hills to follow the laughter, they had said among the trumpets, among the cocks and Chameleons, Ha ha!

When, not long after, she rebuilt her life by publishing, at forty-nine, a book—*Seven Gothic Tales*—that was an instant success and established the beginning of a cult following, she chose as a pseudonym the word Isak: the Hebrew word for laughter.

She went on, as we know, to publish more books before her death at seventy-seven; to become high priestess of her cult, guru to young writers, and public figure in her own country of Denmark; to be elaborately feted on her trips to the US; to turn herself, apparently by an act of will—as she had done in reestablishing her broken life—into the formidable Gothic sybil of her old age, a figure straight from one of her own tales. Her life story should be one of the most moral of fables, extolling the triumph of perseverance, courage, and hard work in the face of adversity. Such rewards, finally! A Book-of-the-Month Club author four times over, standing ovations at public readings, parties, bouquets, photographs.... And yet we cannot help feeling that the laughter she heard in the African hills, and with which she announced herself a writer, was—to say the least—not a comfortable sound.

It is not hard to see a Luciferian quality in Dinesen's life after she had heard the Ha ha! of the gods among the trumpets. Several years ago a Danish author, Thorkild Bjørnvig, published a memoir of his relationship with her when she was in her fifties and he a young writer.[1] It is not a pretty story. She proposed that they should establish an indissoluble covenant by mixing their blood: he was to become son, disciple, and platonic lover in one—and hers forever. She believed they were in telepathic communication, and when she cursed him and he subsequently had an accident she assumed she had exercised witchcraft. She did everything she could to separate him from his wife, even after the wife had made a suicide attempt. Scenes of obsessive

---

1. *Pagten: Mit venskab med Karen Blixen* (Copenhagen: Gyldendal, 1974); in English as *The Pact: My Friendship with Isak Dinesen*, translated by Ingvar Schousboe and William Jay Smith (Louisiana State University Press, 1983).

jealousy alternated with tenderness, and in the end Bjørnvig made a violent break with her.

In his account he described her as proud of what she considered to be a special pact with the Devil. After she had been permanently infected with syphilis by her husband, she said,

> there was no help to be had from God—and you must understand how terrible it is for a young woman not to be allowed to make love—then I promised my soul to the Devil, and in return he promised me that everything I was going to experience hereafter would be turned into tales. And you can see: he has kept his promise.

Allowing for a vivid sense of drama, we must nevertheless accept that she felt there to be a special truth in this—the evidence is in the pattern that runs through her tales. And as early as 1926, when she was still "Tanne" (her Danish nickname), the harassed, self-doubting mistress of a bankrupt African farm, she was writing to her brother: "I'm convinced that Lucifer is an angel who should have wings over me. And the only solution for Lucifer was probably rebellion and his fall to his own kingdom."

In that letter she was ruminating, in particular, a break with the smug, decent values of her provincial Unitarian family in Denmark, values that she entirely repudiates in the cold, patrician fantasies she chose to write. Throughout them runs a theme of common humanity surrendered in exchange for something else—pride? power? above all for the ability to turn life, with its muddle and pain, into art—exquisite where life is confused, heartless where life is passionate. A cardinal, in one of the *Last Tales*, is persuaded to tell his life story to a beautiful penitent; with her life in fragments she had come to him for confession, and "in the course of our talks together all these fragments have been united into a whole.... You have shown me myself."

Who, then, she asks, is he? He replies with an elaborate story. He is one of the twin sons of a princess, fathered literally by the oafish prince, spiritually by a castrato singer the princess loved. The prince had intended to call the child Anastasio, the princess to call him Dionysio; when twin boys are born the roles are divided, and Anastasio is promised to the Church, Dionysio to the arts. But one of the identical boys dies in a fire, and it is uncertain which is the survivor: to the prince he is Anastasio, to his mother Dionysio. He reaches adulthood and is ordained to the priesthood—"left to promenade the high places of this world, in one single magnificently harmonious form, two incompatible personalities."

But to the chosen officeholder of the Lord, certain spiritual benefits are withheld:

> "I am speaking," he said, "of the benefit of remorse. To the man of whom we speak it is forbidden. The tears of repentance, in which the souls of nations are blissfully cleansed, are not for him. *Quod fecit, fecit*!"

She understands, says the penitent; yet she feels she has lost her adviser and friend for someone of whom she is even a little afraid. Art is remorseless: "What you call the divine art to me seems a hard and cruel game, which maltreats and mocks its human beings." But, replies the cardinal, the telling of the story can do for human beings what nothing else can do: "The story only has authority to answer that cry of heart of its characters, that one cry of heart of each of them: '*Who am I*?'"—as his story has done for him, as her confession has done for her. Now it is clear, she says; he is, indeed, a loyal servant of a great master. But she has one last question to put to him:

> "Are you sure," she asked, "that it is God whom you serve?"
>
> The Cardinal looked up, met her eyes and smiled very gently.

> "That," he said, "that, Madame, is a risk which the artists and the priests of this world have to run."

It is something of a relief, after contemplating the diabolic element in Dinesen's fiction and life, to be reminded of her younger self—Karen Blixen—in Errol Trzebinski's life of Blixen's adored friend Denys Finch Hatton, who died in 1931, the same year that her coffee farm went bankrupt.[2] *Silence Will Speak* is all gush and missing punctuation, but it is interesting for the light it throws on her most important relationship and on the life of the East African settler that she lived for seventeen years. Finch Hatton was beyond doubt her great love (she would in any case have divorced Baron Bror Blixen, who gave her syphilis, and whose character would seem to be epitomized in an anecdote related by Trzebinski: "That's mine for the night," he announced after a glance at a rich American girl, and proclaimed his success the next day). In her later life as Dinesen she is said to have made an unfailing habit of looking out, every night, in the direction of Africa and Finch Hatton's grave; but for some reason—Trzebinski suggests her possessiveness, Robert Langbaum in *Isak Dinesen's Art*[3] her syphilis—he did not marry her, though he used her house as home when he was not out on safari.

Trzebinski, also a white settler in Kenya, researched diligently, but her prose brings bathos into the Blixen/Dinesen life story by making the great white hunter sound like a cross between Lord Peter Wimsey and Bulldog Drummond: laughing hazel eyes, exquisite voice, and a legend to all who knew him. As with many another good-looking, upper-class Englishman, Denys Finch Hatton's finest hour seems to have been at his public school; Julian Huxley, no less, recalled him as the handsomest boy at Eton, "standing on top of College Wall in a red silk dressing-

2. *Silence Will Speak: A Study of the Life of Denys Finch Hatton and His Relationship with Karen Blixen* (University of Chicago Press, 1977).

3. *Isak Dinesen's Art: The Gayety of Vision* (Random House, 1965).

gown. An unforgettable Antinous." When he was presented with diamond cuff links and a set of ruby shirt studs by an adorer, "his immediate impulse was to hurl them into the grate" (but he relented and gave them to his sister "as a keepsake," wise boy). He was inclined to drive girls down to Eton to contemplate its beauty in the moonlight.

What emerges from the haze is the portrait of a gifted eccentric with an outsized younger-son complex (his poor brother Toby, heir to the Winchelsea earldom, had only half the glamour); perhaps a melancholic like Blixen's father, who shot himself when she was ten; a man of courage and culture, but restless and self-defeating, a little heartless, a voluntary but uneasy exile from the home he could not inherit. The life of the pioneers in British East Africa, though always close to the primitive, was in some ways like the aristocratic setting of a Dinesen tale: wine in the crystal glasses from home, Stravinsky on the gramophone, good food, talk, and books—and perhaps the roar of a lioness in the dark outside. (There were drugs, too, which Trzebinski suggests may have influenced Dinesen's prose style; but could she also have obtained them once she returned to Denmark?) But when the coffee crop failed and this carefully composed world fell apart, the noble Finch Hatton seems to have had little support to offer, apart from quoting poetry: "You must turn your mournful ditty/To a merry measure,/I will never come for pity,/I will come for pleasure." In effect, Trzebinski suggests, they had parted even before his Gypsy Moth airplane crashed.

Later Dinesen was to fantasize that he might have committed suicide, as her father had done; as she was also to speculate that her father's suicide could have been caused by the shame of having the same disease that she herself had. It is impossible to know, in a life that so successfully made itself myth (she even, Dinesen-like, married Bror Blixen because she was in love with his twin brother), whether there was any truth in her speculations. Trzebinski's book, like the memoir published by Thomas Dinesen about his sister,[4] at any rate wholesomely reminds us of the nonmythical aspect of her life, when she was still a vulnerable and insecure woman unsuccessfully trying to run her farm and find an identity; at forty she was writing, rather touchingly, to her brother:

> Oh, do you think, Tommy, do you think that I can still "become something" or have I neglected my chances in life while there was still time, so that I have nothing left but to fade away and go to seed, to be patient and hope that others will have patience with me for being a complete failure?

The softer side of her character, indeed, coexisted even with the harshness and vanity that grew on her with age: she was always devoted to animals and children, she tried hard to raise money for a hospital in East Africa, and she worked unselfishly during the Second World War in an escape network for Jews in Nazi-occupied Denmark.

Even so, the remarkable transformations from Tanne to Tania (Finch Hatton's choice) to Isak are recorded in her photographs, which show uncommonly little likeness between the conventional prettiness of the young woman, the confident handsomeness of middle age, and the images of the old lady, hooded, painted and powdered, eyes black with kohl, fragile as an insect—but powerful. "Women," says a character in "The Monkey," "when they are old enough to have done with the business of being women, and can let loose their strength, must be the most powerful creatures in the whole world."

In *Carnival* (1975) and in *The Angelic Avengers* (1946), we now have the sweepings of Dinesen's work: the former made up chiefly of stories she discarded as not good enough for publication, the latter an

4. *Tanne: Min Søster Karen Blixen* (Copenhagen: Gyldendal, 1974); in English as *My Sister, Isak Dinesen*, translated by Joan Tate (London: Joseph, 1975).

"entertainment" written under a pseudonym during the Second World War. Robert Langbaum, whose book admirably explains and assesses each of her works in turn, dismisses *The Angelic Avengers* as of no literary value and points out that Dinesen was annoyed when it was chosen by the Book-of-the-Month Club in America, for she considered it a frivol, an illegitimate child, and quoted in correspondence the remark of one of the characters which appears as epigraph to the book:

> You serious people must not be too hard on human beings for what they choose to amuse themselves with when they are shut up as in a prison, and are not even allowed to say that they are prisoners. If I do not soon get a little bit of fun, I shall die.

Nevertheless for those who find the ruthlessness of her more serious work oppressive, *The Angelic Avengers* is a delightful romp, a Daphne du Maurier novel rewritten by Hans Christian Andersen. The sultry presence of evil is there, as usual; embodied in Mr. Pennhallow, who preaches a sermon on the loathsome contagion of the fallen woman, and sells fresh young girls into white slavery. There is a touch of voodoo, a pact with Beelzebub, and some cannibalism; it is a romp nevertheless, for virtue triumphs, the charity of a virgin exorcises evil, and—as a character says—

> "A fairy tale . . . ought to end up with a happy marriage."
>
> "Perhaps it ought to," said Zosine, "but there are so many difficulties and obstacles between the two—as always in fairy tales—that I do not know what to think about it. And I have not quite finished my tale yet."

But a marriage there is, and love and redemption triumph. The book deserves wonderful period illustrations and the status of a children's classic, cannibalism and all. More seriously, the fact that it moves with pace and feeling, unlike some of Dinesen's more ambitious work, might be because she found herself happy with a fable about the redemption of the corrupt, that is, the syphilitic. The effect of her illness on her view of the writer as a dedicated being, yet cut off from common humanity, surely cannot be overestimated.

Carnival is chiefly for the Dinesen devotee, since most of the stories in it were rejected by the fastidious author. The usual ingredients are there, but often without the imaginative fusion of her best stories. The first two, however, written in Danish before she married, are interesting in showing that her early attempts at writing were fully in the vein of her later work: both are lightweight, ironic fables with the barest touch of cruelty. The title story, "Carnival," written in Africa, is important too because in it she is clearly describing her relationship with Denys Finch Hatton and her transition to independence. "All my existence becomes nothing but being in love," says Mimi,

> all my thoughts turn around one single person, there is no sense in it, it is not living.... I have lost everything in life—friendship, hats, ambition—that is quite sad in itself, but it is not what makes me unhappy. No, it is this, that if Julius knew how I feel about it he would dislike it so much.... He wants me to run parallel with him in life. God, Polly, how sorry one ought to feel for all parallel lines which want to intersect as badly as I do.

Do you remember the nuns, and our maiden aunts? she says.

> They lived in God, and threw themselves upon the Lord, and rested in him, and all that. Now say that that was the thing which God disliked most of all, and that in the end he would say to them: "For the love of God" (or whatever words he uses to that effect) "do think of something to do for yourselves, find some interest

> of your own in life. I really should not have created you if I had known that you could do nothing but fall back upon me again."

The wittiest and most characteristic of the stories in *Carnival* is the short fragment which ends it, "Second Meeting." Aboard ship for his last expedition to Greece, Lord Byron has a visitor announced, one who looks remarkably like himself. Fourteen years ago, the visitor, Pipistrello, explains, he saved his Lordship's life by dressing up in his borrowed clothes and presenting himself in Byron's place to three brothers planning to kill him for seducing their sister. The matter was easily settled by the small ransom of a sovereign, which the avengers good-humoredly handed over to Byron's double. With it he bought a marionette theater; everything that has happened to him since, he has turned into a story. And again—

> Certainly it is a great happiness to be able to turn the things which happen to you into stories. It is perhaps the one perfect happiness that a human being will find in life. But it is at the same time, inexplicably to the uninitiated, a loss, a curse even.

What, he now asks, has Lord Byron done with his gift of fourteen years? For he has come to finish the story. (Here, in a typical parenthesis, he tells the story of another, second meeting: the Virgin Mary, at Pentecost, with a blush on her face, calling out, "Oh, is it you, sir? After these thirty-four years, is it you?") Why, he wants to know, have these fourteen years been a series of self-inflicted defeats? There will have to be one great and deadly defeat, says the double, to round off the story. But there will be compensations. You are going to tell me that in a hundred years my books will still be read, says Byron: "I have had it said to me before."

> "But wrongly said, Milord, wrongly said," said Pipistrello. "In

a hundred years your works will be read much less than today. They will collect dust on the shelves."

"I do not much mind," said Lord Byron.

"But one book," said Pipistrello, "will be rewritten and reread, and will each year in a new edition be set upon the shelf."

"Which book is that?" Lord Byron asked.

"*The Life of Lord Byron*," said Pipistrello.

Will Blixen/Dinesen also come to be known more for her life than for her works? Of the books, *Seven Gothic Tales* (1934) and *Out of Africa* (1937), the one with its extreme artifice and the other with its directness, will probably last the longest. But the pattern of her life is at least as remarkable a creation: we look back to the strangeness of the story of the white cock, the chameleon, and the laughter of the gods; to the time when Blixen was leaving everything that mattered to her behind in Africa, learning to fall back on nothing and no one, and to become Dinesen; to the book that followed, in which, as Langbaum says, "we read about people who have passed through a catastrophe to a tragicomic realm of indifference, where all things are alike." He quotes a passage from "The Dreamers" in that first book:

> If, in planting a coffee tree, you bend the taproot, that tree will start, after a little time, to put out a multitude of small delicate roots near the surface. That tree will never thrive, nor bear fruit, but it will flower more richly than the others. Those fine roots are the dreams of the tree. As it puts them out, it need no longer think of its bent taproot. It keeps alive by them—a little, not very long. Or you can say that it dies by them, if you like. For really, dreaming is the well-mannered people's way of committing suicide.

The survivor—*quod fecit, fecit*—is sometimes more frightening than the suicide.

20

ALMOST QUEENLY: REBECCA WEST

REBECCA WEST DIED in 1983 at ninety-one, in a comfortable flat overlooking Hyde Park. She was a Dame Commander of the British Empire, to her amusement and gratification. Will she be remembered more as a character, thoroughly damely and commanding, or for her writings? Eleven novels, of varying literary merit; nine other books on general subjects, of which the most admired (and especially relevant today[1]) is *Black Lamb and Grey Falcon*, on Yugoslavia; a mass of articles on the public affairs of her time. She was an oracle, a pontificator, and unclassifiable, who might have left a more settled reputation if she had written only fiction or only political analysis. She was chagrined to know quite well that she would be remembered for her private life: her affair with H. G. Wells—girl, twenty-one, meets cad, forty-seven—and the birth of their son. The story is not gossip fodder, but tragic and central to her life. When Wells is properly reassessed as a writer, it will be known which of the two leaves the greater literary reputation.

She knew—came to know—everybody who was anybody, so the first selection of her letters, as well as sparkling with wit and malice, is full of the great and famous (the *really* great and famous, such as

1. This essay was written at the height of recent Balkan wars.

the Queen, wearing "something one could buy in a dress-shop in the high street in High Wycombe").[2] The selected two hundred letters are culled from around ten thousand. I imagine that in those left unculled there is more about her endless minor illnesses and much, much more of the paranoia that grew worse with age. Enough is present to show how it went, how the impecunious girl reinvented herself as a very commanding Dame.

The background to the great chip on her shoulder must have come partly from having an illegitimate child, excruciatingly humiliating in her day. Virginia Woolf, another sharp-eyed lady, wrote that all West's difficulty came from "the weals and scars left by the hoofmarks of Wells." (She also had comments about dirty nails and so on; Rebecca, for her part, would not "have fed a dog" from one of Vanessa Bell's plates, and characterized Lytton Strachey's beard as "an extension of his personality in the direction of doubt.") West often, in these letters, ascribes all her troubles to the demon Wells; but her temperament was also formed earlier, as Victoria Glendinning's biography shows.[3]

She was not born Rebecca West but Cicely Fairfield. (The adoption as pen name of one of Ibsen's characters—the mistress of a married man who urges him to joint suicide—is extraordinary.) She had a painfully déclassé childhood which, like unmarried motherhood, was cruel in those days. Spendthrift father left wife and three daughters when Cicely was nine. The girls were clever, money was short, relatives embarrassing, but they got an education. All four women were socialists and suffragists. The young Rebecca, as is well known, got Wells's attention by cheekily calling him "the Old Maid among novelists" in a book review. (Subtext: "Come and disprove it.") He approached but then retreated. (Subtext: "Come and get me.") She threatened to shoot herself; he dropped his current mistress and

2. *Selected Letters of Rebecca West*, edited by Bonnie Kime Scott (Yale University Press, 2000).

3. *Rebecca West: A Life* (Knopf, 1987).

returned, and at their second sexual meeting made her pregnant. And he had only just got over the scandal of doing the same to another lovely young girl! She had captured a truly naughty daddy; he, she said later in a letter to her son, "wanted the panache of having a child by the infant prodigy of the day." Both, we can now see, were fighting the pain of their social origins; but there was love, though he did not leave his marriage, and they stayed (somewhat) together for ten years. The difficulty of bringing up her son, Anthony, alone caused distress and, later, bitter resentment on Anthony's side.[4]

---

4. His novel, *Heritage*, came out in the US in 1956. When he wrote it, in the 1950s, Rebecca West blocked its publication; the characters in it were recognizable to anyone in the know and far from flattering. In his introduction West declares it to be a positive, genial work in view of his mother's later behavior. He gives his leading character the name Dickie Savage, partly, presumably, to represent his own feelings and partly after the poet who, Johnson wrote in his *Lives*, was pursued by a monstrous mother. His own mother, he said, did not actually, like the Countess of Macclesfield, try to get him hanged. But from his puberty onward her aim, he declares, was to "do me what hurt she could, and she remained set in that determination as long as there was breath in her body." According to him, she blocked his career, made public scenes, tried to break up his marriage, tricked him out of his financial inheritance, and wrote hundreds of letters to people denouncing him.

This is horrible stuff, but it does mellow. Dickie's mother is a moody and mendacious actress, and it is not (here differing from real life) clear for some time who his father is. His parents are explained to him by a friend of the family:

> You see they're both so wonderful at making up stories on the strength of a few facts that they don't very often pay very much attention to the humdrum sort of stories that most people live.... They met, they fell in love, and they both made up wonderful stories about what the rest of their lives were going to be, and what the other person was like. And when they started living together they found how different the stories were, and how badly they fitted into each other's stories.

But Dickie Savage ends by concluding that "she's been a loving mother, and an absolutely indifferent one who had a child by mistake, she's been a cold-hearted bully, and a wonderful friend. I wouldn't, now I'm not demanding that she always appear in a particular role, have her any different." Not a few of us, after all, might say the same of our loved ones.

All this is related in letters to Wells, to friends, and, in terms that are painful to read, to her son. She had done everything for him, she says, his father nothing; no, she did not send him to boarding school at two years old, he was *three*: "You have one grievance against me, and one only; that I did not have an abortion and kill you." His grievance, no doubt, was that he had been passed from hand to hand like a parcel far too young. But she had to, or wanted to, earn a living and a reputation. The whole tragedy so shaped her life that it is hard to imagine what form, without it, the life would have taken. A much better one? Or perhaps she would have found storms of love and hate somewhere else.

The effect of these years is visible in the tremendous haughtiness of her *grande dame* years. "I can't reconcile myself to being treated as an inferior scatterbrain by someone with whose crazy behaviour I have been coping all my life, without a word of thanks, or of regret," she wrote of her well-meaning elder sister. "There is a reference to me on page 39 which I wish you had asked me about" is a typical opening to letters to authors and editors. James Joyce, for some complicated reason, "made a long attack on me in *Finnegans Wake*."

When in the 1950s she was mistaken, in her evenhandedness, for a supporter of Joseph McCarthy, the witch-hunter of Reds under the bed, she wrote to the writer J. B. Priestley, "I have never spoken or written a single word in defence of McCarthy.... Can you suggest why...I should suddenly fall for a half-baked gorilla from the Middle West?" Did that mean, she asked, that she could never mention Communist infiltration into certain bodies in the US? As a liberal who had seen enough to detest communism, she felt herself under every kind of attack for speaking out. Her marriage in 1930 to a part-German banker (at first a source of pride, but not entirely successful) and her network of acquaintances in the States meant that she was exceptionally well informed about world affairs. She would have greatly enjoyed outraging our current political correctness.

But the friends she made, as well as unmade! Bonnie Kime Scott, the editor of the *Selected Letters*—a careful selection, though not generous with background information—mentions the eagerness of people to offer material and contribute to the book. Though most recipients of the letters are now dead, I think they would have been glad to share some of their gems: on Ingrid Bergman, for instance, "a nice soul, but...common and mannerless...she might well be a housemaid in a big Hamburg hotel"; on Mary McCarthy, who had "a behind built on the lines of a canal barge." The writer Elizabeth Jenkins was granted a wondrous tribute in a letter to Virginia Woolf:

> ...a disordered blonde, about whom I felt something that could only be expressed by the haughty words I heard a lady use to another at 1 in the morning at the corner of Dover St. "What are you doing here with us? You are the Strand cut, not Piccadilly."

Later she was to concede generously that "I'm sure she is a very nice woman." The wit was not all malicious. The ways of cats are caught well in her grieving letter over Ginger Pounce, a fine marmalade creature:

> He...was always very careful not to make a fuss of me, but in a cagey way let me know that he knew I was doing pretty well for him and there were no hard feelings. He had a very reserved, reluctant way of licking my hand in a way that suggested he was saying to himself, "I hope to God the woman won't start to think I want to marry her."

The above targets were presumably not her friends (apart from the cat), but many, many others were, both men and women. To the latter, she is sometimes heartbreakingly honest about the distresses in her life. Toward men, she tends to show the attitude that is nowadays so popular: that they are unfortunately rather endearing, but quite hopeless. There are, though, examples in the collection of very gentle letters of condolence over deaths. As someone whose pattern was to do battle and then collapse with an illness, there was perhaps a yearning for gentleness that she resisted as others would alcohol or drugs—in the war against humbug, it had to be avoided. Fierceness was all. Fierceness and some fun—even her angry son admitted that she could be a wonderful companion.

Should one dwell so much on the wit and malice, the private life and neuroses of a woman who was made Dame Commander of the British Empire and member of the French Légion d'Honneur? She herself would certainly have disliked it. Did she not write on politics, on travel, literary criticism, history, feminism—on most of the concerns, in fact, of her century? The difficulty is that her range was so wide that it can hardly be represented in two hundred letters; besides, being very feminine (in spite of the alarm she sometimes aroused in men), she did not separate her writing from her feelings and personal experiences—they are part of the oeuvre. Objectivity was not her style. (In this context the unsurpassable put-down of this style by Wells, quoted in Glendinning's biography, has to be brought in: "You have a most elaborate, intricate and elusive style which is admirably suited for a personal humorous novel.... You are ambitious and pretentious and you do not know the measure and quality of your power." As a whole, though, "it is a sham. It is a beautiful voice and a keen and sensitive mind doing 'Big Thinks' to the utmost of her ability—which is nil.... There my dear Pussy is some more stuff for your little behind. You sit down on it and think." The hoofmark of Wells! Who would not be left with a lifelong sense of rage?) In her book on the postwar trials of Nazi war criminals and pro-Nazi British, she found a good channel for her interest in suspicion and betrayal, as well as her way of finding a sharp distinction between black and white, good and evil. "Judgmental" it could be called, by people who like to stick to shades of gray.

The place to see her moral philosophy hammered out most impressively is *Black Lamb and Grey Falcon*—for the reader who can manage it. This study of Yugoslavia just before the Second World War is very long indeed—350,000 words, she estimated—and, as she says in a letter here, is better in the second half than the first. The book gets off the ground very, very slowly. At first, on rereading it, I wondered why it had sent me wandering around Macedonia some years ago, and finding it very different from the country West saw. Such longueurs in the book, so many rather bogus conversations with the husband whom in life she found dull! But as the meaning that she finds in the history and way of life of these small Balkan peoples increases, she finds a declaration of faith of her own there.

West herself wondered at her own dedication to the book. Why, she wrote to Alexander Woollcott,

> should I be moved in 1936 to devote the following 5 years of my life, at great financial sacrifice and to the utter exhaustion of my mind and body, to take an inventory of a country down to its last vest-button, in a form insane from any ordinary artistic or commercial point of view—a country which ceases to exist? I find the hair rising on my scalp at the extraordinary usefulness of this apparently utterly futile act.

For her own needs, it did prove useful. Earlier she had written to her husband that "I have a feeling that once I have done this book all my work & my life will be simpler."

The project began with a British Council lecture tour in 1936. This was followed by a return visit with her husband—"It is more wonderful than I can tell you," she promises him at the beginning of the book—and a third visit. She felt somehow more a natural Balkan, once she had discovered the place, than English; she felt it to be a mother country, a place where "the mode of life was so honest that it put an end to perplexity." Having battled against English grayness all her life, she found a natural home in the beauty and desolation, savagery and hospitality, of this very non-English place where nothing was stifled or denied. This hardly comes out in the letters; it was all poured into the book.

In Yugoslavia, which in spite of its poverty she loved for its richness of color and a "unique sort of healthy intensity," she worked out a philosophy of life—and of her own life, which she felt had gone essentially wrong. It was inspired by two symbols with far-reaching associations. One—the lamb—she saw being carried to a sacrificial stone in Macedonia, a bloodstained altar to which barren women prayed. The falcon was in a famous poem on the Battle of Kosovo (which we all know about now). It was translated for her: Tsar Lazar, leader of the Serbs against the Turks, is visited by a gray falcon with a message. If you want to defeat the Turks, it says, gird on your swords and fight. But if you want a heavenly kingdom, build a fine church here, and let yourself and your army be defeated. The prince chooses the heavenly kingdom, and is indeed defeated. It was in 1389. West was living, of course, in the shadow of Hitler and the approaching war at the time. What got through to her was the wrongness of Tsar Lazar's choice. If people can destroy themselves, can have an innate impulse toward defeat, "then all the world is a vast Kosovo."

From the sacrificed lamb she felt she had learned the ugliness of the principle of sacrifice, and the deep hold it had on the imagination, including her own. It was behind the atrocious Christian doctrine of the Atonement:

> None of us, my kind as little as any others, could resist the temptation of accepting this sacrifice as a valid symbol. We believed in our heart of hearts that life was simply this and nothing more, a man cutting the throat of a lamb on a rock to please God and obtain happiness.

But then, disliking the cruelty, human beings are fatally drawn toward the role of sacrificial victim; again, they choose defeat.

She had written about this before—"The desire to frustrate ourselves, not to be what we are"—but it was Yugoslavia and her book that integrated the knowledge. In the epilogue to *Black Lamb and Grey Falcon*, written after the Second World War had started, she continues the theme, with the suicide of nations and Europe's self-destruction in the ongoing war. After the war, she was convinced that when Britain backed Tito rather than Mihailovitch as leader of Yugoslavia a gross mistake was made. (This is a point where the editor of the letters might have sacrificed some notes and given a fuller account of this crucial decision.) As late as 1972 she addressed a letter to the editor of *The Times Literary Supplement* in which she repeats this view and documents it.

The insights of *Black Lamb and Grey Falcon* felt right for her own life, apparently so successful but, she believed, tragic in personal relationships. She had one more blow to come. When her rather befuddled husband died in 1968, years after their marriage became celibate, she found out that the old man had been pursuing a positive harem of women for years. She wrote to a friend then her most bitter words: "You say 'this has been a bad experience.' But it's been more than that. It's been a bad life; and the only one I have."

This would probably not have been her final, considered judgment. What would she have made of the new millennium's political state? She knew how little federation and cooperation meant to people compared to love of country: "For the last nineteen years," she wrote to Lionel Trilling in 1952, "I have been coming more and more in contact with exiles and refugees as they presented themselves before me in increasing destitution [and] it was nationalism, the pride of a people in their own country and in their own culture" that mattered to them. She might have foreseen a Yugoslavia of nationalist explosion. In Serbia she had seen with shock a cross dedicated to fallen fighters for freedom, 1389–1912. Now the second date would have to be chiseled out and advanced by—a century? Perhaps more.

It may seem unkind after what is—I hope—a reasonable assessment of West's whole achievement to append some thoughts about some of her minor work. In particular the two early novels, *The Return of the Soldier* and *Harriet Hume*,[5] from 1918 and 1929, are now justly forgotten—positively repressed, I imagine, by those who see the author chiefly in relation to the history of feminism. But apart from their being (unintentionally) so deliciously ridiculous, they do show the later Dame Commander of the British Empire struggling in a quite touching way with our age-old difficulty of the relation between men and women. She never cracked the problem, of course; but these early attempts to incorporate sentiment and passion do have to be accepted as part of the picture. Some may like to see in them just those dreadful hoofmarks. As for *The Young Rebecca*,[6] a collection of her earliest journalism from around 1912 and 1913, it is a sparkling and essential read, and without the slightest trace of a hoofmark.

West wrote, she once said in a radio talk, to explore character—an unexceptionable explanation from a writer half of whose oeuvre was fiction, except that it is only outside her novels that she really does so. When she has to invent, she generally flusters and fails; but once she has a theme, whether a journey or a political trial or a critical exposition, her gift for observing character and then fitting it into great sweeping generalizations and moral patterns comes into its own. She needs her characters to be somewhat at a distance: a fourth-century saint (lily-livered Augustine), the peasants and monks and chambermaids and children of her Balkan journey, the human dregs in the dock at Nuremberg. Watching these like a hawk, interpreting them

5. Both republished by Virago, 1980.

6. Viking, 1982.

sub specie aeternitas, she is stunningly magisterial. "Who does she think she is?" we are inclined to ask as she explicates history, sorts out morality, defines our condition and destiny. Someone exceptionally well up to the job of doing so, is the answer.

But then there are tremendous failures. In her early book reviews reprinted in *The Young Rebecca* she is hilariously cruel about what has displeased her, so let me borrow some of her naughtiness (if not her wit) and say that *The Return of the Soldier* and *Harriet Hume* are awful. It is their very awfulness that is endearing: we see that this powerful writer is not in fact the Archbishop of Canterbury and Regius Professor of History and Lord Chief Justice rolled into one, but an uneven writer who spans extremes of brilliance and disaster. *The Return of the Soldier* was made into a film, with Glenda Jackson as Margaret (shabby, with loyal gray eyes and as full of natural goodness as a cup of Ovaltine) and Julie Christie as Kitty (dainty, rosebud-mouthed, very nasty—a recurring figure in West's books). Caught between them is the shell-shocked booby Chris (played in the film by Alan Bates), a powerless hulk up for grabs by the women; for in the trenches he has lost the memory of his marriage to Kitty and thinks he is still Margaret's lover. These two powerful females decide his fate: he must be woken from his shell shock, face the truth, and be handed back to Kitty. The final sentence sees her gloating over her repossession: "I heard her suck her breath with satisfaction. 'He's cured!' she whispered slowly. 'He's cured!'"

It is a curious amalgam of West's themes: the necessity for truth at all costs; the ineffectuality of men as compared to women; the awfulness, however, of a certain kind of woman. But there is another element in her view of the sexes—and this is going to make modern readers squirm, for I assume the following to be serious:

> It was my dear Chris and my dear Margaret who sat thus englobed in peace as in a crystal sphere, [and] I knew it was the

> most significant as it was the loveliest attitude in the world. It means that the woman has gathered the soul of the man into her soul and is keeping it warm in love and peace so that his body can rest quiet for a little time. This is a great thing for a woman to do.

True. But it has been better put (by Shakespeare, John Donne, Ella Wheeler Wilcox . . .).

Harriet Hume is even more of an oddity, given that it was written eleven years later, when West was in her mid-thirties and had meantime published a successful volume of essays and reviews, *The Strange Necessity*. Victoria Glendinning in her introduction to the novel charitably calls it "an exercise in the higher whimsy." If the higher whimsy is what you want, it is your book; if not, it is simply embarrassing. West is nothing if not solid and vigorous and prosy, and this arch fantasy about two manikins (or manikin and womanikin) dances like an elephant. Dialogue such as "You are riding softly down the moments as a snowflake rides down the airs, white, oh, so white, and weightless as anything in this ponderous universe, and you are trembling, trembling, trembling" is neither serious nor a skit, but simply skittish.

"I suspect you of being the embodiment of some principle," says hero Arnold Condorex to heroine Harriet Hume. "Are you love? Are you truth? You are not justice, though you might be mercy. Are you poetry? Or are you philosophy?" No, in fact. Not love, poetry, etc., but the Feminine Principle—"Write me down as all that Arnold Condorex rejected"—while the said Arnold stands for the Masculine. Harriet, who mews and twitters and scampers about on teeny birdlike feet, embodies things it would seem well worth rejecting; Condorex as masculinity, however, is simply a plain shit. They pursue each other through baroque landscapes and through the years, and the moral seems to be that the two principles must complement each other. In fact, though, the female once again has the whip hand, for not only has Harriet the psychic gift of reading Condorex's thoughts instantly—reasonable enough grounds for his eventual murder of her, one would imagine—but she is the one who enlightens him about what the two of them represent:

> Humanity would be unbearably lackadaisical if there were none but my kind alive. 'Tis the sturdy desire you have to shape the random elements of our existence into coherent patterns that is the very pith and marrow of mankind. Think, my love! You must admit that when you were not pursuing the chimera of greatness, you performed many very worthy achievements that enabled our species to establish itself on this globe more firmly.

In spite of this kindly pat on the head the Masculine Principle remains understandably gloomy, and the closing wish for the two ghosts—"A Very Happy Eternity"—seems unlikely to come true.

And this is the author who dismissed *The Waves* as Pre-Raphaelite flummery! It is the crudeness of the revenge fantasy—superior women putting down inferior men—that stifles imaginative vitality in these novels. In *The Thinking Reed* of 1936, a much better book, this has been overcome:

> It struck her that the difference between men and women is the rock on which civilization will split before it can reach any goal that could justify its expenditure of effort. She knew also that her life would not be tolerable if he were not always there to crush gently her smooth hands with his strong short fingers.

These are its closing words—an ending that veers rather endearingly between magisteriality and a touch of the *Forever Amber*s. But perhaps it is a handicap, in writing about the relationship between men and women, to be conclusive. To be aghast and muddled and fascinated is at least a good start.

Of the four novellas published under the title *The Harsh Voice* in 1935, two are about sexual obsession (and both involve flimsy men being dealt with by women, though not so crudely as in *The Return of the Soldier* and *Harriet Hume*). In "There Is No Conversation" a woman tracks down someone she thought had been in love with her own disastrous husband, and discovers that in fact the woman had never cared a pin for him:

> I told you that there was no conversation; that no one listens to what the other one says. But it appears that the inter-silence of the universe is more profound even than this. It appears that even the different parts of the same person do not converse among themselves.... I was utterly desolate, because of a cry from my heart, which was not reasonable, and had not been understood by the rest of me, which is governed by reason.... I had wanted her to lay something before me which I realized I had never ceased to seek, something which would make it right and reasonable that I should have spent ten years of my life with my first husband, enduring unfathomable agony, sustained by unsurpassable pleasure, until I was overcome by a fatigue that seemed like the judgment of a third person.... An insane part of me feels that there is a sanction for my life in that miserable and fruitless time, if only I could lay my hands on it, which transcends all the claims that I can make for myself because of these later years when I have been building up a tranquil home for people who are among the salt of the earth.

Here she has moved on from the earlier novels, clogged with daydreams and anger. Always she celebrates woman as the first sex, the strong sex; but now, with good humor, she acknowledges that everyone is in a fix. Men are insecure creatures with the double burden of physical strength and dependence on women; women are committed to maternity, but vulnerable to men's revengefulness and weakness. And she is starting to acknowledge that human beings of either gender are crucially divided between affirmative and self-destructive passions, Eros and Thanatos. In this, without benefit of jargon, she is at heart a true Freudian.

In *The Young Rebecca*, finally, we go back to the very first version of her feminism, a version genuinely innocent of pain and complexity, the early writings of a prodigiously talented and high-spirited girl just out of her teens. These pieces have the humor and glow of her later work without its dark side: "Submission to unhappiness is the unpardonable sin against the spirit" is their motto. About a third of the collection consists of articles written in 1912 and 1913 for *The Clarion*, a radical socialist weekly edited by Robert Blatchford; another bunch, mainly book reviews, are from *The Freewoman*, a feminist journal so shocking that Rebecca West had been forbidden by her family to read it. It is all irresistibly witty and quotable. Her easiest targets are the antifeminists of the time; they go down like ninepins—the "fluffy yet resistant matter of Dr Saleeby," "Dr Lionel Tayler's interminable sentences," "the fog-like featureless gloom of Sir Almroth Wright." And (since this was before the time of trying to grapple with the strong-tender-fingers problem herself) she has a remorseless way with the sentimental novelist:

> I was held from the very first page, whereon I read: "There were reservoirs of love in her—of wife-love and of mother-love—accumulating reservoirs, which had never been tapped...." The conception of fate as a Metropolitan Water Board regulating the flow of spiritual liquids is immense.

But she is as sharp as a knife, too, over women and the things they get away with. "A little later," runs the summary of a novel, "he discovers that to furnish her house daintily with Bokhara hangings and brass-footed workboxes she has spent every penny of his income of six hundred and frittered away a thousand of his capital. She avoids discussion by having a baby in a sentimental and rather pretentious way." For the middle-class lady "loafing about the house with only a flabby mind for company" West has no mercy, nor for the creed of "virtue" and self-sacrifice:

> Anti-feminists, from Chesterton down to Dr Lionel Tayler, want women to specialize in virtue. While men are rolling round the world having murderous and otherwise sinful adventures of an enjoyable nature, in commerce, exploration or art, women are to stay at home earning the promotion of the human race to a better world. This is illustrated by the middle-class father who never goes to church himself, but always sends his wife and daughter.

For the working woman she fights like a tiger; feminism never distracted from economic injustice. Three vintage essays from *The Clarion*, from 1913, show her at the top of her form. In "The Sheltered Sex: 'Lotos-Eating' on Seven-and-Six a Week," she casts an eye on a politician's pronouncement that something must be done about women drawing too many welfare benefits. In a blazing rage she compares statements about the sanctity of motherhood with the wages that women in "the graceful feminine occupation of chain-making" are getting for an eighty-hour week:

> If we want to make every woman a Madonna we must see that every woman has quite a lot to eat. But the working woman never has even enough to eat.... No civilization has ever burdened woman so heavily before as the capitalist does today by making her a factory-hand by day, domestic drudge by night. The human frame is not built for such a strain.

In "The Sterner Sex" she compares the lot of the government employee in Whitehall—"cool and uncreased young men emerging from the cloister of their offices"—with its other employees, machine sewers of uniforms, whose wages had just been reduced by two shillings to seventeen-and-fourpence a week. And in "Mother or Capitalist? What the World Asks of Women" she attacks the abuse of the working-class mother: "It is so much easier to accuse working women of feeding their babies on pickles and tea than to accuse society of poisoning these babies long before their little bodies came into being...." Her contempt for charitable patronage is rock-firm. Charity is "an ugly trick," "a virtue grown by the rich on the graves of the poor," "cheap moral swagger." And "attempts to poke the sickly and exhausted into unspontaneous gambols" (good phrase! take note, street theaters and community arts centers and neighborhood play schemes) provoke her special scorn:

> Surely everyone can see that a community must be sick unto death before its amusements have to be organized and imposed upon it.... You won't get them to practise art now any more than domestic economy. They're tired and cross and hungry, and they won't play.

A writing career of seventy-one years is a rare phenomenon. What consistency is there between the young journalist and the eighty-nine-year-old author of the text of *1900* (a better-than-average picture book based on that year) and the author of the books and articles in between? Certainly the twenty-year-old who wrote loftily that "the only way to medicine the ravages of this fever of life is to treat sex lightly, to...think no more hardly of two lovers who part soon than we do of spring for leaving the earth at the coming of June" differs from the writer who struggled ambivalently but more realistically with the relations between men and women. The red-hot socialist of

1913 is not the same as the grave indicter of communism and its spies. And she never did succeed with the idea she proposed in 1912:

> Some woman ought to write a novel about a man and the struggle of his soul with the universe, as moving and pathetic as *Tess of the D'Urbervilles*. It would be a great thing for a woman to do as much for one man as Meredith did for all his women.

But in *1900* (a year in which men, "poor stuff" though she once called them, did a lot beyond annexing the Tonga Islands for Britain—discovered Knossos, composed *Tosca*, wrote *Uncle Vanya*, elaborated the quantum theory) the young writer is still clearly visible. The wit is as sharp as ever ("It is extraordinary how dangerous an upright piano covered with mother-of-pearl looks: it seems to be about to shoot the pianist for not doing his best"), and the *hauteur* ("There was too much German *schmaltz*, too much banality about Einstein"), and the empathy for the working woman:

> Looking into doorways one saw dark garments lying in heaps round sewing machines, and thoughtful women looking down at them in a dedicated pose.

And always the wry view of the sex war. "Men and women," she sighs, "do not really like each other very much."

21

GREAT SPACE AND TUNDRA: SLATER, JAMISON, MILLETT, FRANCE, FERGUSON

ALONENESS DOESN'T GET much worse, doesn't push the sufferer farther off the map, than it does in mental illness. A number of women have been able to describe with truth how this feels. The first two to follow write, unusually, from the point of view of working as mental health professionals and also having suffered painfully themselves from such illness. Both of them avoid the dangers of clinical jargon on the one hand and feel-good optimism on the other. Perhaps experiences of extremity clear the clichés out of the brain.

Lauren Slater's *Welcome to My Country*[1] is focused on patients she treated, with a dramatic closing flashback to her own earlier illness; Kay Redfield Jamison's *An Unquiet Mind*[2] is more specifically the account of how, as a badly afflicted manic-depressive herself, she became an authority on the background and treatment of the condition. Both authors write without self-pity and with generosity toward people who helped them. Jamison, after a cheerful childhood marred by her father's eventual mental disintegration, first became ill while still in high school (she makes no bones about words like "ill" and "insane"). The term "manic-depressive" is often thrown about rather

1. *Welcome to My Country: A Therapist's Memoir of Madness* (Random House, 1996).

2. *An Unquiet Mind: A Memoir of Moods and Madness* (Knopf, 1995).

casually; her account makes it clear that this is a crippling illness, with a strong physical basis. As she says, "It is an illness that is biological in its origins, yet one that feels psychological in the experience of it; an illness that is unique in conferring advantage and pleasure, yet one that brings in its wake almost unendurable suffering and, not infrequently, suicide."

At one end of the spectrum is the depression,

> a day-in, day-out, night-in, night-out, almost arterial level of agony. It is a pitiless, unrelenting pain that affords no window of hope, no alternative to a grim and brackish existence, and no respite from the cold undercurrents of thought and feeling that dominate the horribly restless nights of despair.

Some people can recognize this, depression on its own being so much commoner than manic-depression. But mania, at the other end of the spectrum, is from another world:

> There was a definite point when I knew I was insane. My thoughts were so fast that I couldn't remember the beginning of a sentence halfway through. Fragments of ideas, images, sentences, raced around and around in my mind like the tigers in a children's story. Finally, like those tigers, they became meaningless melted pools. Nothing once familiar to me was familiar. I wanted desperately to slow down but could not. Nothing helped—not running around a parking lot for hours on end or swimming for miles.

The curious thing is that Jamison managed to continue through college concealing her illness; and even more curious, that what she was studying was psychology, and that the more she read about psychopathology the more she refused to recognize her own illness. As she says with some humor, she was the exact opposite of the medical student who reads the textbook and thinks she has all the diseases in it.

She did eventually accept the need to take lithium for the rest of her life, but throws a good deal of light on why psychiatric patients hate taking their drugs. The side effects are unpleasant, and it is hard to abandon all hope that "normality"—life without medication—will be reached one day. She expresses nostalgia, as for war or love, for her "highs," when euphoria flowed so easily and before the amusement on friends' faces turned to concern. Even the memory of mania corrodes her excellent prose style: gliding through starfields is mentioned, and lilacs and ecstasy, and peals of riotous laughter. More fun for her, perhaps, than for those around her.

This leads on to the relation of manic-depression to creativity, which Jamison has written about in another book.[3] She describes a class in which the students were asked to give their responses to the ink-blot test; having seen hers, the teacher asked her to stay behind and told her he had never seen such "imaginative"—for which she reads "eccentric"—responses to the test before. This was, she says, her first lesson in appreciating "the complicated, permeable boundaries between bizarre and original thought."

Lauren Slater is also by training a clinical psychologist, and has won literary awards as well. This shows in a certain lushness of language, which sometimes works well and sometimes not so well. She casts her book in the form of studies of the first group of patients she encountered as a professional—mostly schizophrenic men, for whom she feels a sensitive and respectful empathy. Her theme, she says, is separation and connection; so she looks beyond clinical jargon and the patients' garbled schizo-speak to see that their real condition is a terrible loneliness:

---

3. *Touched with Fire: Manic-Depressive Illness and the Artistic Temperament* (Free Press, 1993).

> I go to the library one evening after work and look up the literature on delusions. There are articles on delusions of grandeur and paranoia, but nowhere does the literature mention delusions that weave around the themes of longing and loss, of great space and tundra. Why? I wonder. Is it that the schizophrenic experience seems so bizarre to us, we can't imagine such a patient might be suffering from something as common as loneliness? As highbrow as existential anomie?

In the great classic of the literature of madness, *Memoirs of My Nervous Illness*, Judge Daniel Schreber describes how he saw the world when he was incarcerated in Sonnenstein Asylum in 1893: he became convinced that the entire world had been depopulated and was inhabited only by temporary shadows.

One would have liked to hear more from both writers about how psychotherapy worked for them; both are writing about experiences that are considered almost beyond its reach, but both acknowledge the importance of the help they got. Both have thought deeply about the dilemma of coming clean about their own histories while also working in the mental health field. Slater declares that American confessionalism, the Oprah Winfrey style of public self-abasement, can be nauseating. But she leads up to her own disclosures by describing the time when she had to meet a patient at the very hospital where earlier she had spent many stays for anorexia and self-mutilation. She was terrified of being recognized, and made herself exchange jargon with colleagues about "borderline personalities" and "antisocials." It was, as she says, a betrayal—and in a profession that ostensibly pursues honesty.

Jamison too describes her misgivings: misgivings about her professional prospects, about family privacy, even about whether self-disclosure could make her experiences clinical and unreal. Both writers struggle with the feelings of shame and guilt that are peculiar to mental illness as opposed to, say, multiple sclerosis or diabetes. She does not even mind the label of psychotic, Jamison says, as much as she minds being thought weak or inadequate. But she also says, "I am tired of hiding, tired of misspent and knotted energies, tired of the hypocrisy, and tired of acting as though I have something to hide." And she quotes from fellow manic-depressive Robert Lowell: "*Yet why not say what happened*?"

The question raised is: How far should those who treat mental illness have had personal experience of it? Alcoholics are generally given help by ex-alcoholics; marriage counseling is not dispensed by virgins; bereavement counseling is unlikely to be offered by someone who had never had a bereavement. If it is somewhat different with mental illness, this could be because few sufferers are as lucky as Slater and Jamison in getting the support that helped them through their struggles to their careers. Most patients, I think, would far rather be helped by someone with such a history than by one with the defects that do not get labeled and treated and medicated: pomposity, unimaginativeness, defensiveness. Both these courageous writers should do a lot to bridge gaps, and warm those of us who feel, rightly or wrongly, rather shamefully different from the rest of the world.

Kate Millett's illness—manic-depression—was diagnostically the same as Jamison's, though the course of her experiences ran differently. Again, in spite of a record of such miseries, one has to say that, like Jamison and Slater, she was paradoxically lucky. Few return from the loony-bin trip with the energy or articulateness to describe what it was like[4]; some never return at all. It is this majority that Millett understands and identifies with:

> In the corridors of St. Vincent's I am one with the mad.... One of the shabby who waste eternity staring at the lighted numbers

4. *The Loony-Bin Trip* (Simon and Schuster, 1990).

> and reading discarded newspapers, forbidden to smoke.... Madwomen who mumble, men who pace, nervous people who use the phone all the time to tell whomever they are that they are still stuck down here, won't be done for another couple hours.

Having some years earlier been forcibly hospitalized for manic-depression and put on lithium medication, she decided in 1980 to go off the drug, to "belong to myself at last." The result—as she saw it—was that friends began to pick on her, to gang up on her to persuade her to take her pills, and eventually to plan to lock her away. Rightly, she does not make a final judgment of how disturbed she actually was, but tells it as it felt to her (and perhaps still does). It is the omnipresent sense of persecution that she re-creates, the fear of a trapped animal that has to placate and outwit its captors, keep an eye on the door in hope of a breakaway, silently calculate chances of rescue. But she is honest enough to include a letter from a friend that suggests that it is also difficult for other people to handle someone apparently becoming irrational and hard to recognize.

Millett describes the awful helplessness of the ill person, in relation not only to what the world may do to her but also what her own mind may do to her—"Has something happened inside my skull which will unfold quickly or even slowly but which will be my downfall? My God, if anything should happen to my mind"—realizing only too late how precious it is, and now how fragile. The essence of the plight is condensed in one detail of her description of an attempted forcible hospitalization: she signals for a taxi to make her escape but, curiously, none of them stop; then she sees that her sister, farther down the road, is tapping at her temple to indicate "crazy." From this situation she did escape through knowledge of her legal rights, but some time later, at Shannon airport in Ireland, the frightened jokes we all make about funny farms and men in white coats come true, and she is taken to a grim Catholic barracks in the Irish countryside.

In the end, later and back in the States, it is the depressive rather than the manic phase of her illness that defeats her—the "pitiless, unrelenting pain" without a window of hope that Jamison describes. After much suffering, she accepts the wretched necessity of going back on medication, and a combination of courage, hard physical work, and help from friends and a doctor get her back to health—and to writing the book. Writing it must have been of the greatest value, because, as she says, during depression "the world disappears. Language itself.... One's real state of mind is a source of shame. So one is necessarily silent about it, leaving nothing else for subject matter." She is telling it here for all the other people who still are shut up in this silence.

Millett argues, like Jamison, that mania is creative and might be left to run its course, that people are far more sympathetic to the person who is depressed—even punitively so:

> Depression—that is what we all hate. We the afflicted. Whereas the relatives and shrinks, the tribal ring, they rather welcome it: you are quiet and you suffer.... You should shut up because you talked too much before, you should close down all your capacities because you were boastful and extravagant about them before.

This is perhaps unfair; it is easier to sympathize with sorrow than with false elation and its consequences.

But given—and Millett might not agree with this—that in a minimum of cases people must be in psychiatric care, must it so rarely be an asylum in the real sense of the word? Should not, for instance, psychiatric staff take antipsychotic medication for a time as part of their training in order to know what it feels like? (A psychiatrist friend of mine who was given haloperidol when she was "mad" now does not prescribe it.) Analysts and therapists (sometimes) manage to offer empathy and affection because they are protected by the fifty-minute hour, the selection of "well-behaved" patients, and the support of a prestigious profession; but within institutional psychiatry there seems very much less of this humaneness. I should like to see, as a parallel to Millett's book, one by, say, a psychiatric nurse who can write as articulately as Millett and can explore what it is that, so often, gets in the way of compassion and real human contact.

Others who have to go through these hells remain outside hospital walls, and work through psychotherapy. But they too have not left enough records of their experience. *Consuming Psychotherapy*, the account by "Ann France" (a *nom de plume*), is an exceptional one.[5] The dedications that preface her book are to acquaintances "whose friendship was more therapeutic than any professional counseling," and to her therapist "who made it all possible, and often impossible." Her own experiences in psychotherapy were a mixture of good and bad, and she tries, with the help of wide reading around the subject, to sort out what she believes to be harmful and helpful practices. On the one hand she is, she says, still quite surprised that she is alive to tell the tale[6]; on the other, she ends the book on a reconciliatory note by comparing her therapy to the reading of Proust—"It opened my eyes and ears to the life inside me and around me."

In between, she covers many points raised by this curious modern adventure in introspection. A therapist who read her manuscript commented that she was stronger on the rights of patients, or consulters as she prefers to call them, than of therapists[7]; of course, she replies—if we don't stand up for ourselves, who will? The vast literature is nearly all by professionals, which is why the personal accounts by

---

5. Free Association Books, 1988.

6. She is not. She committed suicide after the book's publication.

7. Perhaps we should, though, have more sympathy with the therapist's dilemma. The late Sarah Ferguson wrote in memory of her analyst, who died during her treatment:

> You were my mother, and father, and husband, and lover. You were my wife, and the times when I was a boy, a man, or a hermaphrodite, you were my brotherly

Slater, Jamison, and Millett are also so welcome. (What about at least a token contribution by a consulter in every professional journal?)

Ann France's history was, first, a fairly successful psychotherapy with therapist no. 1; a second one a few years later during which she fell into very deep waters; and a rescue operation by therapist no. 3, helped by friends and a Samaritan befriender. Her therapists were in fact unusually tolerant and flexible; they raised no objection to her seeing nos. 2 and 3 concurrently for a time, and in the end she survived a suicidal depression that was worse than anything she had experienced before beginning therapy. The danger she sees is that consulters may be led into places where the therapist cannot follow and cannot help. When she was depressed her therapist could only say, "You have come up against my limitations." Something the professionals should perhaps discuss is what they really feel about profound pain when it does appear in their patients. Suicide, as Ann French points out, is often a real preoccupation, but tends to be tabooed as a subject by therapists.

The issues she discusses center around the strange and fraught relationship between consulter and therapist—how much of it is "transference" (leftover feelings from childhood), how friendly or aloof the therapist should be, how much frustration the consulter should have to accept. She sees that transference emotions are vividly present on the consulter's side, but argues that they should exist against the background of a solidly real relationship—people who have been

---

> friend. You were more than all these too. More than doctor, teacher, and stalwart supporter.... Surely I should now be able to carry on and make the best of my life, even though you are not visible here beside me. I try, and try, and I cannot. [Sarah Ferguson, *A Guard Within*, Pantheon, 1974]

"Transference" seems an inadequate, almost a silly word for this depth of emotion. And yet she describes pulling out the analyst's books onto the floor, hiding under his desk, biting off a piece of glass from the drink he offered her, taking off all her clothes (all "transference," too, and one cannot help feeling that it was, truly, impossible work for him).

confused in childhood need to distinguish phantasm from reality, and a mysteriously silent therapist only thickens the mystification.

She is particularly emphatic about the unproductiveness of therapists' silences. In Ann France's childhood, silence was used as a punishment, and although she had a therapist who was unconventional—who lent her books, offered her coffee, sent postcards—France found any lack of response agonizing. She discusses also silence's opposite, the imposition of "interpretations" on everything the consulter says. One of her therapists attributed France's childhood passion for ballet to pleasure in wearing a unisex leotard. France was too shy to tell her that in fact diaphanous dresses were worn.

She argues therefore for as natural a relationship as possible, rather than concealment on one side and revelation on the other. But this in itself is of course not enough, any more than probity in a solicitor or sobriety in a dentist. The therapist with whom she fell into a depression was a cheerful person who tended to say "That's all right" to much of what France said; it was not all right, she now feels, it needed probing and pursuing. The core of psychotherapy she defines as "the creation of a space where you are entitled to be just as you are, however defective." It does not sound very difficult; but it must imply a surrounding of the space by keen understanding as well as by ordinary support.

Her book points to two particular problems in the therapeutic enterprise which those in the so-called caring professions might think more about. One is a kind of double bind in the enterprise itself. The consulter is urged to excavate his or her most intense feelings—anger, despair, infantile dependency—and keeping them back is censured. But in fact they are not very acceptable when they do turn up; throwing the furniture around is not popular, nor is ringing up at midnight, nor even—as Ann France shows—being despairing. The aim of psychotherapy is ostensibly to produce a free spirit, but the rules about being cooperative and punctual—and not too ill—are really rather strict.

The other dilemma is whether psychotherapy's aim is that the consulter relive the bad experiences, or be solaced by good ones. France quotes one of her therapists saying, "A sense of deprivation is not cured by more deprivation, but by the feeling of security and gratification derived from a need having been met"; but professionals would hardly claim to supply all the love that consulters should have had from their parents. On the other hand, just going back to the traumas, according to France, can leave the consulter horribly stuck.

Good psychotherapy might seem to be always balancing on a knife-edge, and to demand more empathy, patience, and skill than most people possess. Perhaps it is the "impossible profession," in Janet Malcolm's phrase[8]; but there is no shortage of people anxious to learn to "care" and confident they can do it. In the absence of religious and communal support, the formal therapeutic dialogue is here to stay, and both parties to it need to be heard.

8. *Psychoanalysis, the Impossible Profession* (Knopf, 1981).

VI

TRAPPED

22

CONSPICUOUS GALLANTRY: MARGARET OLIPHANT

MARGARET OLIPHANT (born in 1828, died in 1897) was a literary phenomenon who is thankfully being rescued from a long spell of oblivion. Publishing her first book at twenty-one, she wrote well over a hundred novels and books of short stories, half a dozen biographies, a score of books on literary and historical themes, and innumerable ephemeral articles on subjects ranging from Scottish national character to the condition of women to Savonarola to Victor Hugo. The quantity of her work was at the expense of quality, and ensured that all of it would unfairly be lumped together as third-rate, as she well knew. She wrote and wrote not only because it came naturally to her but because she was the sole support of seven people.

In her autobiography[1] she muses with much honesty and just a little bitterness on her literary fate. In particular she compares herself with George Eliot:

> Should I have done better if I had been kept, like her, in a...mental greenhouse and taken care of?... It is a little hard sometimes not to feel with Browning's Andrea, that the men who have no wives, who have given themselves up to their art,

1. *The Autobiography and Letters of Mrs. M. O. W. Oliphant* (Dodd, Mead, 1899).

> have an almost unfair advantage over us who have been given perhaps more than one Lucrezia to take care of.... Curious freedom! I have never known what it was.

If there is a touch of self-pity or self-approbation in this, she rounds on it very quickly:

> I know I am giving myself the air of being *au fond* a finer sort of character than the others. I may as well take the little satisfaction to myself, for nobody will give it to me. No one even will mention me in the same breath with George Eliot. And that is just.

(She remained, however, just a little feline about her fellow writer: "These superior heroines are very awful people and of course poor Miss Brooke has got to have her heart broken.")

The tragedy in this life of a very untragically disposed person was that her sacrifice of what she might have written was in vain; all but two of her children and adopted children predeceased her. The bitterest thought was that

> now I think that if I had taken the other way, which seemed the less noble, it might have been better for all of us.... Who can tell? I did with much labour what I thought the best, and there is only a *might have been* on the other side.

She was, she added, "in very little danger of having my life written... for what could be said of me?" Fortunately, her life and her novels are now being brought back to our attention.[2]

---

2. Merryn Williams, *Margaret Oliphant: A Critical Biography* (St. Martin's, 1986); Elisabeth Jay, *Mrs. Oliphant: "A Fiction to Herself"* (Clarendon Press, 1995).

She came from a Scottish family that moved south (her Scottish backgrounds and dialogue are always impeccable), a matriarchal family whose pattern was to be repeated with her own children. Her father "took no particular notice of me or of any of us," and her brothers were to live failed and broken lives, but her mother was a formidable Scottish lady from whom her daughter must have picked up much learning—enough to write on an astonishing variety of subjects without benefit of examinations.

Even before her engagement to Frank Oliphant at twenty-three she had written two novels. The first, published much later, curiously foretold her own life—a noble sister cares for orphaned children, a brother goes to the bad. The second, *Margaret Maitland*, appeared in 1849, and was unconventionally the story of a sturdy Scottish spinster—"we are not aware that the Maiden Aunt has ever before found so favourable a representative in print," said the *Athenaeum*. Margaret Oliphant was always to avoid when she could the vapidities of boy-meets-girl plots. Life, as she said, was "full of broken threads and illogical conclusions, and lacks altogether the unity of the regularly constructed fiction, which confines itself to the graceful task of conducting two virtuous young persons through a labyrinth of difficulties to a happy marriage."

Within a few years of her marriage she had sustained several of the hard blows fate was to deal her; she lost two babies, falling into a serious depression after the second; her husband, an artist, died in Rome of tuberculosis; some time later she lost her eldest and favorite daughter. Those who argue that children were not cared for until this century and that the Victorians were inured to their loss should read her description in *Sir Tom* of parents caring for a dangerously ill child:

> He went out upon the terrace in the misty chill morning, all damp and miserable, with the trees standing about like ghosts. There was a dripping thaw after a frost, and the air was raw and

> the prospect dismal; but even that was less wretched than the glimmer of the shaded lights, the muffled whispering and stealthy footsteps indoors. He took a few turns up and down the terrace, trying to reason himself out of this misery. How was it, after all, that the little figure of this infant should overshadow earth and heaven to a man, a reasonable being, whose mind and life were full of interests far more important?

Mrs. Oliphant wrote of her own daughter's death:

> Here is the end of all. I am alone. I am a woman. I have nobody to stand between me and the roughest edge of grief.... I have to bear the loss, the pang unshared. My boys are too little to feel it, and there is nobody else in the world to divide it with me.

The irony was that so many tragedies should strike someone so intrinsically cheerful and resilient; throughout the worst of times she always wrote on—"I am a wonder to myself, a sort of machine... always fit for work whatever has happened to me." Her husband's death left her with the children, debts of £1,000, and her skill as a writer. With eighteen novels by now behind her (in general her poorer ones), she set out at once on a new novel, a seven-volume translation from the French, and a biography. It is not surprising that she wrote a little tartly of a more famous widow,

> I doubt whether *nous autres* poor women who have had to fight with the world all alone without much sympathy, can quite enter into the "unprecedented" character of the Queen's sufferings. A woman is surely a poor creature if with a large happy affectionate family of children around her, she can't take heart to do her duty whether she likes it or not.

Hateful Henry! This is a gross misunderstanding, a collision between two utterly opposed artistic temperaments—the one tortured and perfectionist, the other fluent and tough. Of course they cannot be compared as writers; but words like "fatuity" are totally inappropriate. Even the least of Oliphant's novels have taste and spirit; not for her the woodenness and sentimentality of Rhoda Broughton or Ouida or Mrs. Humphry Ward at her worst. (Their heroines were always ready to "throw their glorious hair over the breast of any chance companion," she remarked tartly. "What need has a woman for a soul when she has upon her head a mass of wavy gold?") Of course period charm is part of the pleasure in her books—silver tea-things in the firelight, sunshine on mossy English lawns; but the mild humor that plays about the Victorian props is quite modern. A bereaved young lady closets herself with *In Memoriam*, but decides that much as she loved her father, Lord Tennyson's words are not quite appropriate to him; a vicar's wife waters her maidenhair ferns, brooding that the shade of carpet her predecessor left in the drawing room is not the lightest cross the Lord has asked her to bear. Mrs. Oliphant was a religious woman ("there is nothing else which makes any response at all out of the awful darkness in which, one time or another, every living soul loses some precious thing") but she has a certain amount of fun with churchiness, from Dissent to High Church.

She takes much trouble with her subsidiary characters—older women, aunts (sometimes Wodehousian), children (nice and quite nasty). Spears the socialist leader in *He That Will Not When He May* is sympathetically drawn, though it becomes clear that socialism is something that one is courteous toward but does not take seriously. Though she does not write much about the poor, Mrs. Oliphant was, like so many Victorians, sharply aware of their existence and at a loss for a solution. She seems to have hoped, like Mrs. Gaskell, that restraint and goodwill on the sides of both labor and capital would suffice. The difficulty of redistributing money comes up in both *Sir*

Tom and *The Greatest Heiress in England*, where a naive heiress tries to give her wealth away, causing much offense and scandal.

The novels' mildness is nearly always spiced by some unconventionality. Mrs. Oliphant is not fond of straightforward happy endings. The last words of *Hester* are:

> And as for Hester, all that can be said for her is that there are two men whom she may choose between, and marry either if she pleases—good men both, who will never wring her heart. Old Mrs Morgan desires one match, Mrs John another. What can a young woman desire more than to have such a possibility of choice?

The words are ironical; Hester does not much care for either, and longs to work and travel.

In *The Perpetual Curate*, one of Oliphant's mellowest works, the lovers are allowed a happy ending—but there is a satirical comment:

> "How a young man like you, who know how to conduct yourself in some things, and have, I don't deny, many good qualities, can give in to come to an ending like a trashy novel, is more than I can understand. You are fit to be put in a book of the Good-child series, Frank, as an illustration of the reward of virtue," said the strong-minded woman, with a little snort of scorn; "and, of course, you are going to marry and live happy ever after, like a fairy tale."
>
> "It is possible I may be guilty of that additional enormity," said the Curate, "which, at all events, will not be your doing, my dear aunt, if I might suggest a consolation. You cannot help such things happening, but, at least, it should be a comfort to feel you have done nothing to bring them about."

The Ladies Lindores has Lady Caroline married off by her parents to a brute (unusual—her men tend to be weak rather than brutal); when he dies Caroline is quite plainly depicted as being overjoyed. Even then Mrs. Oliphant was evidently dissatisfied with the happy ending that reunited Caroline with her true love, for she wrote a sequel about her disappointment with her gentle second husband.

She was not unable to write real love stories, though. Lucy Woodhouse's feelings when she thinks her curate does not love her are caught very exactly:

> She sat down on the sofa, in a kind of dull heaviness, looking into vacancy. She was not positively thinking of Mr Wentworth, or of any one thing in particular. She was only conscious of a terrible difference somehow in everything about her—in the air which choked her breathing, and the light which blinded her eyes.... The world altogether had sustained a change.

And in the old couple Captain and Mrs. Morgan in *Hester* she draws a remarkable but unsentimental portrait of a long-lasting love.

One of the themes of the novels is responsibility, its acceptance and evasion—and the majority of her responsible characters are women. Nettie in *The Doctor's Family* decisively takes on her ne'er-do-well brother's family—"I should scorn to cry about it. It is simply *my business*. That is what it is. One is sorry, of course, and now and then it feels hard, and all that"—but she is given a close scrutiny:

> To fancy this willful imperious creature a meek self-sacrificing heroine, was equally absurd and impossible. Was there any virtue at all in that dauntless enterprise of hers? or was it simply determination to have her own way?

Though Nettie is presented as a tremendous character, she is at first totally dismayed when her burden is taken away and she is free to marry her lover.

Women in Oliphant's novels generally accept men as they are, but with moments of scorn or rebellion ("You are only a man," says Nettie, with "a certain careless scorn of the inferior creature"). In her short stories Margaret Oliphant seems to have felt freer to explore the serious dilemmas of her women contemporaries: in one, a respectable middle-aged family man is discovered to have set up a "wife" in another district; in another a new bride, appalled by marriage, jumps off the train during her honeymoon and never goes back; in another a young widow struggles with feeling for a man who has compromised her:

> She had seen him all round in a flash of awful reality and perception, and hated him—yet loved him all the same.... It did not matter to her, it did not affect the depth of her heart, any more than it would have affected her had he lost his good looks or his beautiful voice. Ah yes! it did matter. It turned her very love, herself, her life, into things so different that they were scarcely recognisable. The elements of hate were in her love, an opposition and distrust ineradicable took possession of her being: and yet she belonged to him, and he to her, almost the more for this contradiction.

This more serious vein she might have developed further if she had had time to write as she wished. It is impossible to know whether in other circumstances she might have become a major novelist. The wonder is that of her voluminous output so much is supremely enjoyable.

23

HER OWN STRAITJACKET: ALICE JAMES

ALICE JAMES'S LIFE was tragic but she dares us to pity her. "You poor child," wrote her brother William, with the uneasy condescension that characterized his relationship with her, "stifling slowly in a quagmire of disgust and pain and impotence." She fought back grimly; his letter, so amusing, had made her roar with laughter: "I may not have a group of Harvard students sitting at my feet drinking in psychic truth, [but] I shall not tremble, I assure you, at the last trump."[1] She might prefer honest dislike to pity from posterity; and indeed this gallant and intelligent woman was spiteful, bitter, and very easily dislikable.

Since her literary remains consist only of letters and her short and uneven diary, there is irony in the very fact that interest is now taken in her life. What she passionately wanted, and never was granted, was recognition for herself on her own merits; yet the diary might not have survived[2] if she had not been sister to two famous men, and the excellent first biography of her owes something to the fact that she so painfully embodies the thwarted Victorian woman who is being

---

1. Quoted in *The Death and Letters of Alice James*, edited and with a biographical essay by Ruth Bernard Yeazell (University of California Press, 1981).

2. *The Diary of Alice James*, edited by Leon Edel (Dodd, Mead and Co., 1964).

rescued from obscurity.[3] She was a victim, but it would be a pity simply to keep her in that role and sanctify her—for one thing, the James family also produced two male casualties in the younger brothers we never hear of.

The James family pattern was in fact extraordinary in an extravagant pre-Freudian way that is now hard for us to grasp. Though outwardly generous and permissive, it produced five damaged children of whom two were geniuses; devoted to honesty and the pursuit of happiness, it was united by a deep concern with illness. A recent biography of the father of the clan[4] reveals convolutions dating back to the grandfather who arrived in the United States in the 1790s. He was a tough Ulsterman overloaded with Presbyterian notions of sin, suffering, and damnation; though the five children of Henry Senior never knew him, his influence filtered down through his son. This father of the five, a bafflingly contradictory relative to have to handle, was determined to be a completely different kind of father when his own time came; but, as may more often be the case than we realize, the imprint of a forceful ancestor hung around, and a spectral voice boomed loudly down the years. Alfred Habegger suggests that William Junior's fascination with conversion and Henry Junior's with secrets may both point back to hidden Calvinism. The concept of will was important to all three men—yet, looking at such family patterns, one is led to wonder whether the role of free will wasn't in fact very small.

Little is known about the mother of the family. "She was the perfection of a mother—the sweetest, gentlest, most beneficent human being I have ever known," Henry could write, and with real conviction, on his mother's death, while portraying mothers in his fiction as strong and dangerous. ("A large florid stupid seeming lady" was how a New England neighbor described her.) Like all the Jameses, she

3. Jean Strouse, *Alice James: A Biography* (Houghton Mifflin, 1980).

4. Alfred Habegger, *The Father: A Life of Henry James, Sr.* (Farrar, Straus and Giroux, 1994).

had the dreadful family habit of jocularity when she wanted to touch on hostility or anxiety. "My daughter a child of France!" she wrote to Alice when she heard she was enjoying herself abroad:

> What has become of the high moral nature, on which I have always based such hopes for her for this world and the next? That you should so soon have succumbed to this assault upon your senses, so easily have been carried captive by the mere delights of eating and drinking and dressing, I should not have believed.... Indeed I see it all now, to be merely the effect of a little cerebral derangement produced by the supernatural effort you made in crossing the Channel.

Henry Senior lost a leg as a boy trying to put out a fire; the mysterious injury of Henry Junior's that has puzzled biographers may have been acquired in the same way. The father's conversion to Swedenborgianism, after a youth of sin, repentance, and New England evangelism, was prompted by the terrible "vastation" that came upon him out of the blue, a "damnèd shape" in the corner of the room that reduced him to helpless terror. William, after years of depression and hypochondria, experienced a similar vision—"an epileptic patient whom I had seen in the asylum, a black-haired youth with greenish skin...moving nothing but his black eyes and looking absolutely non-human.... *That shape am I*, I felt potentially." Robertson, the youngest James, was a lifelong depressive and alcoholic who spent periods in an asylum, and Wilky James, wounded in the Civil War, died bankrupt and desolate at forty.

As Jean Strouse points out in her biography of Alice James, the family assumed a "bank account" model of health and happiness: when one member of the family was well he or she was robbing another of his portion. At the same time sensibilities were so acute that there was constant danger of falling ill through sheer sympathy.

Intelligence, too, was stored in some central fund, and Alice, Robertson, and Wilky were aware that there was little left in the bank for them. Alice, passionate and demanding by nature, found only one way left to distinguish herself: she became the most spectacular of the family invalids. Behind William's half-conscious cruelty there was perhaps a sense that his sister was ill on his behalf, that potentially "that shape am I."

Habegger's account shows how biased even by the standards of the time father Henry's view of the sexes was. An opponent of women's suffrage, he had described woman in an article as man's "inferior in passion, inferior in intellect, and inferior in physical strength." It was in fact the delightful inferiority that made her so appealing to man. And "no woman had a right to be plain," the great thinker had ineffably said in a lecture; "her nature entitles her to be beautiful only." Alice was plain.

Henry James Senior herded the family around Europe to expose them to half a dozen cultures, and he encouraged them above all "just to *be* something, free and uncommitted." All five children wrote glowingly at various times about childhood and family life, but occasionally a different picture is glimpsed. It was the unremembered Wilky who wrote that his problems seemed to stretch back to infancy; he "never saw infants now without discerning in their usually solemn countenance a conviction that they are on their guard and in more or less hostile surroundings." Henry recalled that "we wholesomely breathed inconsistencies and ate and drank contradictions." Perhaps the diet was not entirely wholesome, and the command just to be something free and uncommitted was not easy to follow. Uncle's philosophic talk, cousin Minny Temple noted, was in fact "ignoble and shirking" and "didn't give me the least comfort or practical help."

Henry Senior's total surrender to Swedenborgianism in young adulthood clearly released him at a stroke from the conflicts imposed by a severe Calvinistic upbringing. A curious mixture of the occult and the sensible, it offered a benign deity in place of implacable Jehovah and an assurance that all shall be well in spite of our sinful nature. Essentially the Swedenborgians believed that the new Kingdom of God is irresistibly establishing itself, through a nucleus of the enlightened; meanwhile—as James Senior evidently saw it—our good and bad impulses will work themselves out in their own way, prompted by the spirits of all kinds that surround us (Swedenborg, an eminently sane man in many ways, conversed fluently with them for years). For a man crushed since childhood by fear of damnation this came as a life saver; he could sit back, he felt, and leave the battle to God. Writing to Robertson, who confessed to unclean desires and recurrent despairs, he explained that

> I learned to separate myself, as an entirely disinterested party, from the great conflict raging in my bosom, and leave it to God's perfect providence to settle it as it may for the welfare of all mankind.... I let angel and devil chase each other about the empty chambers of my mind as they will...without my pretending to join in.

The head of the James clan was bringing his children up in full reaction against the narrowness of his own childhood; but the very things that are reacted against tend to rebound back on the next generation, and perhaps his sympathetic explanations left them less than consoled. They grew up under a double bind that enjoined them to live the freest of lives, so long as they were not unhappy—for unhappiness did not really exist. And though it did not exist, it was of the deepest interest to them all.

Alice recalled an incident when she was nine years old as being crucial in her life. The James children, who were being dragged around Europe in search of the ideal education, were out on a visit in the French countryside. They were sent to play in a dusty yard:

> Harry [Henry] was sitting in the swing and I came up and stood near by as the sun began to slant over the desolate expanse, as the dreary hrs, with that endlessness which they have for infancy, passed, when Harry suddenly exclaimed: "This might certainly be called pleasure under difficulties!"

She felt, she wrote in her diary many years later, that in that moment she acquired a "new sense whereby to measure intellectual things." She and Henry, in fact, had begun to crack the family code. There remained a sense of alliance between them; Wilky and Robertson's alliance was one of common failure; while William uneasily but definitely held on to the position of leader, and to the end of his days patronized "dear old, good, innocent and at bottom very powerless-feeling Harry."

Alice James was seven when the family began its wanderings around Europe, and twelve when they came back to New England. While her brothers were being deposited in one progressive *pensionnat* after another, she was taught by governesses; she had no chance to meet other American girls or to put down roots. Her first experience of school was when the Jameses settled, in 1860, in Newport for four years. "Alice is a dear little girl" was a visitor's report. The dear little girl, however, had already begun what she herself considered a slow self-murder.

She recalls in her diary the "low, grey Newport sky in that winter of 62–63 as I used to wander about over the cliffs, my young soul struggling out of its swaddling-clothes as the knowledge crystallized within me of what Life meant for me." What it meant for her—and why it should have been so at this heartbreakingly young age is obscure—was "absorbing into the bone that the better part is to clothe oneself in neutral tints, walk by still waters, and possess one's soul in silence." She had, clearly, a passionately imperious nature which refused compromise and which, thwarted, turned in on itself.

Henry—who loved and helped her—wrote after her death that

> the extraordinary intensity of her will and personality really would have made the equal, the reciprocal life of a "well" person—in the usual world—almost impossible to her—so that her disastrous, her tragic health was in a manner the only solution for her of the practical problem of life—as it suppressed the element of equality, reciprocity, etc.

Clothed in neutral tints, then, she acted the part of the quiet Bostonian girl of the 1860s. What was actually going on, as she recollected years later in her diary, was that

> as I used to sit immovable reading in the library with waves of violent inclination suddenly invading my muscles taking some one of their myriad forms such as throwing myself out of the window, or knocking off the head of the benignant pater as he sat with his silver locks, writing at his table, it used to seem to me that the only difference between me and the insane was that I had not only all the horrors and suffering of insanity but the duties of doctor, nurse, and strait-jacket imposed upon me, too.

At nineteen she had her first serious breakdown. The twelve years between that and an even deeper collapse into illness were punctuated by a trip to Europe, when she astonished all by her robustness, but were otherwise twelve years of waiting: waiting for "offers" that did not come. The letters of these years are a catalog of friends' engagements and marriages—and an insidiously spiteful one:

> What do you suppose I heard the other day? Nothing less than that those dreadful Loverings had had no end of offers! It was insulting, but satisfactory as explaining the mystery of why

> the article had been so scarce in Quincy Str., for if such ragged growth as the Miss L-s are what's courted, its no wonder that a rare exotic like—modesty forbids my saying who—is left unplucked upon its stem, to reach a bloom bordering, to put it delicately, on the full-blown.

This is already the tone of the diary: dreadfully jocose, self-wounding, poisonous with pain.

At thirty came breakdown again—"that hideous summer of '78 when I went down to the deep sea, its dark waters closed over me, and I knew neither hope nor peace." Jean Strouse suggests that William's marriage (to another Alice) contributed to it; and being thirty, perhaps, marked a kind of official end to "offers." She was too ill to go to her brother's wedding; her father sat at her bedside, still serenely "untroubled about the issue of Alice's troubles.... It is only the burden of the mortal life that she groans under." This was not the lightest of burdens, and she ruminated suicide. There were recoveries and relapses; Alice's "attacks" were now the linking theme of her existence.

When Mrs. James died in 1882, Alice (less surprisingly to us than to her contemporaries) rose well to the occasion; "her Mother's death seems to have brought new life to Alice," wrote her aunt. Robertson, too, in a letter reported that "I sleep beside [father] in mother's empty bed and we have quiet happy talks at night about mother's nearness and about our pride in her. The last two weeks of my life have been the happiest I have known." Curious tributes to this "perfection of a mother." A year later Henry Senior died and the spinster daughter, on her small inheritance, endured two years of alternating "nerve cures" and torturing solitude:

> Those ghastly days, when I was by myself in the little house in Mt. Vernon Street, how I longed to flee in to the firemen next door and escape from the "Alone, Alone!" that echoed through

> the house, rustled down the stairs, whispered from the walls, and confronted me, like a material presence, as I sat waiting, counting the moments as they turned themselves from today into tomorrow.

In the autumn of 1884, she sailed for England and Henry.

The third volume of Henry James's letters (1883–1895)[5] covers the years in which brother's and sister's lives most closely overlapped. In 1884 when she arrived in London he was forty, she thirty-six, with seven and a half years to live—years of rapidly growing invalidism in lodgings, with a nurse for company. Henry's behavior toward her was faultlessly gentle: "His kindness and devotion are not to be described by mortal pen," she wrote; he turned over his share of their father's income to her, kept William in touch with her progress, canceled holidays when "attacks" demanded it, visited her, and entertained her. He put something of her brittle gaiety into the invalid Rosy of *The Princess Casamassima*. There was a small world that they shared; but the larger one of literary bachelordom is far from hers. What is common to his letters and hers is a deep guardedness about the private self.

By the time his sister settled in England Henry James was a success both socially and professionally; his first five novels were behind him, and during the years she was living there he wrote *The Bostonians*, *The Princess Casamassima*, *The Tragic Muse*, and stories and plays. The third volume of his selected letters also encompasses (mostly after Alice's death) the dreadful debacle of the stage ventures. It shows James reaching the crest of the wave—of a wave, rather—and starting to decline from it. In 1887 he is writing to William that

> I am able to work better, and more, than I have ever been in my life before; it isn't much, but it's enough, and at any rate it is so

5. *Letters, Volume III: 1883–1895*, edited by Leon Edel (Harvard University Press, 1980).

> much more than has been the case in former years that I look back with wonder and pity to the wretchedly bad basis I have always been on.... Little by little I have grown less *sick*.... Now I can do the essential.

Only eight years later, resenting the smallness of his earnings, the magazines' lack of interest in his short stories, and the humiliations of the stage, he had, he felt, "fallen upon evil days—every sign or symbol of one's being in the least *wanted*, anywhere or by anyone, have so utterly failed. A new generation, that I know not, and mainly prize not, had taken universal possession." These two glimpses are as much as he ever allows of his feelings; and the letters, with their upholstered urbanity, their *voyons un peu* and their *que diable*, their evocation of "the British coal scuttle, the dark back-bedroom, the dim front sitting-room, the *Times*, the hansom cab, the London dinner" are somewhat stifling in large doses.

His sister's are stifling in a different way. What we see in the letters she wrote home from England is a desolating picture of endurance, on the invalid couch, "within three feet of the fire. I have 2 suits of winter underclothing a flannel lined wrapper, 2 very warm shawls over my shoulders, a very heavy rug over my legs & these constantly supplemented by a duvet & fur cloak." A window is left open a crack, and she has "rheumatism in the head" for twelve hours. Sometimes she is wheeled out in her bath-chair. She faints as regularly as clockwork—over a dogfight, a coarse expression of Nurse's, the results of a local election. And a succession of doctors comes and goes with a succession of diagnoses—"These doctors tell you that you will die, or recover! But you don't recover." What they agreed on, in the main, was that her disorders were nervous rather than organic.

Words that describe mental pain regularly acquire a pejorative meaning: Alice James's symptoms were "hysterical." Jean Strouse gives a sympathetic and acute account of hysteria and never condescends to her subject's illness, which was, in essence, despair. Alice James was too intelligent not to know that her sufferings were a protest against her whole life, that she was "an emotional volcano within"; "the difficulty is my inability to assume the receptive attitude," she wrote to William, "that cardinal virtue in women, the absence of which has always made me so uncharming to & uncharmed by the male sex." Later on, after reading his paper "The Hidden Self," she was to make a remarkable analysis in her diary. It is, in a way, reminiscent of her father's description of his cure through Swedenborgianism—deliberately "separating himself, as an entirely disinterested party, from the great conflict raging in my bosom"—but Alice's account is secular and more honest:

> William uses an excellent expression when he says... that the nervous victim "abandons" certain portions of his consciousness.... I have passed through an infinite succession of conscious abandonments and in looking back now I see how it began in my childhood, altho' I wasn't conscious of the necessity until '67 or '68 when I broke down first, acutely, and had violent turns of hysteria. As I lay prostrate after the storm with my mind luminous and active and susceptible of the clearest, strongest impressions, I saw so distinctly that it was a fight simply between my body and my will, a battle in which the former was to be triumphant to the end.... When all one's moral and natural stock in trade is a temperament forbidding the abandonment of an inch or the relaxation of a muscle, 'tis a never-ending fight.... So, with the rest you abandon the pit of your stomach, the palms of your hands, the soles of your feet, and refuse to keep them sane when you find in turn one moral impression after another producing despair in the one, terror in the other, anxiety in the third and so on until life becomes one long flight from remote suggestion and complicated eluding of the multifold traps set for your undoing.

From the diary and the letters we see how complete was the split between the two sides of her that were at war. She was brave, and wished to be accepted as such; Henry did so, writing to William that she gave "a very good account of herself.... That she has been able to do it is a proof of strength. But of that sort of strength she has much" (she herself meanwhile described this period as the "long desolate 'keeping up'"). One side of her certainly is all stoicism, contemptuous of those weaker than herself. But then there are the amused, detached references to her "goings-off"; the body that fainted, screamed, raved might have been simply a rather tiresome companion that she had to take about with her. Fortitude was a strictly demarcated area; as she comments in the diary, "Which of us has not given within a faint paralytic smile over her 'Courage,' however careful her vanity may have been not to dispel the superficial illusion."

The diary was begun nearly three years before her death; ironically, it seems that by the time she became unmistakably and fatally ill the writing of it had begun to add something to her life, perhaps because it enabled her to look back on her experiences, as in the passage quoted above. It is not primarily self-exploratory—she discusses books, politics, and the small happenings of the sickroom—but there is a sense, in spite of its waverings between archness, self-congratulation, and self-contempt, that she is steadily affirming an identity. What is painful for the reader is the grim, jocose tenacity with which she urges on her death. "I am working away as hard as I can to get dead...," she writes to her sister-in-law; "The trouble seems to be there isn't anything to die of, but there are a good many jokes left still, and that's the main thing after all."

Eighteen months later there was, after all, something to die of. She had long since been edged into choosing death as the only project she could succeed at; so she died well, calmly recording Henry's playwriting ventures and the hypocrisies of the British beside the progress of her decline. William wrote telling her how happy he was for her, and she replied in the same vein. Nobody, it seems, wrote to say that they would have liked her to live. This did not escape her: "The universal tendency 'to be reconciled' to my passing to the summer land, might cause confusion in the mind of the uninitiated!" It was not all darkness, though: the very end was peaceful; she had found a voice in the diary; and she had recorded in it that the winter before her cancer was diagnosed she had been happy, having both Henry and her friend Katharine Loring in constant attendance. She had even softened enough to write benignly of her nurse, whom she had long nagged on paper and in action—there was such security, she wrote, in anchoring herself to her "long narrow Fra Angelico surface."

Her literary brother was truly saddened by her death. Fastidiously he changed "the last breath" to "the breath that was not succeeded by another" in his letter to William. Two years later, his letters record, he was deeply shaken by the death of another woman, the writer Constance Fenimore Woolson. She says in one of her letters, discussing Isabel Archer of *The Portrait of a Lady*, that for women,

> one gets hopeless enough sometimes (while watching them) to think that a duller mind, a more commonplace character, is the better gift. Simple goodness, and a gentle affectionate unjudging nature, seem the high prizes for a woman to gain in this lottery of life.

Unlike Alice James, who would have spat at "a gentle affectionate unjudging nature," Constance Woolson seems to have half taken the role upon herself: her letters to James, with whom she was in love, are intensely, reproachfully obsequious. He had valued her company very much, and had made it quite clear he had no sexual interest in her; she committed suicide, at fifty-three, by jumping from her bedroom window in Venice.

24

AN ICE-COLD WREATH: KATHERINE MANSFIELD

WHEN SHE PONDERED in her diary the glorious future for women, Katherine Mansfield was nineteen and at home with her family in New Zealand, after three years at an English school that she had been sorry to leave. It was 1908; she was writing that she now knew "what women in the future will be capable of." They would throw off their self-made chains, and get rid of the insipid doctrine that love is all in all to them. Then she would be able to have what she wanted: power, wealth, and freedom. (So little?) At about the same age, we remember, Rebecca West had been writing confidently that the only way to manage life was "to treat sex lightly, to... think no more hardly of two lovers who part soon than we do of spring for leaving the earth at the coming of June." Do we pity or admire, laugh or cry?

It started well enough, when she was back in England, making literary contacts, beginning to get published, "ready to try *all* sorts of lives." She tried them—traveled to Europe, made love to men and to women, became pregnant, married and immediately left her husband, lost a baby, acquired a terrible disease.[1] The trouble with trying to—in our current phrase—"have it all" is that it demands a firm sense of self.

---

1. Systemic gonorrhea, which may have been a factor in her acquiring the second, fatal illness (TB)—perhaps from D.H. Lawrence. Both illnesses were incurable at the time; gonorrhea

Mansfield, in her insecurity, struggled against dreadful excursions into falsity, as everyone who met her was aware: the thread running through her journal is her haste to get free of them before her approaching death. Virginia Woolf wrote regretfully of her "small lies and treacheries, the perpetual playing & teasing, or whatever it was." And yet, Woolf felt, she was able to "get down to what is true rock in her, through the numerous poses which sicken or bewilder most of our friends."

Mansfield grew up in a well-to-do but unsympathetic family, evidently a plain, sulky, and unpopular girl ("Well, Katherine, I see you're as fat as ever," was her mother's greeting after a trip) who nevertheless had the advantage of unspoiled countryside and a big extended family to grow up in. At fourteen, already "in love" with a boy her age, she was sent over to school in England, read Oscar Wilde, fitfully hated her family, wrote little sketches ("'You adorable creature,' whispered Rudolf.... She felt the room sway and heave"). Boringly ordinary today, but coming on a bit strong for an age when adolescence had not yet been invented. Antony Alpers points out in his biography,[2] without making too Freudian a fuss about it, how presciently strong was the death-wish theme in her juvenilia. At seventeen, she ended a story: "'O—o—I want to live,' she screamed. But Death put his hand over her mouth."

To the New Zealand editor who printed her first few sketches she described herself as "poor—obscure—just seventeen years of age—with a rapacious appetite for everything and principles as light as my purse." It is, obviously, the self-portrait of any flushed teenager (as the child of a prosperous man, she was not even particularly poor); but about the predatory lack of principle she was pretty accurate. Virginia Woolf's first reaction—"an unpleasant but forcible and utterly

---

that had spread caused infertility. Claire Tomalin's *Katherine Mansfield: A Secret Life* (Knopf, 1988) gives the clearest account of these illnesses.

2. *The Life of Katherine Mansfield* (Viking, 1980).

unscrupulous character"—is in line with a good many other reactions appearing in biographies. Coldly regarded as a child, she perhaps had only the choice between victim's role and victimizer's—though in the end it was life that made a victim of her. "True to oneself! which self?" she pondered in her diary:[3]

> What with complexes and repressions and reactions and vibrations and reflections, there are moments when I feel I am nothing but the small clerk of some hotel without a proprietor, who has all his work cut out to enter the names and hand the keys to the wilful guests.

Just as Beryl, in *Prelude*, sees

> Her false self running up and down the stairs, laughing a special trilling laugh if they had visitors, standing under the lamp if a man came to dinner, so that he should see the light in her hair, pouting and pretending to be a little girl when she was asked to play the guitar.

Leonard Woolf declared that no one had ever made him laugh so much—quite a tribute from the austere Leonard. Another friend recalled Katherine flouncing into a restaurant and eliciting murmurs of "Oh là là!" from the men.

Katherine Mansfield's diaries cannot be considered the equal of Virginia Woolf's—she died too young for that, for one thing—but there was a strong bond between them. They were in search of the same kind of writing, the same kind of honesty, in spite of a difference

---

3. *The Letters and Journals of Katherine Mansfield: A Selection*, edited by C. K. Stead (Penguin, 1977). The editor makes clear that the "journals" were abstracted from a mass of unsorted material, first by Murry and then by himself.

in age and experience; and—notwithstanding ambivalences—they recognized it. In her diary Mansfield wrote:

> I do not think I am a good writer; I realize my faults better than anyone else could realize them. I know exactly where I fail. And yet, when I have finished a story and before I have begun another, I catch myself *preening* my feathers. It is disheartening.... And anything that I write in this mood will be no good; it will be full of *sediment*.

This is reminiscent of Woolf's "reprimand" to herself:

> The dream is too often about myself. To forget this, & to forget one's own sharp absurd little personality, reputation & the rest of it, one should read; see outsiders; think more; write more logically; above all be full of work; & practise anonymity.[4]

One might have expected Woolf to have been interested in, for instance, the novelist Elizabeth Bowen, who revered Woolf's work and was a friend; but Woolf in her diaries returns to Mansfield, to the fact that there was "a certain understanding between us.... I can talk straight out to her."

By the time the two writers met in 1912, Katherine was living—rather fitfully—with the editor and critic John Middleton Murry. These later years are obviously better chronicled in letters and diaries than the louche early ones. Poor ineffectual Murry, whom she eventually married, does not emerge too well from the record. As T. S. Eliot remarked of the pair, two sentimentalists together more than double the falsity. To most eyes, Katherine was a sharp, worldly, witty person, and this is the person she projects in her writings, but the on-and-

---

4. *The Diary of Virginia Woolf: Vol. 3, 1925–1930* (Harcourt, Brace, Jovanovich, 1980).

off relationship with Murry brought out a rash of soppism in both. Aldous Huxley had them in mind in his *Point Counter Point* (1928), which ends:

> That night he and Beatrice pretended to be children and had their bath together. Two little children sitting at opposite ends of the big old-fashioned tub. And what a romp they had! The bathroom was drenched with their splashings. Of such is the Kingdom of Heaven.

Over these years, nevertheless, she was writing determinedly though sporadically. *Prelude* was published by the Woolfs in 1918 and *Bliss* in 1920; but "The Garden Party" was not finished until fifteen months before her death, and it was toward the end that her writing had started to gather momentum. A certain amount of time had also had to be put into potboiling journalism.

The interest of the last period of her life, as it is recorded in journals and letters, is in a heroic effort to make something solid out of this restless and contradictory nature, at the same time facing an inevitably approaching death, and of course writing. A resigned turning away from Murry was eventually an important part of the process, and seems to have been so well accomplished as to leave affection rather than bitterness. Before this, what we have seen is someone at the mercy of her own histrionic versatility. There were so many poses that the real Katherine, like her friends, comes to suspect them all: "I'm possessed by a sort of Fate"; "I am become a little child again"; "You have transformed me utterly"; "Friendless, hopeless, loveless alone"—and so on. She had called herself variously, to different people, Kass, Kassie, Katie, Katherine, Käthie Schönfeld (Beauchamp), and Katharina (her Russian phase). "I suppose her gifts as a Novelist led her to imagine herself as the heroine of several Romances," wrote an acquaintance tartly. More charitably, we can see her as the child of a cold mother, striking innumerable anxious poses before the mirror. Sentimentality about her mother and her home, running alongside the dramatic currents in her life, are reminiscent of Sylvia Plath's unbearably cheery letters to *her* mother. But Mansfield was continually working to clean and sharpen her style, and to clear her vision.

In a very early letter it appears that her elder sister had said of her that "nothing but a great trouble would ever put her right." An odd thing for a sister to say—yet in a way it came true, when she had to come face-to-face with her illness. In the meantime we often see flashes of the brave and inquisitive woman who wrote in her diary that "to be alive and to be a 'writer' is enough." "Sitting at my table just now," she said, "I saw one person turning to another, smiling, putting out his hand—speaking. And suddenly I clenched my fist and brought it down on the table and called out—There is *nothing* like it!" Even in the letter to Murry announcing the doctor's verdict of tuberculosis she is searching curiously for the right phrase for this change in her life: "Its like suddenly mounting a very fresh, very unfamiliar horse—a *queer queer* feeling," she wrote.

The winters that she had to spend, following the medical custom of the time, in the warmer climate of the French Riviera were a torment. Murry, most of the time, was working in England. In 1918 she spat blood: "I spat—it tasted strange—it was bright red blood.... How unbearable it would be to die—leave 'scraps,' 'bits'...nothing real finished." She observed the tubercular fits of blind rage:

> My deadly deadly enemy has got me today and I'm simply a blind force of hatred.... It fills you with death and corruption, it makes you feel hideous, degraded and old, it makes you long TO DESTROY.

And the long nights of the tubercular patient:

> The man in the room next to mine has the same complaint as I. When I wake in the night I hear him turning. And then he coughs. And I cough. And after a silence I cough. And he coughs again. This goes on for a long time. Until I feel we are like two roosters calling to each other at false dawn. From far-away hidden farms.

Murry's letters, too concerned with himself, maddened her: "I've scarcely any time.... Talk to ME. I'm lonely. I haven't ONE single soul." Her letters to her distant and, she felt, uncaring husband are simultaneously sentimental and enraged at this time. Then she had a very powerful dream:

> I must put down here a dream. The first night I was in bed here, i.e. after my first day in bed, I went to sleep. And suddenly I felt my whole body *breaking up*. It broke up with a violent shock—an earthquake—and it broke like glass. A long terrible shiver, you understand—and the spinal cord and the bones and every bit and particle quaking. It sounded in my ears—a low, confused din, and there was a sense of flashing greenish brilliance, like broken glass. When I woke up I thought there had been a violent earthquake. But all was still. It slowly dawned upon me—the conviction that in that dream I died. I shall go on living now—it may be for months, or for weeks or days or hours. Time is not. In that dream I died. The *spirit* that is the enemy of death and quakes so and is so tenacious was shaken out of me. I am (December 15, 1919) a dead woman, and *I don't care*. It might comfort others to know that one gives up caring; but they'd not believe any more than I did until it happened. And, oh, how strong was its hold upon me! How I *adored* life and *dreaded* death!

After it, she wrote *The Man Without a Temperament*, about the dreary lot of a man who gives up everything to nurse a sick wife—a kind of forgiveness of her unsatisfactory mate, and preoccupied, like so much of her work, with the distance between people.

The following summer, when she was in England and met Woolf again, Woolf wrote in her diary:

> I said "You've changed. Got through something"; indeed theres a sort of self command about her as if having mastered something subterfuges were no longer so necessary. She told me of her terrific experiences last winter—experiences of loneliness chiefly...in a stone house with caverns beneath it into which the sea rushed: how she lay in bed alone all day with a pistol by her.... She went to Murry for assurance; didn't get it; & will never look for that particular quality again.

The posing, the subterfuges, indeed start to disappear from her diary and letters. When the journal fragments philosophize, they carry conviction, and the style strengthens. "Charm," coyness, drop away. "We only live," she writes, "by absorbing the past—changing it. I mean really examining it and dividing what is important from what is not.... I used to think this process was fairly unconscious. Now I feel just the contrary."

The closing episode of Mansfield's life—the stay in the eccentric Gurdjieff community, where she died—is put into perspective by Alpers' biography: by no means a crazy escapade, but the choice of a dying person with nothing to lose, and which for her last months provided a wonderfully lively escape from the glum alternatives of living with Murry or with her devoted but irritating friend Ida Baker. Now that the romantic haze wafted around her by Murry after her death has long since dissipated, we can see and admire the real struggle put up by this wretchedly unlucky girl: a struggle for more honesty both in living and writing (compare the way that Lawrence, incomparably more important as a writer, let illness sour rather than strengthen him). What she aimed at, in the words of the narrator of "A Married Man's Story," was "just the plain truth, as only a liar can tell it."

Some weeks after her death Virginia Woolf looked back at it. At the morning when Nelly had run in to say over the breakfast table that "Mrs Murry was dead—it said so in the paper!" Confused feelings, then a depression—no point in her writing, because Katherine wouldn't be there to read it, Katherine only thirty-three. She seemed to be wearing a white wreath, an ice-cold one, reluctantly.

> And I could see her before me so exactly, & the room at Portland Villas. I go up. She gets up, very slowly, from her writing table. A glass of milk & a medicine bottle stood there. There were also piles of novels. Everything was very tidy, bright, & somehow like a dolls house. At once, or almost, we got out of shyness. She (it was summer) half lay on the sofa by the window. She had her look of a Japanese doll, with the fringe combed quite straight across her forehead. Sometimes we looked very steadfastly at each other, as though we had reached some durable relationship, independent of the changes of the body, through the eyes. Hers were beautiful eyes—rather doglike, brown, very wide apart, with a steady slow rather faithful & sad expression. Her nose was sharp, & a little vulgar. Her lips thin & hard. She wore short skirts & liked "to have a line round her" she said. She looked very ill—very drawn, & moved languidly, drawing herself across the room, like some suffering animal. I suppose I have written down some of the things we said. Most days I think we reached that kind of certainty, in talk about books, or rather about our writings, which I thought had something durable about it.

Probably, Woolf thought, "we had something in common which I shall never find in anyone else."

Conclusion

by the Author

I DON'T, of course, think there *is* a conclusion.

These women! They have baffled me by falling into such different groups. What has the rapscallion Helena Blavatsky in common with Lady Churchill, or the hallucinating Ruth with down-to-earth Dora Russell? In puzzlement, and skimming through one of my favorite books, *Roget's Thesaurus of English Words and Phrases*, I have dredged up "castaway," "aloof," "outsider," self-determining," "marooned," "individualist," "recluse," "nonconforming," "rarity," "visionary"—and I'm sure a home could be found here for every one of these labels. Some women, willingly or not, sacrificed much of themselves to other people's needs, and others to an art—writing, painting, singing. Others built entire fantasy worlds that got them through life but nevertheless estranged them somewhat from ordinary humanity. I think of Blavatsky in old age, feeling herself surrounded by dupes and longing for her Russian homeland, and Enid Blyton in her fairy-tale woodsy cottage with the elves and pixies and gnomes. Some (perhaps even most?) were in search of a "self": Blixen/Dinesen, Eddy/Eadie, Mansfield ("I want to be *real*"). Some might even protest, justifiably, against being included with loners: Verdi's dedicated Giuseppina, for instance, or the cheerful and sociable witches. And there are some who had simply been hit too hard by misfortune.

A surprising number had known bereavement in childhood, and some of these had a real core of isolation within themselves. When there is such a sense of void at the center, all the stronger is the stockade that protects it. On the map of solitude, defenses are prominent. Some, the fantasists, are interesting because they successfully stifled any misgivings under an unstoppable flow of words. Brazil and Blyton did, of course, both being committed worshipers of themselves and their work—which annoyed librarians, and any parents who hoped to foster good taste in their offspring.[1] Blavatsky might be crowned queen of fantasists, yet I suspect that she had one foot in reality, which makes her more uneasy and more of a marvel. Those of the women who committed themselves to a real art with real standards, such as Gwen John and Katherine Mansfield (and of course Virginia Woolf) had a struggle to the death. With the Brazils and Blytons, we feel that at some point in childhood they were not *noticed* enough, and so there they stuck and blew up their fantasy balloons. (And for a moment, let's hear it for fantasists: Didn't they all give pleasure, sometimes more? Don't we all, child or adult, sometimes need to avoid the great masters of solitude—Kafka, Beckett—in favor of junk reading?)

So many of these women *learned* from isolation. Lauren Slater, writing as someone who has been mentally ill and also worked professionally with mental illness, describes a search through the academic literature on schizophrenia. She found no mention anywhere of loss, or separation, or loneliness. "Is it that the schizophrenic experience seems so bizarre to us, we can't imagine such a patient might be suffering from something as common as loneliness? As highbrow as existential anomie?" Nobody else had noticed.

---

1. Agatha Christie belongs here. My son asked for *The Mousetrap* for his eighth birthday; he is now of an age to worry about his weight and his hairline. This hugely boring play has been running for fifty-two years.

Indeed, "loneliness" is something of a taboo word, like "sad" or "pathetic," used now with contempt or *Schadenfreude*. Perhaps there's fear behind it. Saturday night and no date? Nobody phoned today? Get a diet book and a how-to-live book, and keep quiet about it. To feel aloneness has come to imply humiliation: but I don't think these women cared two pence for appearances.

Out of all these life experiences, I have been most drawn to the plain declarations of aloneness, no fantasy hiding place allowed. Ottoline Morrell: "It is no fun being an oddity for it makes one eternally lonely"—short and simple. Comical Stevie Smith, who cheered herself by thinking of suicide and declared that all children should be taught about its usefulness: "*Ah night space and horror, keep my dreams from me.*" Kate Millett on silence: "[In depression] one's real state of mind is a source of shame. So one is necessarily silent." Mansfield coughing, coughing, coughing through the night as her death came nearer. Gwen John alone with her cats, painting ever smaller and fainter pictures. Karen Blixen making her sinister pact with the devil. And of course Alice James, who "went down to the deep sea, its dark waters closed over me." This is the sense of isolation that goes right through the personality, to its very beginnings.[2]

So it does with the two men of genius who appear in chapter 10. Both Leos Janacek and Luigi Pirandello, musician and playwright, quite separately used their two women correspondents as a kind of inner mascot, such as students might take into examining rooms. Janacek "put" his creativity into safekeeping in Kamila Stosslova's mind (though she was thirty-seven years younger and musically illiterate)—he could "know that it's as safe in your mind as if it were hidden in mine." He

---

2. Andrew Solomon, in his *The Noonday Demon: An Atlas of Depression* (Scribner, 2001), recalls a particular moment in childhood when he was first aware he could fall through the safety net. And later, observing his weeks-old nephew, he thought he could see depression striking in the very moments before a feeding.

warmed himself at the idea of her, composed his best works: *together* they were triumphing, he said. Pirandello wrote to "his" young actress, Marta Abba, with even more possessive desperation: "You are my creature, my creature, my creature, in which all my spirit lives with the very power of my creation, so much so that it *has become your thing and you are all my life.*" The relationship was platonic; she was *his* not in any bodily sense, but because she had played *his* Ersilia, *his* Stepdaughter, *his* Evelina Morli, and to see any other actress play them was excruciating to him. The long passage quoted on pages 104–105 is an extraordinarily precise description of his creative process: he too puts her inside his brain, his self, and she does the work for him; if she leaves him or, more literally, he loses his inner grasp of her, the writing stops, his writing hand turns to stone. Though here the fearful isolation is more on the part of the two men, being a muse of this kind was not, at the least, pleasurable for the women. It was as if their souls had been annexed.

This leads into deep waters: the ways in which personalities can form and split and re-form, feed off one another or die for one another, divide and reinvent themselves, reinvent others as pixies or ageless Tibetan masters. Dissociation can take no end of forms, useful or pathological. And the life of creators being so edgy and isolated, it may be helpful just to declare that the whole power of the writing hand lies with a young woman many miles away. Blyton didn't inquire who sent her the stories of Little Noddy and Big Ears: they just came. Blavatsky claimed her messages came from the ageless Tibetans and sometimes, perhaps, she convinced herself that was true. Olive Schreiner and Havelock Ellis gave each other life-saving support by letter, but ran out of conversation when they were together—the "real" person and the inner image were out of balance, as though one had exhausted the other. Indeed, Blyton and Brazil, though they wrote their reams of tosh, seem to have had rather dull and depleted personalities in their ordinary lives. Margaret Oliphant of course had to write as many reams, but the difference was that she didn't write through fairy-tale arrangement but by her own hard-working hand and to pay the bills. Consequently her work was real and good—though not as good, she knew, as it could have been if she had been given more time.

Do we all function by means of some inner mascot or mascots (internalized objects, if you prefer the jargon)? Probably, yes. Gwen John and Bertrand Russell—who said that he had loved a ghost all his life and had become spectral—were both of them pursuing the mother lost so early and hardly known? I think so. But most of us either cannot delve that far, or don't want to or need to. What is clear is that it is best, if aloneness is to be borne, to have an inner world as orderly as that of an old-fashioned doll's house: everything in its proper place and everyone pleasant and contented. No "great space and tundra," in Lauren Slater's words, but a safe and solid world somewhere. (I see it as right in the middle of the brain, sending out a cheerful light.)

So if there is any conclusion to be reached about our theme, it has simply to do with the lament of a thousand pop songs: Don't leave me. Loneliness might be said to be lack of human nourishment in the ordinary world; aloneness the lack of even the safe, inner doll's house with its tiny population.

But what, finally, about aloneness that is not pain, that is gallantry or self-sufficiency? Must all be doom and disaster? What about courage? Looking back at the lives described here, I cannot see a single one lacking in courage or fighting spirit. All shall have medals. I think in particular of Simone Weil's unfathomably brave life, turning the oozing wounds of neurosis and self-disgust into . . . into something far better, at any rate.

And then there is the recovery from isolation, the return from great space to solid ground. Nobody can have known more or written better about this than Virginia Woolf (this is from *The Waves*):

> How then does light return the world after the eclipse of the sun? Miraculously. Frailly. In thin strips. It hangs like a glass cage. It is a hoop to be fractured by a tiny jar. There is a spark there. Next moment a flash of dun. Then a vapour as if earth were breathing in and out, once, twice, for the first time. Then off twists a white wraith. The woods throb blue and green, and gradually the fields drink in red, gold, brown. Suddenly a river snatches a blue light. The earth absorbs colour like a sponge slowly drinking water. It puts on weight, rounds itself, hangs pendant, settles and swings beneath our feet.
>
> So the landscape returned to me.

The *horror vacui* that Mansfield glimpsed in Augustus John's mind, the crippled trees and extinct fires, give way to life again.

Conclusions

by the Subjects

And then suffering, bodily suffering such as I've known for three years. It has changed for ever everything—even the *appearance* of the world is not the same.... It has taken me three years to understand this—to come to see this. We resist, we are terribly frightened. The little boat enters the dark fearful gulf and our only cry is to escape—"put me on land again." But it's useless. Nobody listens. The shadowy figure rows on. One ought to sit still and uncover one's eyes.

—KATHERINE MANSFIELD

Impose your style. Let it be simple and strong. The short strong stalks of flowers. Don't be afraid of falling into mediocrity. You would never.

—GWEN JOHN

You see, we belong *here*! I wrote a review of a book recently on man's responsibility for nature, and I said that now that we've had a look at the cold moon, and our own earth in contrast, we realize what a precious thing we have here. We should be taking care of it, and enjoying it, and *loving* it; and to me this is worth everything else in the world that anybody could invent.

—DORA RUSSELL

Sometimes the Holy Ghost is a woman, but whether He, She, or It, always there, holding the disintegrating structure together (or so we hope in our agnostic hearts) and will not, must not, withdraw.

—PATRICK WHITE

On reaching a certain degree of pain we lose the world. But afterwards comes peace, when we find it again. And if the paroxysm returns, so does also the peace which follows it.

If we realize this, that very degree of pain turns into an expectation of peace, and as a result does not break our contact with the world.

—SIMONE WEIL

Ah me, only
In heaven's permission
Are creatures quiet
In their condition.

—STEVIE SMITH

INDEX